Industry and Policy in Independent Ireland, 1922–1972

Industry and Policy in Independent Ireland, 1922–1972

Frank Barry

OXFORD
UNIVERSITY PRESS

OXFORD
UNIVERSITY PRESS

Great Clarendon Street, Oxford, OX2 6DP,
United Kingdom

Oxford University Press is a department of the University of Oxford.
It furthers the University's objective of excellence in research, scholarship,
and education by publishing worldwide. Oxford is a registered trade mark of
Oxford University Press in the UK and in certain other countries

Published in the United States of America by Oxford University Press
198 Madison Avenue, New York, NY 10016, United States of America

British Library Cataloguing in Publication Data
Data available

Library of Congress Control Number: 2023902252

ISBN 978-0-19-887823-0

DOI: 10.1093/oso/9780198878230.001.0001

Printed and bound in the UK by
Clays Ltd, Elcograf S.p.A.

To Ciara, to the Barrys of Currow and Mallow, the Feigherys of Banagher, and the ghosts of Gardiner Place.

Preface

Around twenty years ago, when I was lecturing in economics at University College Dublin and specializing in the role of foreign direct investment (FDI) in the modern Irish economy, I became engrossed in historian Mary Daly's work on industrial development in the early years of the Irish Free State. By the early 2000s, foreign-owned firms accounted for close to 50 per cent of manufacturing employment. For most of them, Ireland served as an export platform from which to produce for the European Union and other neighbouring markets. I had not considered until then the role that FDI had played in the industrial economy of earlier times. Mary Daly's work was replete with references to British firms—and some of other nationalities—that had avoided the tariff barriers of the era by establishing in Ireland to service the protected local market.

The anonymized database currently maintained by the Department of Enterprise, Trade and Employment contains the longest time series on the nationality of ownership of Irish industry. Its coverage extends back only to 1972. It should be possible, I thought, to work out reasonably precisely how extensive this older type of FDI had been if the nationality of ownership of the largest manufacturing firms of the earlier protectionist era could be identified.

Naively, I guessed that it might take only a few months to complete this task. I would soon discover that there were no comprehensive lists of the largest firms in operation in Ireland over the period. (This proved also to have been the case for the United Kingdom, though much research had already gone into doing for the United Kingdom what is done here for Ireland.) The few lists that surfaced on occasion in newspapers and magazines focused almost exclusively on companies traded on the Dublin stock exchange. Privately owned firms, semi-state companies, creamery cooperatives and the like were not included. Nor were most of the foreign-owned firms that I knew to have been in operation at the time.

The earliest research publication to emerge from this project finally saw the light of day in 2016. It focused on the sectors surveyed by the Committee on Industrial Organisation in the early 1960s. The names of the firms that the Committee had surveyed were listed in its reports, though firm-specific employment numbers had to be pieced together from other sources, and certain major industries were underrepresented or not included.

I continued to work to identify the largest firms in operation over earlier and later time periods and across the entire manufacturing sector. Nationality of ownership was no longer the characteristic of sole or even of primary interest. Chapter 2, which extends the analysis back to the decades prior to the establishment of the state in 1922, reveals the extent of Protestant and unionist control of the leading businesses of the time.

The search for the largest firms involved drawing on official reports, industry and academic studies, books, magazines, and newspaper articles to construct 'long lists' of candidate firms by time period and by industrial sector and then seeking to unearth employment numbers for these firms. I could not have competed the mammoth task of narrowing down these long lists without the assistance of my students at Trinity Business School, where I was appointed to the chair of International Business and Economic Development in 2007. (Many reported that their research assignments for a final-year undergraduate course on Economic Policy and Business History that I had been invited to develop proved a popular discussion topic at subsequent job interviews.)

I owe a debt of gratitude to them and to my research assistants Michael Scholz and Benn Hogan who organized all of the results accumulated over the years into a comprehensive firm-level database. The data reported here have been extensively cleaned and cross-checked for consistency. To provide a sense of the variety of sources from which they have been derived, those pertaining to the decades prior to 1922 are reported in Chapter 2. Primary sources for later periods are available at: https://doi.org/10.25546/101139 (Barry Project: Firm-Level Data on Irish Industrial History). It is planned to make the entire database of several thousand firms available to the public at some stage in the future, though many of my notes are written in a shorthand that may be difficult to decipher.

The other element of the research on which the book is based pertains to economic and industrial policy and the policy formation process. Former Taoiseach Garret FitzGerald once observed that even democratically elected governments are subject to such strong pressures from vested interests that many of the policies they adopt are detrimental to society as a whole. This research seeks to identify the combination of political beliefs, electoral and interest-group pressures and other constraints that lead to the adoption of particular policy stances. It also tracks the origins of some of the policy innovations that have proved of major significance to the economic well-being and development of the country.

Much of my knowledge of Irish economic history was picked up by osmosis from my then colleagues in the University College Dublin economics department, Cormac Ó Gráda and Kevin O'Rourke, and from Mary Daly in the nearby history department. The interest that leading British economic historian Nick Crafts took in my work from an early stage provided huge encouragement. These have all continued to be major sources of inspiration.

Random conversations with friends and colleagues, and sometimes even simple questions raised at particularly opportune moments, contributed significantly to the development of my thinking on these matters. I took note over the years of insights that emerged from interactions of these types with John Bradley, Louis Cullen, Tommy Graham, Finola Kennedy, Frances Ruane, and Brendan Walsh. The business history element of the research builds on the work of Andy Bielenberg of University College Cork. I have benefited too from the infectious enthusiasm of local historians, particularly James Madigan of the Liberties Cultural Association and Matthew Potter and Sharon Slater in Limerick. Joe Durkan first drew my attention to the potential value of the reports of the Committee on Industrial Organisation. Jim Quinn was responsible for my developing the Trinity Business School undergraduate course referred to earlier. Robin Adams, John FitzGerald, Patrick Honohan, Seán Kenny, Eoin McLaughlin, Cormac Ó Gráda, and Frances Ruane kindly read and commented on various draft chapters.

I am indebted also to Eunan O'Halpin for his invariable willingness to accommodate my requests to present early drafts of my work to the Trinity Research Seminar in Contemporary Irish History. The comments and feedback of the participants at these and other seminars are gratefully acknowledged.

Contents

List of Tables

List of Abbreviations

AIFTA	Anglo-Irish Free Trade Area Agreement
CIO	Committee on Industrial Organisation
CIP	Census of Industrial Production
CKD	completely knocked down (motor vehicles)
CRH	Cement Roadstone Holdings
DDC	Dairy Disposal Company
DETE	Department of Enterprise, Trade and Employment
DUTC	Dublin United Tramways Company (later Dublin United Transport Company)
EEC	European Economic Community
EFTA	European Free Trade Association
ESB	Electricity Supply Board
FBU	fully built up (motor vehicles)
FDI	foreign direct investment
GSR	Great Southern Railways
IAOS	Irish Agricultural Organisation Society
ICC	Industrial Credit Company
IDA	Industrial Development Authority
MNC	multinational corporation
NAI	National Archives of Ireland
NATO	North Atlantic Treaty Organization
NESC	National Economic and Social Council
NIEC	National Industrial Economic Council
OECD	Organisation for Economic Co-operation and Development
OEEC	Organisation for European Economic Co-operation
PDDE	Parliamentary debates, Dáil Éireann (lower house)
PDSE	Parliamentary debates, Seanad Éireann (upper house)
PRONI	Public Records Office of Northern Ireland
SFADCo	Shannon Free Airport Development Company Ltd
TD	Teachta Dála (member of lower house of the Irish parliament)
UCDA	University College Dublin Archives

Two canals head westward out of Dublin. The Grand Canal hugs the city's arteries, the Royal Canal bisects them. For those unfamiliar with the route, walking the Royal Canal can be disorientating. Neighbourhoods that one might have thought some distance apart huddle close together. This book is about history more than geography, though the two are inextricably linked. My hope is that it might track the mind map of the Royal Canal.

1

Vantage Point, 1972

In 1972, on the eve of Ireland's accession to the European Economic Community, the Guinness brewery at St James's Gate and the biscuit factory of W. & R. Jacob off Aungier Street remained Dublin's largest manufacturing establishments. The more than 200-year-old brewery employed a workforce of 3,500. The biscuit factory, which dated from 1853, still employed around 1,500, though production had already begun to shift to the suburbs. The Jacobs workforce was predominantly female, Guinness's almost exclusively male. The broader Guinness Group was, along with Cement Roadstone Holdings, the largest manufacturing employer in the state.

Having concentrated almost since its inception on the production of stout and porter, Guinness had responded to the first indications of the emerging 'lounge bar society' by launching a new lager at its bicentenary in 1959. Brewed mainly in Dundalk, *Harp* had become the best-selling lager brand in Britain and Ireland. In combination with various industry partners, Guinness had gone on to acquire the Smithwicks brewery in Kilkenny, producer of the country's most popular ale, and the former Magners in Clonmel, which held the rights to the Bulmers cider brand in Ireland. The lime cordial with which lager was frequently flavoured was produced by Cantrell & Cochrane (C&C), in which the brewer held close to a half share. The two companies between them were buying up many of the local soft drinks brands that remained popular throughout the country.

The Guinness Group's Irish workforce numbered around 5,000. The brewer—formally a British company since its incorporation in 1886—employed a further 1,500 at Park Royal in London and had recently opened plants in Nigeria and elsewhere for which the 'concentrated essence' was produced at St James's Gate. Cement Roadstone Holdings (CRH) employed several hundred more than the Guinness Group in Ireland. The Jefferson Smurfit Group was somewhat smaller. Though formed only in 1970, CRH's origins—like those of Smurfit—lay in the Ireland of the 1930s. Both firms remained predominantly domestically oriented in 1972, though one UK acquisition by Smurfit in 1973 would double the size of its workforce and extend its operations into the developing world. At peak production in the

Industry and Policy in Independent Ireland, 1922–1972. Frank Barry, Oxford University Press.
© Frank Barry (2023). DOI: 10.1093/oso/9780198878230.003.0001

early Free State era, the Ford plant in Cork had been by far the largest manufacturing employer. It would remain in operation into the 1980s. The most significant new export-oriented foreign multinational was US firm General Electric (GE). GE had established the first of its Irish operations at Shannon in the early 1960s and opened another in Dundalk several years later.

Identification of the largest employers of the early 1970s provides us with more than just a snapshot of the era. Because the pace of change in industry was much more gradual then than it has since become, all of the major structural and economic changes that had occurred since Ireland's integration into the United Kingdom in the early nineteenth century had left a legacy. Though few sectors would be unaffected by European Economic Community (EEC) membership, the industrial foundations of the expansion of subsequent decades are also in evidence.

1.1 Industrial History of the Free State Area

Southern Ireland was one of the many regions in Europe and beyond—including others in the United Kingdom of the time—to deindustrialize in the wake of the British Industrial Revolution. Cottage textile industries in particular were unable to withstand the competition from cheap factory-produced imports. The Irish Free State at its birth in 1922 remained predominantly agricultural, as shown in Table 1.1. Manufacturing output was far more complex

Table 1.1 Numbers employed in agriculture, industry, and services (thousands), 1926–1971

	Agriculture	Industry	Services
1926	653	162	406
1936	614	206	415
1946	568	225	432
1951	496	282	438
1961	370	255	410
1971	272	320	457

Note: Agriculture includes forestry and fishing. Industry comprises mining, manufacturing, construction, and utilities. *Source*: Kieran Kennedy, Thomas Giblin, and Deirdre McHugh. *The Economic Development of Ireland in the Twentieth Century* (London: Routledge, 1988), 143, based on adjusted population census data.

in structure even then, however, than might be suggested by the '4 Bs': beer and biscuits in Dublin, butter and bacon beyond the Pale.

The economic history of the state up to EEC accession is conventionally divided into three phases. The first comprises what is generally character- ized as the laissez-faire era of the Cumann na nGaedheal governments of the 1920s, the second the *dirigiste* and protectionist policy regime of the Fianna Fáil administrations that followed from 1932. The beginning of the third phase is typically dated to the late 1950s when Seán Lemass took over from Eamon de Valera as Taoiseach and leader of Fianna Fáil. Though Lemass had been the chief architect of protectionism, he adopted the broad principles of a plan prepared by the head of the civil service, T. K. Whitaker, who had feared during the severe economic crisis of the mid-1950s that 'the achievement of independence would prove to have been a futility'.[1] Protectionism was abandoned, an application to join the EEC submitted, and a Free Trade Area Agreement (AIFTA) signed with the United Kingdom in 1965. The growth in manufacturing employment and labour productivity over these and several sub-phases is depicted in Table 1.2.

Though there had been some convergence in economic structure (as seen in Table 1.3), Ireland, despite decades of protection, remained under- industrialized by Western European standards when EEC membership was finally achieved in 1973.

The conventional historical account requires substantial refinement, how- ever. A number of the large manufacturing employers of the early 1970s date from Cumann na nGaedheal-era policy initiatives, including some of the

Table 1.2 Growth rates of manufacturing employment and labour productivity, 1926–1973

	Employment	Productivity
1926–1931	1.6	0.0
1931–1936	8.6	−1.3
1936–1946	1.5	−0.3
1946–1950	5.9	4.6
1950–1960	0.8	2.3
1960–1973	2.3	4.0

Source: Kennedy et al., *Economic Development*, 228; data drawn primarily from Census of Industrial Production (CIP).

[1] T. K. Whitaker, *Protection or Free Trade: The Final Battle* (Dublin: Institute of Public Administration, 2006), 8.

Table 1.3 Industrial and manufacturing employment as a share of the labour force, Western Europe and Ireland, 1920s and 1970s

		Early-to-mid-1920s	Early-to-mid-1970s
Industry as share of labour force	Ireland	15	32
	Western Europe	31	41
Manufacturing as share of labour force	Ireland	10	20
	Western Europe	26	30

Note: Western Europe refers to country average for twelve states other than Ireland. Industry is as defined in Table 1.1.
Source: Peter Flora, Franz Kraus, and Winifried Pfenning. *State, Economy and Society in Western Europe, 1815–1975*: The Growth of Industrial Societies and Capitalist Economies, Vol. 2 (Chicago, IL: St James Press, 1987).

'experimental' protectionist measures adopted at the time. The other predominantly agricultural states that newly appeared on the map of Europe in the aftermath of the First World War had adopted a strategy of extensive import substitution as soon as independence had been achieved. It was not simply an attachment to laissez-faire principles that caused the Free State not to follow suit. William Martin Murphy, the leading nationalist industrialist of his day, had noted at the Irish Convention in 1917 that the products of Irish agriculture 'are exported in normal times to a greater value than the products of all the Ulster industries combined' and that 'Great Britain is at the present time the best and practically the only market.' Though a strong advocate of fiscal independence, 'it would be folly', he concluded, to depart from free trade in 'articles of home produce'.[2] The great British economist, John Maynard Keynes, in a sympathetic lecture delivered in Dublin in 1933, advised that 'those who seek to disembarrass a country of its entanglements should be very slow and wary. It should not be a matter of tearing up roots but of slowly training a plant to grow in a different direction.'[3]

Economies of all types—industrial as well as agricultural—turned away from free trade in the 1930s as export markets collapsed. Where Ireland differed from most of the rest of Western Europe was in remaining protectionist into the 1950s and 1960s. Here in particular the conventional account needs to be revisited. Tariff barriers began to be reduced only in 1963, by

[2] Horace Plunkett, *Report of the Proceedings of the Irish Convention* (Dublin: HM Stationery Office, 1918), 39, para. 21.
[3] John Maynard Keynes, 'National Self-Sufficiency'. *Studies: An Irish Quarterly Review* 22, 86 (1933): 181.

which time EEC membership had become the strategic long-term goal of Irish diplomatic and economic policy. Given the surprise nature of the UK application submitted in 1961, this could not have been envisaged at the time of the Whitaker Report. The trade-offs faced in the case of EEC membership were substantially more benign than those that had been on offer in 1958.

The conventional account, furthermore, conflates the new export-oriented foreign direct investment (FDI) strategy of the 1950s and the trade liberalization of the following decade. The Industrial Development Authority was established by the first Inter-Party government in 1949, the nationwide industrial grants and export profits tax relief regime of the mid-1950s by the second. The Shannon Free Zone, in turn, which *was* Lemass-sponsored, differed in its aims and outcomes from the Inter-Party initiatives. While the latter achieved early success in attracting British and Continental European firms, Shannon was targeted particularly towards US companies and the North American market. That the new FDI strategy facilitated the trade liberalization of the Whitaker–Lemass era—by bolstering confidence that the economy could survive the eventual dismantling of protectionism—identifies it as an early example of what has come to be known since the Chinese liberalization process of the late 1970s as 'dual-track reform'.

Existing writing on Irish economic and business history has been criticized as being overly focused on the role of the state. Many of the changes in industrial structure, particularly from 1948 when the new post-war world began to take shape, were not directly ascribable to changes in the trade regime. The first phase of rural electrification began in 1946: the increased demand for electrical equipment and the labour-saving household appliances that it facilitated (and that would transform the lives of Irish women in particular) was reflected in an expansion in the size of the firms that produced them. Growing purchasing power abroad led to the emergence of new export industries producing what would have been considered luxuries or quasi-luxuries at the time: carpets, crystal glass, processed beef, and whiskey liqueur. The rural economy benefited from the demand for raw materials by new foreign-owned operations engaged in the production of infant formula and chocolate confectionery. Youghal Carpets, the most successful Irish carpet producer, dated from 1954: by 1972, it employed 1,500 in Ireland and a further 1,000 overseas. Waterford Glass dated from 1947: on the eve of EEC accession, it employed 2,000 in its Irish manufacturing operations and a further 2,000 overseas and in the Dublin department store (Switzers) that it had acquired to facilitate its retail sales. Beef processing also emerged as a significant export industry only from the late 1940s.

Much of the literature on the subsequent transformation of the economy has focused on the contribution of the new foreign-owned export-oriented ventures of the period, of which Liebherr in Killarney and Standard Pressed Steel in Shannon were early examples. The new export-oriented FDI strategy helped to diversify the economy in ways that could not have been imagined in earlier decades. Political independence, as elsewhere, had been associated with a desire for reduced economic dependence on the former dominant power. Though early Fianna Fáil had striven for increased self-sufficiency, the United Kingdom accounted for the same share of Irish exports in the mid-1950s as it had when Fianna Fáil first came to power, while British multinationals accounted for a higher share of manufacturing jobs than at the foundation of the state. The new multinationals of the 1950s and beyond came from a much broader range of countries and exported to more diverse destinations.

The 'brownfield' FDI of the period, comprising the acquisition and restructuring of existing businesses, has attracted relatively little attention. US firm Grace & Co. acquired the leading indigenous confectionery producers H. B. Ice Cream and Urney Chocolates in the 1960s before selling them on to Unilever in 1973. US firm St Joe Paper acquired two of the surviving Irish paper mills. Each of these firms employed more in early-1970s Ireland than pharmaceuticals giant Pfizer, one of the highest-profile greenfield foreign investors of the period. British firms such as Courtaulds, Lyons, and others also entered the ranks of large employers through their acquisitions of the 1960s and early 1970s.

The share of foreign firms in Irish manufacturing was already high by European standards at the time of EEC accession, as shown in Table 1.4. This is sometimes interpreted as a reflection of the success of the new export-oriented FDI regime, which had also by this time attracted the likes of Krups, Ferenka, and Killarney Hosiery ('Pretty Polly'). While this would be true of later decades, the explanation is different for this earlier period. Foreign firms could avoid the tariff barriers of the protectionist era by establishing operations inside the protected market. Major employers among this class of 'tariff jumpers' included Irish Dunlop, Rowntree–Mackintosh, Fry–Cadbury, Players–Wills, and Clarks Shoes. A decision to close the Ford plant in Cork had been reversed when the new Fianna Fáil government of the early 1930s prohibited the importation of fully built-up cars. The plant had, from that time, assembled cars and trucks primarily for the domestic market. Most of these firms would exit within ten to fifteen years of EEC entry. The high share of foreign firms in Ireland seen in Table 1.4 reflects an amalgam of FDI of different types. These include the 'tariff factories' of the protectionist era, the

Table 1.4 Share of foreign firms in manufacturing employment, selected European countries, early-to-mid 1970s

	Early to mid-1970s
Austria	20 (1973)
Finland	3 (1976)
France	15 (1973)
Ireland	**34 (1972)**
Norway	7 (1975)
Portugal	7 (1975)
Sweden	6 (1975)
United Kingdom	11 (1973)

Note: Data pertain to firms with minimum 50 per cent foreign ownership.
Sources: OECD (Organisation for Economic Co-operation and Development) Penetration of multinational enterprises in manufacturing industry in member countries. (Paris: OECD, 1977, 1978 update); Irish data from Department of Enterprise, Trade and Employment.

brownfield acquisitions of the 1950s and 1960s, and the new export-oriented greenfield projects on which most economic analyses of the period have focused.[4] Guinness, whose registered office had been in London since its incorporation, would also have been included within this group.[5]

Mergers and acquisitions form an important part of the process by which economies adjust to the onset of freer trade. Increased scale, enhanced access to capital, and broader management skills are required if firms are to survive in the new more competitive trading environment that ensues. These and other developments associated with the economic liberalization of the era were significant drivers of change in the Irish industrial environment. Protectionism, paradoxically, by providing a safe haven for traditional family business practices, had facilitated the survival of significant elements of the pre-1922 southern business establishment. As will be seen in Chapter 2, the business elite inherited by the new state was predominantly Protestant in religion and unionist in political orientation. It is not coincidental that the *Irish Times* would note in 1965—as protectionism was being dismantled— that 'the day of the identifiably "Protestant" or "Catholic" firm is passing,'

---

[4] Sweeney was one of the few to draw attention to this point at the time: John Sweeney, 'Foreign Companies in Ireland'. *Studies: An Irish Quarterly Review* 62, (1973): 273–286.
[5] Its registered office, initially at Birchin Lane and later at Salisbury House, would transfer to the Park Royal brewery after the Second World War.

a view echoed in an Economic and Social Research Institute survey of the perspectives of contemporary business leaders published several years later.[6]

Among the other effects of the wave of mergers and acquisitions was an increase in concentration levels, as measured by the share of output accounted for by the largest firms. In the creamery sector, the more innovative cooperatives that had diversified early out of butter expanded both organically and by acquisition. The workforce at Mitchelstown, the largest cooperative of the era, more than trebled to 1,600 in the twenty years to 1973. By the 1960s, its *Galtee* brand had become the most popular bacon on the Irish market, outstripping Henry Denny & Sons and the other long-established private producers. Ballyclough, with which Mitchelstown would merge to form Dairygold in the 1990s, expanded through contracts to supply UK firms Rowntree and Cow & Gate with the raw materials for their export-oriented operations. The second great wave of creamery-sector concentration would occur in the decades following EEC accession; the first occurred in the decades that preceded it.

1.2 Census of Industrial Production

The data employed in Tables 1.1 and 1.3 are derived from the census of population. Population-census data are relatively standardized and widely used in cross-country comparisons. Data from the Census of Industrial Production (CIP) are more useful for the purposes of the present book. The CIP is based on questionnaires relating to enterprises rather than to individuals and provides greater insight into the evolution of industrial structure.[7] The first Free State Census of Industrial Production was conducted for 1926. Table 1.5, which provides details for 1926 and other selected years, shows a three-to-fourfold increase in manufacturing employment between 1926 and 1972.

Table 1.6 depicts the change in industrial structure over this period. Food, drink, and tobacco accounted for almost half of manufacturing employment in 1926; by 1972 its share had declined to a little over one-quarter, though the extensive backward linkages of agri-food industries substantially increase their overall significance to the economy. Textiles, clothing, footwear, and

[6] *Irish Times*, 23 March 1965; Michael P. Fogarty, 'Irish Entrepreneurs Speak for Themselves'. Economic and Social Research Institute Research Series, ESRI Broadsheet No. 8 (1973).

[7] The first CIP for 1926 provides a sector-by-sector comparison of the number of industrial workers recorded in the CIP and the population census for that year. As micro businesses and the self-employed are not included in the CIP, the number of industrial workers recorded is substantially lower than that reported in the population census.

Table 1.5 Manufacturing employment as recorded in CIP, 1926–1972

Year	Manufacturing employment
1926	56,535
1929	62,439
1931	60,943
1938	97,285
1939	98,822
1942	89,762
1945	97,433
1948	119,662
1960	156,588
1972	197,315

Note: Includes 'all other industries' (e.g. sector 35 in the 1926 CIP).
Source: CIP.

leather expanded to a little under one-quarter, while the share accounted for by the metals and engineering sector—which, along with chemicals, includes most of what might be considered 'modern' industry—trebled.

Data on establishment size are reported in the census only intermittently. Establishments—though sometimes confusingly referred to as firms—are more akin to individual factories, plants, creameries, bakeries, etc. There is no necessary relationship between the number of large establishments and the number of large firms.[8] There were nine establishments with workforces of 500 or more in 1929; by the late 1960s, the number had risen to more than fifty (Table 1.7).

The CIP also provides information on the female share of the workforce. Across all of manufacturing, 32 per cent of wage earners in 1926 were female, ranging from a high of 87 per cent in clothing to a low of 2 per cent in clay, glass, and cement. The overall proportion remained unchanged in 1972, as seen in Table 1.8.[9] The decline in the female share in some sectors was counterbalanced by a strong increase in metals and engineering, within which there was a substantial change in sectoral structure. The electrical machinery

[8] The term 'firm' is sometimes used here to refer to an enterprise (the smallest separate autonomous legal unit) and sometimes, more broadly, to the totality of activities in common ownership or control. The Irish operations of US firm General Electric referred to earlier for example consisted of two separate enterprises—EI at Shannon and Ecco in Dundalk. (Horgan reports that 'Lemass was so unhappy about the shamrockery' implicit in the name Emerald Isle that he succeeded in having it referred to only as EI: John Horgan, *Seán Lemass, the Enigmatic Patriot* (Dublin: Gill and Macmillan 1999), 249.)
[9] The female share differs between the CIP and the population census. It also depends on the categories of workers focussed upon (e.g. whether administrative and clerical staff are included alongside wage earners).

Table 1.6 Sectoral breakdown of manufacturing employment, 1926 and 1972

	Numbers employed		Shares (%)	
	1926	1972	1926	1972
Food	18,399	42,760	33	22
Drink	7,000	7,450	12	4
Tobacco	2,096	2,230	4	1
Building materials (clay, glass, and cement; wood and furniture)	5,113	19,090	9	10
Metals and engineering	3,804	41,390	7	21
Of which: motor vehicles	*1,447*	*7,770*	–	–
Basic metals	*1,276*	*13,890*	–	–
Engineering and implements	*1,081*	*15,700*	–	–
Ship and boat building and repairing and railroad equipment	*	*4,030*	–	–
Textiles and clothing	8,840	39,605	16	20
Of which: textiles other than hosiery	*3,990*	*14,415*	–	–
Hosiery	*849*	*8,170*	–	–
Clothing	*4,001*	*17,020*	–	–
Footwear and leather	967	7,370	2	4
Paper and printing	5,739	16,690	10	8
Chemicals and miscellaneous	4,577	20,730	8	11
Totals	56,535	197,315	100	100

Note: *Separate details not provided for 1926 and not included under 'Metals and engineering'.
Sources: CIP (1926, 1972).

and appliances segment had scarcely existed in 1926: females made up 55 per cent of the workforce in this segment in 1972. The absence of male-dominated heavy engineering in Ireland, and the consequent prominence of food, textiles, and clothing, resulted in the female share across all of manufacturing exceeding that in Britain.[10]

[10] The comparison, which is not completely straightforward because different sectoral categories were employed in the two jurisdictions, was conducted for 1966: Brendan M. Walsh, 'Aspects of Labour Supply

Table 1.7 Number of establishments employing 500 or more, 1929–1975

Year	No. of establishments
1929	9
1931	7
1938	13
1944	13
1947	21
1958	31
1963	45
1968	51
1975	52

Source: CIP.

Table 1.8 Female share of wage earners in manufacturing industries, 1926 and 1972

Industry	Irish Free State, 1926	Ireland, 1972
Food	29	29
Of which: chocolate and sugar confectionery and jams	78	64
Drinks	3	8
Tobacco	67	55
Textiles	61	49
Of which: hosiery	85	69
Clothing	87	83
Footwear and leather	37	46
Wood and furniture	9	9
Paper and printing	37	27
Chemicals and miscellaneous	27	26
Clay, glass, and cement	2	12
Metals and engineering	8	18
Of which: electrical machinery and appliances	–	55
Total	32	32

Source: CIP.

1.3 Firms and Establishments

While there were only nine manufacturing establishments employing 500 or more in 1929, there were almost twice as many manufacturing firms of this size (as many large firms operated more than just one plant or factory).

and Demand, with Special Reference to the Employment of Women in Ireland'. *Journal of the Statistical and Social Inquiry Society of Ireland* 22, 3 (1971): 88–123.

The number of firms in this size category had risen to seventy or so by the time of EEC accession.[11] These firms are listed in Table 1.9. In dealing with the early history of the state some attention is paid to department stores, builders' providers, and milk distributors as some of their activities were industrial in nature. Many department stores produced clothing, furniture, and furnishings; builders' suppliers were major producers of timber; and the Dublin milk distributors began to pasteurize and bottle their milk supplies and produce their own brands of ice cream in the early 1920s. Developments in these sectors are not tracked comprehensively over later decades as the relative significance of their manufacturing activities declined as the economy industrialized. Five of the substantial employers in Table 1.9 were state or largely state-owned enterprises: the Dairy Disposal Company dated from the 1920s, Irish Sugar from the early 1930s, and Irish Steel, Verolme Dockyard, and Nítrigin Éireann from later periods.[12] Around half of the remainder of the firms in Table 1.9 were foreign-owned.

There is an ambiguity, it should be noted, to the dates of establishment appended to many of the firms on the list in Table 1.9 and throughout the book. The Ford plant in Cork is variously dated to 1917, when work on the factory commenced, and 1919, when it came into regular production. Even for Guinness, 1759 may not necessarily be exact: an early official guidebook states that the brewery 'was founded about the year 1759 by ancestors of the Guinness family buying the brewing plant of a Mr. Rainsford'.[13] Similarly, though Jameson whiskey is conventionally dated to 1780, the distillery came into John Jameson's ownership only in 1810 when he acquired it from his wife's family. Accuracy as to when businesses ceased operating is even more difficult. Many of the smaller local breweries transitioned into bottling or soft drinks production over a period of years, while whiskey might be released from bond long after a distillery had closed. The significance of many of the other dates will become clearer later.

A substantial number of the largest manufacturing employers of 1972 predate the establishment of the state. Guinness, Jacobs, Gouldings, and Ford were already significant employers by 1922. The workforce at metals and engineering company Hammond Lane, cigarette and pipe tobacco manufacturer

---

[11] The industrial holding companies of the era (Braids, Fitzwilliam, Joshua Watson, and the like) are not included unless one or more of the individual manufacturing firms within the group were significant employers.

[12] The focus here is on large *manufacturing* firms. Though Bord na Móna and Gaeltarra Éireann also employed large workforces, Bord na Móna was primarily a resource extraction company, while the industrial developments sponsored by Gaeltarra Éireann were individually all relatively small in scale.

[13] *Guidebook to Guinness's Brewery* (Visit of members of the Irish Convention, 20 September 1917), mss 7357, fols 232–99: Hopwood Papers, Bodleian Library, Oxford. I am grateful to Anne Dolan for alerting me to this source.

Table 1.9 Manufacturing firms employing 500 or more in Ireland in 1972

Sector	Workforce	Sector	Workforce
Food, drink, and tobacco		**Metals and engineering**	
Guinness (1759)	2,000+	General Electric (1960, 1966)	1,000+
Irish Sugar (1933)		Brittain Group (1913, 1932)	
W. & R. Jacob (1851)		Ford Motor Company (1919)	
Fry–Cadbury (1932)		Hammond Holdings (1902)	
Cork Marts Group (1967)		Unidare (1949, 1957)	
Clover Meats Group (1936)	1,000+	Verolme/Cork Dockyard (1959)	
P. J. Carroll (1824)		Ferenka (1972)	
Mitchelstown Creameries (1919)		Becton Dickinson (1963, 1970)	500+
Ranks (1930)		Electrical Industries of Ireland (1938, 1966)	
Grace & Co. (1963)		Irish Steel (1938, 1947)	
Dairy Disposal Company (1927)		Philips (1957, 1962, 1967)	
Rowntree–Mackintosh (1925, 1926, 1960)		Krups (1964)	
Odlum Group (1845)		Solus Teoranta (1935)	
Waterford Co-op [1964)		Masser–Waterford (1936, 1955)	
Irish Distillers (1966)	500+	Standard Pressed Steel (1960, 1967)	
Players–Wills (1924)		Technicon (1966)	
Bolands (1823)		Liebherr (1959)	
Ballyclough (1908)		**Clay, glass, and cement**	
Golden Vale (1948)		CRH (1936, 1949, 1970)	2,000+
Cantrell & Cochrane (1868)		Waterford Glass (1947)	
Lyons Irish Holdings (1962)		Irish Glass Bottle (1932)	500+
Batchelors (1935)		Arklow Pottery (1935)	
Nestlé (1960)/Williams & Woods (1856)		**Paper and printing**	
Textiles, clothing, footwear & leather		Smurfit Group (1934)	2,000+
Sunbeam (1928)	2,000+	Clondalkin Paper Group (1936)	1,000+
Seafield-Gentex (1936, 1946, 1965)		Independent Newspapers (1905)	
Halliday/Clarks (Ireland) Group (1928, 1938)	1,000+	Irish Press Ltd (1931)	
Youghal Carpets Group (1954)		St Joe Paper (mid-1960s)	
Irish Leathers (1938, 1972)		*Irish Times* (1859)	500+
J. & L. F. Goodbody (1865)	500+	**Chemicals and miscellaneous**	
Courtaulds (1954)		W. & H. M. Goulding (1856)	1,000+
Glen Abbey (1939)		Irish Dunlop (1934)	

Continued

Table 1.9 *Continued*

Sector	Workforce	Sector	Workforce
Jonathan Logan (1960, 1968)		Unilever (pre-1920s)	500+
Irish Ropes (1933)			
Navan Carpets (1937)		Pfizer Group (1971, 1972)	
Killarney Hosiery (1967)		Nítrigin Éireann (1961)	
Doreen (1946)		Semperit (1969)	
Janelle (1952)		Snia (1972)	
Blarney Woollen Mills (1750, 1824)		De Beers (1961)	
Bond Worth (1967)			

Note: The employment figures in the table refer generally to a firm's manufacturing operations in Ireland. Details of overseas operations are provided in the text.
Source: author.

Carrolls, grain miller Odlums, and the *Irish Independent* newspaper group would expand to 500 or more only at a later date. With the demise of the rival *Freeman's Journal*, the latter would employ 500 by the late 1920s.

Firms dating from the Cumann na nGaedheal era include the Dairy Disposal Company and the massive indigenous textiles firm Sunbeam. Several British firms avoided the tariffs of the era by establishing operations in the Free State. The constituent firms of Players–Wills and Rowntree–Mackintosh entered the Irish market separately in the mid-1920s and later amalgamated their local operations. UK firm Crosse & Blackwell acquired the major Dublin confectionary and jam producer Williams & Woods in 1928 and was itself acquired by the Swiss firm Nestlé in 1960. Ranks took over the large Limerick flour milling operation Bannatyne in 1930, though an Irish subsidiary was formed only several years later to conform with legislation introduced by the new Fianna Fáil government.

Firms dating from Fianna Fáil's first unbroken period in office from 1932 to 1948 include, among many others, the state company Irish Sugar, British tariff jumpers Fry–Cadbury and Irish Dunlop, and indigenous firms Smurfit and Clondalkin Paper Mills. Firms dating from the post-war era include the Cork Marts Group, the largest beef processor at the time of EEC accession. Among the largest of the new export-oriented foreign firms was the Dutch company Ferenka, which opened in Limerick in 1972.

Unsurprisingly, many of the firms diversified their Irish operations over time. Even prior to the establishment of the state, the Dutch and British companies that would later merge to form Unilever had acquired the largest Irish soap, margarine, and candle-making firms. Lever Brothers opened a major soap factory on Sheriff Street in Dublin in the 1920s, and Unilever's Irish operations were already of substantial size before it acquired much of the formerly indigenous confectionery and ice cream sector from US company W. R. Grace in 1973. The industrial foundations of the expansion of the post-EEC accession era are also to be glimpsed within the list of firms in Table 1.9. This theme is taken up in the closing chapters of the book.

2

The Pre-1922 Southern Business Establishment and Its Legacy

The vast bulk of industry on the island of Ireland in the early twentieth century was located north of the future border. The experiences of the two parts of the country had differed sharply over the course of the previous century. Strong export-oriented linen and shipbuilding industries had emerged in North-East Ulster alongside a substantial engineering sector, while the rest of the country had deindustrialized and become specialized as a supplier of largely unprocessed agricultural output to the British market.[1]

Belfast had seven manufacturing establishments with workforces of 3,000 or more in 1907 compared to only St James's Gate in Dublin.[2] Though two other Dublin-based companies—the Irish Lace Depot and the Hibernian Lace Company—are occasionally referred to as employing thousands at this time, they are identified as wholesale agencies in a contemporary publication which points out that 'lace making can form the occupation only of leisure hours or of those members of a family who are unfit for more strenuous work'.[3] The female patron of the Tyrconnel Hand-Embroidery Industry described in the 1920s how 'the peasant women' sit on the hills 'minding the cows and doing this fine embroidery'; they had a thousand such women on their books, she reported, 'but, unfortunately, we have not enough work to keep them busy'.[4] Such textile industry 'out-work' continued into the 1960s, particularly in Donegal. Pay was low and outworkers, who were almost exclusively women, were not generally recorded in the Census of Industrial Production. Regular employment in linen alone in the

---

[1] Free State income per head stood at around 50–55 per cent of the UK level in the mid-1920s: Kieran Kennedy, Thomas Giblin, and Deirdre McHugh, *The Economic Development of Ireland in the Twentieth Century* (London: Routledge, 1988), Table 6.2, 124. Northern Irish income per head was significantly higher, though Northern Ireland would long remain the poorest of the UK regions: Frank Geary and Tom Stark, '150 Years of Regional GDP: United Kingdom and Ireland', in *The Economic Development of Europe's Regions*, ed. Joan Ramón Rosés and Nikolaus Wolf (Abingdon: Routledge, 2018), 330–62.
[2] Frank Barry, 'The Leading Manufacturing Firms in the Irish Free State in 1929'. *Irish Historical Studies* 42, 162 (2018): 293–316.
[3] William Townley Macartney-Filgate, *Irish Rural Life and Industry* (Dublin: Hely's 1907), 128–129.
[4] *Irish Times*, 18 October 1927, 6.

Industry and Policy in Independent Ireland, 1922–1972. Frank Barry, Oxford University Press.
© Frank Barry (2023). DOI: 10.1093/oso/9780198878230.003.0002

future Northern Ireland exceeded the entire Free State area manufacturing workforce in 1912.[5]

The North differed also from the rest of the country in its ethno-religious identity and its politics. As a 1926 publication of the Northern Ireland Ministry of Finance explains, the displacement of the native population by English and Scottish settlers from the 1600s had 'undoubtedly operated to introduce bitter animosities, since the incoming colonists differed both in religion and nationality from the original inhabitants, and, in addition, were regarded with all the odium attaching to supplanters'.[6] Protestants across the country were, for the most part, strongly committed to the status quo. The Irish business establishment—disproportionately concentrated in Ulster—was also predominantly Protestant and unionist.[7] The largely Catholic population of the island, by contrast, had long favoured a form of devolved government known as Home Rule but would be radicalized by a series of missteps by government in the aftermath of the 1916 Rising.

The focus here is on the specifically *Free State area* business elite. As was the case in the North, it too is found to have been predominantly Protestant and unionist. That the business establishment inherited by the new state differed from the majority of the population in these respects would impact on economic policymaking well beyond the formation of the first Fianna Fáil government in 1932. There was a danger that taxable income could be driven overseas and business contacts and experience lost. There would have been an understandable desire too for any new government to demonstrate that the scepticism that had been expressed as to the fiscal competence of nationalists was unwarranted. The sectarian divisions in Irish business life would persist for many decades into the future.

2.1 The Free State Area Business Elite

The criterion used here to determine the composition of the business elite is the size of the workforce under a proprietor's control. The chapter first seeks to identify the largest manufacturing employers of the decades prior to independence, as well as the most significant firms in individual industrial

---

[5] Frank Barry, 'Business Establishment Opposition to Southern Ireland's Exit from the United Kingdom'. *Enterprise & Society* (2022), 23, 4, 984–1018. Though Northern Ireland had a significantly smaller population, it had more than twice as many manufacturing workers as the Free State according to the censuses of production produced for the two jurisdictions in the mid-1920s.

[6] *Ulster Year Book* (Belfast: H.M. Stationery Office, 1926), x.

[7] Fergus Campbell, *The Irish Establishment, 1879–1914* (Oxford: Oxford University Press, 2009), ch. 5.

segments.[8] The list of the largest non-manufacturing employers is unlikely to be as comprehensive, as these categories are less well codified. Evidence as to the unionist allegiances of proprietors is provided in an appendix. Religious affiliation is generally determined by reference to the online population censuses of 1901 and 1911.

By the early twentieth century, the industrial elite was converging in wealth and influence on the traditional ascendancy class, as reflected in the leadership of southern unionism, whose principal spokesmen were Lord Midleton and the Presbyterian businessman Andrew Jameson, and in the history of the Guinness family, two of whose members—Lords Ardilaun and Iveagh—had been raised to the peerage.[9]

Guinness was by far the most substantial manufacturer outside Ulster. Lords Ardilaun and Iveagh were conservative unionists, and two of Iveagh's sons sat on the Tory benches at Westminster. The Guinness brewery at St James's Gate employed more than 3,500 in 1912. Around half of the other breweries, all tiny in comparison, were also under Protestant unionist ownership. These included Beamish & Crawford in Cork; Watkins, Jameson & Pim in Dublin; the Great Northern Brewery in Dundalk, and the Cairnes breweries at Castlebellingham and Drogheda in County Louth.

Irish whiskey had been outcompeted by Scotch by the early 1900s and the distilling industry would remain in the doldrums for many decades. Given the capital-intensive nature of the sector and the debilitated condition it was in at the time, none of the distillery companies were major employers. Of the four largest indigenous southern producers, the Dublin Distillers Company—an amalgamation of firms of diverse origins—was ailing and would largely cease production in the 1920s. Of the other three, only Cork Distilleries was in Catholic nationalist ownership. The chairman of the Jameson distillery, Andrew Jameson, also served as governor and director of the Bank of Ireland. Powers was owned by a Catholic unionist family, the Talbot Powers.

[8] Some large employers might nevertheless be overlooked if their business interests were spread across a range of relatively small operations. The various enterprises of distiller D. E. Williams of Tullamore, for example, were said to employ 700–800 workers in total in 1921 (*Freeman's Journal*, 11 July 1921). The McDonagh family, similarly, had interests in a range of ventures across the west of Ireland (*Irish Times*, 26 November 1934). This pattern was not confined to Catholic proprietors.

[9] Rigid class distinctions continued to persist within the establishment, as attested to by W. B. Yeats, who noted of his maternal family in Sligo that 'we were merchant people of the town. No matter how rich we grew, no matter how many thousands a year our mills or our ships brought in, we could never be "county".' (*W. B. Yeats Memoirs*, ed. Denis Donoghue (New York: Macmillan) 1973, 77–8.)

Quaker biscuit company W. & R. Jacob had a 1914 workforce of around 3,000 in Dublin and a further several hundred at its recently established branch plant near Liverpool. The chairman and managing director, George Newson Jacob, was a member of the Dublin Unionist Association and one of a group of businessmen to issue a critique of the economics of Home Rule in 1913.[10] Through the success of another Quaker firm, J. and L. F. Goodbody, the midlands town of Clara had emerged as a jute-processing centre in the mid-nineteenth century. The Clara plant employed close to 1,000 in 1920. Goodbody family members were prominent across a range of professional and business sectors and served on most of the unionist committees of the era.

Other large exporting firms included the Condensed Milk Company of Ireland, chemicals and explosives manufacturer Kynochs, bacon curer Henry Denny & Sons, and fertilizer producer W. & H. M. Goulding.[11] The Condensed Milk Company, by far the largest of the private creameries to survive the emergence and expansion of the cooperative creameries from the 1890s, was estimated by the early 1920s to process one-thirtieth of the entire dairy produce of southern Ireland.[12] With a workforce of 2,000 across Munster in 1898 and an estimated 3,000 in 1922, it was controlled from its Lansdowne base in Limerick city by the Canadian-born Church of Ireland businessman, the 'strongly unionist' Sir Thomas Henry Cleeve.[13] Birmingham firm Kynochs was owned by Arthur Chamberlain, brother of the prominent British Liberal Unionist MP who had split with Gladstone upon the latter's conversion to Home Rule. Some 3,000 jobs were lost when its cordite, explosives, and chemicals plant at Arklow closed in 1918.[14]

Denny & Sons was one of the most significant firms in the UK bacon trade. It employed around 500 in peacetime and perhaps substantially more in 1914–1918 when it was a major supplier to the wartime British military.[15] The chairman, Charles Edmond Denny, served on the General Council of the Irish Unionist Alliance. W. and H. M. Goulding, by far the largest fertilizer producer, employed some 1,200 workers across the nine Irish operations

[10] *Irish Independent*, 11 November 1913.

[11] Gouldings exported in excess of 50 per cent of its output in the 1890s but would later become almost exclusively home-market oriented.

[12] *Cork Examiner*, 9 January 1924.

[13] *The Condensed Milk Co. of Ireland (Cleeve Bros.): A Monster Irish Industry Reviewed* (Limerick: McKerns Printers, 1898); *Cork Examiner*, 13 May 1922; Shaun Boylan, 'Cleeve, Sir Thomas Henry', in *Dictionary of Irish Biography*, https://www.dib.ie/ (Cambridge: Cambridge University Press, 2009).

[14] Kynochs had also recently disposed of the paper mills at Inchicore and Clondalkin that it had operated for a number of years.

[15] There were 350 employed at two of its several Irish factories in Waterford and Limerick in 1895 (*Cork Examiner*, 12 October 1895). Employment at its Cork plant stood at 'well over 100' in 1909 (*Weekly Irish Times*, 10 July 1909).

under its control in 1912, six of which were south of the future border. Sir William Goulding was a leading southern unionist and his brother, Lord Wargrave, sat as a unionist member of the House of Commons until raised to a peerage in 1922.

Most of the substantial export-oriented textile and clothing companies were also under Protestant unionist control. Limerick Clothing had developed an international reputation as a producer of military uniforms under its founder, Scottish expatriate Peter Tait. It was taken over in the 1890s by a group of Limerick businessmen, the most prominent of whom was the unionist milling magnate J. F. G. Bannatyne. Though much diminished in size since its peak, it continued to employ a workforce of more than 600 during the First World War.

Another firm with a substantial international reputation was Balbriggan hosiery manufacturer Smyth & Co. By the early twentieth century, it was owned by local Church of Ireland unionist family, the Whytes. Balbriggan also hosted the 'Sea Banks' hosiery factory of English firm Deeds, Templar & Co., which was burnt down when the town was ransacked by British forces during the War of Independence.[16] The hosiery firms each employed around 400, the majority of whom were out-workers.[17] Balbriggan hosiery was in high demand, however, and excess work had occasionally to be outsourced to Donegal.[18]

Though linen production was concentrated in North-East Ulster, there were several large linen firms elsewhere in the country. The largest, Cork Spinning & Weaving, employed around 1,000 and was owned by a local Presbyterian unionist family, the Ogilvies. Greenmount Weaving of Harold's Cross in Dublin and Boyne Weaving of Drogheda were the largest in Leinster. Greenmount was owned by the Quaker unionist family the Pims (owners of Pim Brothers department store), Boyne Weaving by an Ulster Presbyterian who may have been among a small group of Protestant Home Rulers.[19] Smaller linen producers on the coastline north of Dublin, some under Catholic ownership, were fearful of the disruption of the linen supply chain that partition would entail and viewed the establishment of the Free State with disquiet.

Domestically oriented sectors hosted a number of significant Catholic nationalist firms, including the wholesale drapery, furnishings, and footwear operations of the Cork firm, Dwyer & Co. The only manufacturing segments

---

[16] *Irish Times*, 1 February 1921.
[17] Barry, 'The Leading Manufacturing Firms in the Irish Free State in 1929'.
[18] *Irish Times*, 27 September 1898.
[19] Barry, 'Business Establishment Opposition to Southern Ireland's Exit from the United Kingdom'.

in which the largest firms were in Catholic nationalist ownership, however, were bread production (in which their dominance was marginal), woollen and worsted textiles (in which Blarney Woollen Mills was the only firm with a workforce of 500 or more), and the tiny leather tanning industry.[20]

Flour milling was dominated by the Bannatyne group, which came under the control of the Goodbodys from the 1890s. Employment in Bannatyne and its various subsidiaries is likely to have exceeded 700 in the decades prior to independence.[21] Other Church of Ireland unionist flour millers included the Odlums and the Pollexfens.

There were four industrial-scale bread bakery chains, of which Dublin firms Bolands and Johnston, Mooney & O'Brien were the largest.[22] John Mooney, principal of the latter, was a leading local unionist politician, the largest shareholder was Sir Robert Gardner (one of the partners of accountancy firm Craig Gardner), and the long-term chairman was a member of the Pim family. Cork firm F. H. Thompson was also in Protestant unionist ownership. The proprietors of Bolands and the third major Dublin firm, Kennedys, were Catholic nationalists.

Most of the jam and confectionery producers of the time were Protestant-owned, as was the case also in sectors cognate to brewing, where the influence of Guinness loomed large. One of the most significant maltsters was John H. Bennett & Co. of Ballinacurra, Co. Cork, with which Guinness worked closely in developing new strains of barley. The Bennetts, like the Guinnesses, were Church of Ireland unionists. E. & J. Burke had been established in business in the 1840s as export bottlers for their Guinness cousins, and by 1892 their Liverpool house, under the management of Sir John Nutting, was said to be the most important bottling establishment in the world.[23] Nutting, who would become sole proprietor, was a prominent unionist, as was Sir Henry Cochrane, proprietor of Cantrell & Cochrane, the largest mineral water producer. Other than the industrial bakers, these all employed fewer than 500, as did the leading local tobacco manufacturers, T. P. & R. Goodbody and the Catholic nationalist firm P. J. Carroll of Dundalk.

---

[20] On the leather industry, see Edward J. Riordan, *Modern Irish Trade and Industry* (London, New York: Metheuen, E. P. Dutton, 1920), 178; Andy Bielenberg, *Cork's Industrial Revolution 1780–1880* (Cork: Cork University Press, 1991), 82.

[21] Barry, 'The Leading Manufacturing Firms in the Irish Free State in 1929'; *Irish Times*, 23 January 1923.

[22] Daly reports an employment level of 800 for Bolands in 1888: Mary E. Daly, *Dublin: The Deposed Capital, 1860–1914* (Cork: Cork University Press, 1984), 32. By 1925, this had declined to 420 (*Irish Times*, 22 May 1925). Johnston, Mooney & O'Brien employed around 600 in 1904 (*Freemans Journal*, 16 May 1904).

[23] *Strattens' Dublin, Cork and South of Ireland: A Literary, Commercial and Social Review, with a Description of Leading Mercantile Houses and Commercial Enterprises* (London: Stratten & Stratten, 1892), 36.

Footwear and bulk paper were largely imported prior to the establishment of the Free State. Customized service was important in the cases of printing and paper products, in which there were two firms—Helys and Alexander Thom & Co.—with workforces of 500 or more. There is evidence of the Hely family's support of conservative unionist causes. Thom's was chaired by a member of the Pim family.

The largest engineering firm in 1920 was Henry Ford & Son. Ford's business interests would be affected adversely by the establishment of the Free State as the United Kingdom's 'McKenna tariffs' became applicable to trade in vehicles and car parts between the two jurisdictions. The largest engineering firm after Ford was the Dublin Dockyard Co., which employed around 1,000 in 1919, shortly before its closure.[24] Phillip Pierce & Co. of Wexford was the largest Catholic nationalist firm. Its agricultural machinery factory, the Mill Road Ironworks, employed 300–400 in 1911.[25]

Two advanced engineering firms of the era are also deserving of mention. Though neither were major employers (Grubb had a workforce of 200 in 1919), both had significant international reputations. The Rathmines Observatory Works of father and son Thomas and Howard Grubb had designed and built telescopes for leading observatories in the UK and further afield and were engaged in the design and production of submarine periscopes for the Royal Navy during the First World War. Howard, a Church of Ireland unionist, was knighted in 1887. The Grubb operation relocated to England in 1919.

Edmundson Engineering, too, had largely relocated to England by 1922, where it was reborn as Edmundson's Electricity Corp. Its reputation derived from the gas-lit safety buoys and lighthouse beacons invented by its Scottish-born proprietor, John Wigham, who served as President of the Dublin Chamber of Commerce in the 1890s. These were produced in Dublin and exported across the world. Wigham's Quaker faith led him to turn down the offer of a knighthood for his services to maritime safety. (Thomas Grubb too had been a Quaker.) Wigham was described by the *Irish Times* at his death in 1906 as a 'strong and uncompromising Unionist'.[26]

The Dockyard Company case, however, warns of the danger of assuming an exact overlap between religion and political allegiance. Its principal, Scottish Presbyterian John Smellie, was among a group of Protestant Home Rulers within the business community. Others included various members of the Quaker flour-milling family the Shackletons (though the proprietor

---

[24] Employment at the Rushbrooke and Passage West dockyards in Cork, purchased in 1917 by British firm Furness & Withy, occasionally exceeded 500 but fluctuated with the number of ships under repair.
[25] *Irish Times*, 28 August 1911.
[26] *Irish Times*, 17 November 1906.

of the Anna Liffey mill, George Shackleton, was a committee member of the Irish Unionist Alliance); the Unitarian proprietors of the largest brush making firm I. S. Varian & Co.; bacon curer Alexander Shaw of Limerick; and Robert Woods, proprietor of the largest southern jam and confectionery manufacturer Williams & Woods.

Families other than the Shackletons also displayed evidence of political divisions within their ranks. Though the Smithwicks of Kilkenny were a well-known nationalist family (one had been a leading Repealer with Daniel O'Connell, another a Home Rule MP), John Smithwick, principal of the brewing company, was a signatory to the 1893 Catholic petition against Home Rule.[27] Another signatory was O'Connell's younger son, owner of the Phoenix Brewery in Dublin, who stated in a letter to the *Irish Times* that he was sure that if his father were alive, he would not consent 'to hand over Ireland to the tender mercies of the so-called Nationalist leaders'.[28]

Table 2.1 lists the largest manufacturing employers of the decades prior to independence. Greater reliance is placed on stock-market listings in the construction of Table 2.2, which seeks to identify the largest firms in non-manufacturing sectors. The railway companies and the banks accounted for the vast bulk of Irish stock market capital. The Great Southern & Western Railway Company was the largest private-sector employer south of the future border: its workforce of some 9,000 in 1913 was more than twice that of Guinness. Its long-term chairman was Sir William Goulding. The Gouldings would be criticized by Presbyterian bookseller J. C. M. Eason for the reticence that they and the Arnotts (owners of the *Irish Times* newspaper) displayed in reconciling to the new political dispensation.[29]

The rail transport sector had long been accused of anti-Catholic bias, though a group calling itself the 'Society for the Protection of Protestant Interests' had argued that the sectarian wage disparities then in evidence were ascribable to differences in educational attainment rather than discrimination.[30] The second largest rail company was the Great Northern, whose lines ran from Dublin to Belfast and across the future Northern Ireland. It

---

[27] *Irish Times*, 24 March 1893, 28 March 1893.

[28] *Irish Times*, 31 March 1893.

[29] Louis M. Cullen, *Eason & Son: A History* (Dublin: Eason & Son, 1989), 390. The *Irish Times*, by contrast, described Sir John A. Arnott at his death in 1940 as 'one of the first of his class to accept the new dispensation, and to give the Irish government his whole-hearted support': *Irish Times*, 27 July 1940. Goulding, Arnott, and Sir Harold Nutting had been prominent supporters, along with Lord Iveagh, of Midleton's Unionist Anti-Partition League, which split with the more hard-line Irish Unionist Alliance in 1919: R. B. McDowell, *Crisis and Decline: The Fate of the Southern Unionists* (Dublin: Lilliput Press, 1997), 65.

[30] Society for the Protection of Protestant Interests, *Reply to the Catholic Association and Its Allies, 'the Leader' and 'The Irish Rosary'*, (Dublin: Society for the Protection of Protestant Interests, 1903), 6–8. Unsurprisingly, given their higher average incomes, Protestants continued to have a much higher rate

Table 2.1 Manufacturing firms in southern Ireland employing 500 or more in the decades to independence

Firm	Sector	Religion and political allegiance (or overseas company)	Employment in Free State area	Employment: source
Guinness	Brewing	Protestant unionist (formally foreign-owned)	3,550 (1912)	*Whitaker's Red Book of Commerce* (1912)
W. & R. Jacob	Biscuits	Protestant unionist	3,000 (1914)	*Weekly Irish Times*, 1 August 1914
Condensed Milk Company of Ireland	Dairy produce	Protestant unionist	2,000 (1898) 3,000 (1922)	See references in text
J. & L. F. Goodbody	Jute textiles	Protestant unionist	800 (1920)	Riordan, *Modern Irish Trade* (1920), 140
Kynochs	Chemicals	(British)	2,500 (1918)	*Irish Times*, 16 February 1918
Denny	Bacon	Protestant unionist	*c.* 500 (1900)	See references in text
Bolands	Bread	Catholic nationalist	*c.* 500 (1900)	See references in text
Johnston, Mooney & O'Brien	Bread	Protestant unionist	*c.* 600 (1904)	See references in text
W. and H. M. Goulding	Fertilizer	Protestant unionist	*c.* 800 (1912)	*Whitaker's Red Book of Commerce* (1912)
Dwyer & Co.	Clothing, footwear, furnishings	Catholic nationalist	700 (1918)	*Weekly Irish Times*, 7 December 1918
Bannatyne	Grain Milling	Protestant unionist	*c.* 700 (1920)	See references in text
Blarney Woollen Mills	Woollen textiles	Catholic nationalist	750 (1892) 600 (1919)	*Strattens' South of Ireland* (1892), 199; *Cork: Its Trade and Commerce* (1919), 171
Limerick Clothing Factory	Clothing	Protestant unionist	600 (1914)	*Evening Herald*, 23 September 1914

Cork Spinning & Weaving	Linen	Protestant unionist	1,000 (1919)	*Cork: Its Trade and Commerce* (1919), 173
Greenmount Spinning & Weaving	Linen	Protestant unionist	550 (1922)	*Irish Times*, 7 October 1922
Boyne Weaving	Linen	Protestant, possibly Home Ruler	900 (1910)	*Freemans Journal*, 19 May 1910
Hely	Paper products and printing	Protestant unionist	500 (1916)	*Irish Times*, 10 May 1916
Alexander Thom	Paper products and printing	Protestant unionist	500 (1912)	*Whitaker's Red Book of Commerce* (1912)
Ford	Tractors	(US)	1,429 (1920)	Grimes, *Ford in Cork*, Vol. 1 (2008), 184
Dublin Dockyard Company	Shipbuilding and repair	Protestant Home Ruler	1,000 (1919)	Riordan, *Modern Irish Trade* (1920), 99

Source: author.

employed over 5,000 in 1913 and almost 3,000 in the Free State alone in 1925. Its long-term chairman, Fane Vernon, was a member of the executive committee of the Irish Unionist Alliance. The other large railway companies prior to the amalgamations of the early Free State era were the Midland Great Western (MGW) and the Dublin & South Eastern, both of which were also chaired by unionists.[31] Frank Brooke, chairman and managing director of the Dublin & South Eastern, was assassinated during the War of Independence on suspicion of passing information to the military authorities.

Six of the nine banks operating in the Free State area—the Bank of Ireland, the Provincial, the Royal, and the three Belfast-headquartered institutions— were also unionist in ethos. The other three—the National, the Hibernian, and the Munster & Leinster—were broadly nationalist.[32] A historian of the

of participation in education post-independence: *Investment in Education: Report of the Survey Team appointed by the Minister for Education in October, 1962* (Dublin: Stationery Office, 1965), para. 6.116.

[31] The MGW was chaired for almost forty years by Sir Ralph Cusack, upon whose death the position passed to his son-in-law (*Irish Times*, 4 March 1910).

[32] Campbell, *The Irish Establishment, 1879–1914*, 195. The Bank of Ireland had a complement of 550 officials in 1914: Oliver MacDonagh, 'The Victorian Bank, 1824–1914', in *Bank of Ireland, 1783–1983: Bicentenary Essays*, ed. F. S. L. Lyons (Dublin: Gill and Macmillan, 1983), 41. The National had a more extensive branch network and employed around 600 in 1919: Emmet Oliver, 'The Business of Dublin in the Early 20th Century: An Overview of the Retail and Financial Sectors', *Dublin Historical Record* 71, 2 (2018): 236–50. The National Bank also had a number of branches in Britain.

Table 2.2 Non-manufacturing firms in southern Ireland employing 500 or more in the decades to independence

Firm	Sector	Religion and political allegiance (or overseas company)	Employment in Free State area	Employment: source
Great Southern & Western Railway Company	Rail	Protestant unionist	8,893 (1913)	*Railway Companies: Staff and Wages* (London, 1913)
Great Northern Railway Company	Rail	Protestant unionist	5,460 in Ireland (1913)	*Railway Companies: Staff and Wages* (London, 1913);
			3,000 in Free State alone (1925)	*Returns of Railway Companies* (Dublin, 1926), 61
Midland Great Western	Rail	Protestant unionist	3,451 (1913)	*Railway Companies: Staff and Wages* (London, 1913)
Dublin & South Eastern	Rail	Protestant unionist, (Catholic nationalist from 1921)	1,373 (1913)	*Railway Companies: Staff and Wages* (London, 1913)
Bank of Ireland	Banking	Protestant unionist	550 (1914)	See references in text
National Bank	Banking	Catholic nationalist	*c.* 600 (1919)	See references in text
Pim Brothers	Retail	Protestant unionist	600 (1894)	*Irish Times*, 14 November 1894
Eason & Son	Printing, retail, and wholesale	Protestant nationalist	*c.* 500 (1915)	Cullen, *Eason & Son* (1989), 283
Alliance and Dublin Consumers Gas Company	Gas	Mixed unionist and nationalist	≥ 750 (1917)	*Freemans Journal*, 7 November 1917
Dublin United Tramways Company	Tramways	Catholic nationalist	750–2,000 (1913)	See references in text

Source: author.

Bank of Ireland points out that 'even in the Catholic south, there were fair-sized branches where, as late as the 1890s, the entire staff belonged to the Church of Ireland'.[33] The directors of the bank in the pre-independence era 'were unionists to a man, and the great majority of staff would have regarded themselves as "loyalists"'.[34] A similar situation prevailed across the rest of the financial sector. Both the president and secretary of the Institute of Chartered Accountants were Protestant, as were most of the council and all of the partners of the dominant firms, Craig Gardner and Stokes Brothers & Pim.[35] Robert Stokes and Sir Robert Gardner were among the 150 southern business leaders to criticize the Home Rule bill in 1913.

Of the seven major Dublin department stores of the period, only Clerys was under Catholic nationalist control, though Brown Thomas was purchased in 1919 by the London-based US entrepreneur Harry Gordon Selfridge.[36] Pim Brothers' drapery and furniture store on South Great George's Street, which had a workforce of 600 in 1894, appears to have been the largest among the group.[37] Easons, a major wholesaler and retailer of printed materials, had a Free State area workforce of 500 or so in 1915. Though Presbyterian, the Easons were nationalist in their sympathies.[38]

The builders' suppliers sector would remain Protestant-dominated until at least the 1960s. By the end of the nineteenth century, Brooks Thomas and Dockrells had emerged as the leading incumbents. Maurice Brooks, founder of the former, was described at his death in 1905 as having been a Liberal MP in the days before Home Rule became the defining political issue. He was succeeded as chairman by his son-in-law, Richard Gamble, a member of the City of Dublin Unionist Association. Sir Maurice Dockrell, Brooks's nephew, would serve as one of the few unionist MPs elected for a southern Irish constituency in 1918. Leading firms in cognate sectors included the Dublin timber firm T. & C. Martin, whose proprietors were Catholic unionists. The principals of J. & P. Good, one of the largest building contractors, and of Heitons and Tedcastle McCormick, the largest coal-distribution companies, were prominent unionists, as were the Findlaters, proprietors of a well-known

---

[33] MacDonagh, 'The Victorian Bank, 1824–1914', 44.

[34] Ibid., 44.

[35] Tony Farmar, *The Versatile Profession: A History of Accountancy in Ireland since 1850* (Dublin: Chartered Accountants Ireland, 2013), 65.

[36] Frank Barry, 'The Life and Death of Protestant Businesses in Independent Ireland', in *Protestant and Irish: The Minority's Accommodation with Independent Ireland*, ed. Ian d'Alton and Ida Milne (Cork: Cork University Press, 2019), 155–70.

[37] Its nominal capital was bigger than both Arnott's and Clery's (Oliver, 'The Business of Dublin in the Early 20th Century: An Overview of the Retail and Financial Sectors'). Arnott's employed around 200 at the time: Ronald Nesbitt, *At Arnotts of Dublin, 1843–1993* (Dublin: A. & A. Farmar, 1993), 37.

[38] Cullen, *Eason & Son: A History*, 138–39.

chain of retail stores and other businesses. The Findlaters, Tedcastles, Heitons, and Hewats (who controlled Heitons from the time of the founder's death) were of Scottish Presbyterian stock.

The Alliance & Dublin Consumers Gas Company and the Dublin United Tramways Company were among the few large businesses not to conform to this general pattern. The gas company was a quasi-regulated monopoly provider of public lighting whose origins as an 1866 amalgamation of existing gas companies left a legacy of political diversity on its board. It was chaired until 1914 by William F. Cotton, a Home Rule MP. Cotton was succeeded in the role by John Murphy, a member of a leading Catholic unionist shipping family.[39] The Gas Company employed at least 750 and perhaps substantially more in 1917. The Dublin United Tramways Company (DUTC) was part of the business empire of the leading Catholic nationalist industrialist, William Martin Murphy. Murphy was also proprietor of the best-selling newspaper, the *Irish Independent*, and part-owner of Dublin department store Clerys. His various enterprises are likely to have employed at least 1,500 in the late 1910s.[40]

Tables 2.1 and 2.2 show, in summary, that of the 44,000 workers employed in the large firms identified, more than three-quarters were in businesses under Protestant and unionist control. The claim made by an anti-Home Rule writer in 1912 that few among the large employers 'are in a position to help the Unionist cause effectively, for they have to deal with strike makers and possible boycotters' would appear to have been without foundation.[41] The political sympathies of the large business owners were well known, and even smaller unionist employers made little if any effort to hide their politics. The first strike in the Guinness brewery's history was in 1974, and though Jacobs was centrally involved in the bitter industrial relations dispute of 1913, union leader James Larkin's main antagonist was the nationalist industrialist William Martin Murphy.

That most of the firms, and all of the larger ones, would have had predominantly Catholic nationalist workforces would have shielded them from political or religiously motivated boycotts. Attacks on Goodbody properties ceased when the family warned that their operations might be closed down. Boycotts could be more effectively directed against retailers and distributors, and fear

[39] Cornelius F. Smith, *The Shipping Murphys: The Palgrave Murphy Shipping Line 1850–1926* (Dublin: Albany Press, 2004), 117. John Murphy's father, Michael, had attended the Dublin Unionist Convention of 1892 and was a signatory to the 1893 Catholic petition against Home Rule.

[40] The DUTC employed close to 2,000 in 1929, by which time it operated bus as well as tram services (*Weekly Irish Times*, 24 August 1929). Its workforce numbered at least 750 in 1913 (*Weekly Irish Times*, 30 August 1913).

[41] Simon Rosenbaum, ed., *Against Home Rule: The Case for the Union* (London: F. Warne, 1912), 186.

of antagonizing nationalist customers is understood to have conditioned the behaviour of the retail banks. In the case of manufacturing, the boycott was a blunter instrument. It proved impossible, for example, to discriminate other than by geography in the 1920–1922 nationalist boycott of Belfast goods, and though the Prime Minister of the new Northern Ireland administration believed that 'a boycott of stout would be impossible', handbills advocating a counter-boycott urged the local population to 'cease purchasing all southern goods' including stout, whiskey, and biscuits, even though these were produced almost exclusively by firms in southern unionist ownership.[42]

The data in Table 2.1 also tell us something about the degree of concentration in southern manufacturing, and, by extension, the degree of power in local labour markets these firms would have possessed. The top twenty employers accounted for some 35 per cent of manufacturing employment in the Free State area. In Britain, the top 100—though of vastly greater average size—accounted for only 13 per cent of the equivalent workforce.[43]

2.2 Political and Economic Perspectives on the Union, Home Rule, and Secession

The ethno-religious divide was clearly the major determinant of the overwhelmingly unionist disposition of the business establishment of the time. One future Northern Ireland Finance Minister observed in 1911 that 'the feeling against Home Rule is more religious than economic'.[44] Unionism and Protestantism were intertwined with a sense of class and cultural superiority. One prominent southern unionist described the residences of the landed elite as 'oases of culture, of uprightness and of fair dealing, in what will otherwise be a desert of dead uniformity [where] lofty ideals, whether of social or imperial interest, will be smothered in an atmosphere of superstition, greed and chicanery'.[45]

Southern Protestants were fearful of the hostile environment they might face under a new political dispensation. Sir William Goulding was part of a Church of Ireland delegation that met with Michael Collins and William T. Cosgrave in May 1922 to inquire whether 'the Government was desirous

[42] David S. Johnson, 'The Belfast Boycott, 1920–1922', in *Irish Population, Economy, and Society: Essays in Honour of the Late K. H. Connell*, ed. J. M. Goldstrom and L. A. Clarkson (Oxford: Clarendon Press, 1981), 294–97.

[43] Barry, 'Business Establishment Opposition to Southern Ireland's Exit from the United Kingdom'.

[44] Liam Kennedy, *Colonialism, Religion and Nationalism in Ireland* (Belfast: Institute of Irish Studies, 1996), xiii.

[45] J. M. Wilson, cited in Patrick Buckland, *Irish Unionism 1: The Anglo-Irish and the New Ireland, 1885–1922* (Dublin: Gill and Macmillan, 1972), xxi.

of retaining them or whether, in the alternative, it was desired that they should leave the country'.[46] A changing of the guard would obviously hold little appeal for any class that faced displacement: the middle-class Catholic nationalists who were readying themselves for power in a Home Rule administration felt similarly aggrieved when they perceived their position to be usurped by the interlopers of Sinn Féin after the 1918 general election.[47]

The 1893 Catholic petition against Home Rule demonstrates, however, that there was a more general economic and business dimension to the political divide. Though Catholic merchants had played an important role in the Limerick Chamber of Commerce since its foundation, a history of the organization notes that its ethos was fundamentally unionist until the 1920s.[48] Similarly, the Dublin Chamber of Commerce, while noting that 'as a corporate body we have no politics', described itself in 1892 as 'essentially a unionist chamber [. . .] solely and simply because in defending the union we are defending the commercial interests with which we are identified'.[49]

Nationalists and unionists differed in their assessments of the economic consequences of the Union. Nationalists had come to blame southern deindustrialization on the economic integration that followed the passage of the Act of Union, while the inadequate response to the Great Famine of the 1840s was ascribed to a distant and uncaring government. Though some unionists accepted that the arrangement may not have worked perfectly in the past, they pointed to the benefits that had been delivered since the 1890s, by far the most significant of which was the extensive land redistribution that had been funded by loans from the British Treasury. None of the other constituent parts of the United Kingdom had benefited from such a policy, much to the chagrin of politicians in Scotland and Wales.[50] Democratic local government had also been established, as had bodies such as the Congested Districts Board and an Irish Department of Agriculture and Technical Instruction. Educational provision had been improved and subsidies granted to the post office, housing, and other areas.[51]

Though the UK Pensions Act of 1908 had been designed with the industrial population of Great Britain in mind, the same rates were payable across the United Kingdom under the unified system of administration. As Ireland was

---

[46] *Weekly Irish Times*, 20 May 1922.

[47] John M. Regan, *The Irish Counter-Revolution, 1921–1936: Treatyite Politics and Settlement in Independent Ireland* (Dublin: Gill and Macmillan, 2001), 245.

[48] Matthew Potter, *Limerick's Merchants: Traders and Shakers* (Limerick: Limerick Chamber, 2015), 76.

[49] Cited in Enda MacMahon, *A Most Respectable Meeting of Merchants, Dublin Chamber of Commerce: A History* (Dublin: Londubh Books, 2014), 140.

[50] Seán Kenny and Eoin McLaughlin, 'The Political Economy of Secession: Lessons from the Early Years of the Irish Free State'. *National Institute Economic Review*, 261, 1 (2022): 48–78

[51] Kennedy, *Colonialism, Religion and Nationalism in Ireland*, 58–59. These arguments are presented in detail in the 1912 publication, Rosenbaum, *Against Home Rule: The Case for the Union*.

substantially poorer than Britain, pension payments accounted for a much higher share of Irish national income.[52] Such financial support, unionists argued, rested on the fiscal capacity of the British state, which Ireland on its own could never hope to match. The Irish stock market, furthermore, had fallen on occasion with news of progress towards the enactment of Home Rule, lending credence to the 1913 warning by 150 'Tory business leaders' that it would raise the cost of finance and drive capital and industry from the country.

The costs and benefits of prospective trade protection were a further major point of divergence between the two sides. Edward Carson, the Dublin-born leader of northern unionism, warned in 1921 that concerns over the potential industrial consequences of fiscal autonomy, which it was presumed would lead inexorably to trade barriers between Ireland and Britain, meant that Ulster 'would not agree to it'.[53] Southern unionists had expressed similar fears at a meeting chaired by Lord Ardilaun in 1911.[54] Horace Plunkett, chairman of the Irish Convention, the body established by the British in 1917 to try to secure agreement on an all-Ireland Home Rule solution, stated that the difficulties encountered 'may be summed up in two words: Ulster and Customs'.[55] Britain too wished to retain control of trade policy and conceded fiscal autonomy only towards the end of the Anglo-Irish Treaty negotiations of 1921.

Unionists differed from the majority of nationalists in their commitment to the imperial project. They argued, furthermore, that 'to ignore imperial security [. . .] is to prejudice Irish as well as imperial interests'.[56] Southern unionists proposed at the Irish Convention that customs revenue be retained by Westminster as a contribution to war debt and defence. This would have achieved other of their aims as well, however, including ensuring continued representation in the imperial parliament. In an apparent conciliatory response to nationalists, they made the unorthodox suggestion that control of excise be separated from customs and delegated to any prospective new Irish parliament. By a happy coincidence, this would have protected the Irish brewing and distilling industries from the temperance-oriented British parliamentarians of the era.[57]

---

[52] Cormac Ó Gráda, '"The Greatest Blessing of All": The Old Age Pension in Ireland'. *Past & Present* 175, 1 (2002): 124–61.

[53] Cited in Barry, 'Business Establishment Opposition to Southern Ireland's Exit from the United Kingdom'. On the resistance of Ulster industry, see also Horace Plunkett, *Report of the Proceedings of the Irish Convention* (Dublin: HM Stationery Office 1918).

[54] McDowell, *Crisis and Decline: The Fate of the Southern Unionists*, 46. See also Buckland, *Irish Unionism 1: The Anglo-Irish and the New Ireland*, 326.

[55] Plunkett, *Report of the Proceedings of the Irish Convention*, 5.

[56] Buckland, *Irish Unionism 1: The Anglo-Irish and the New Ireland, 1885–1922*, 106.

[57] Ibid., 109–18. Buckland reports that unionists at the Convention 'talked over fiscal problems with the Guinnesses' (99).

Southern unionists were fearful of possible expropriation by a radical, vengeful, or sectarian Dublin parliament. They also feared the enactment of 'hasty legislative proposals at the expense of the 350,000 loyalists who will be practically unrepresented but who pay most of the taxes'.[58] They professed themselves sceptical of nationalist competence on fiscal matters. Southern unionist business leaders had argued in 1893 that Home Rule would place businessmen at the mercy of 'professional politicians without [. . .] any experience of affairs except what may be acquired in the constant practice of sending round the hat'.[59] Lord Midleton complained to Churchill in 1922 that

> The people are exceedingly ignorant [and] morally cowards [. . .] Greatest extravagancies will probably be proposed and the proceedings in the Dail Eireann [sic] show you how the government are likely to have their hands forced.[60]

That Ireland was overtaxed had long been an article of nationalist faith. Though supported by the findings of a British parliamentary committee in the 1890s, a follow-up report of 1912 found that the balance between expenditures and revenues had since been reversed. The old-age pension was the subject of particular comment. The 1912 report regarded it as 'absolutely certain' that a pensions act designed by an Irish Parliament 'would not have been of such a costly character as to absorb at one stroke nearly one-third of the total revenue of the country'.[61]

Many, or most, on the nationalist side appear to have assumed that self-government would rapidly bring prosperity. Tom Kettle, one-time Home Rule MP and first professor of national economics at University College Dublin, argued that much of the fiscal burden was the result of past misgovernment. Arthur Griffith, founder of Sinn Féin, saw no reason why the island could not provide a living for a population of 15 million. Erskine Childers was one of the few to acknowledge publicly the financial difficulties that would have to be faced, particularly with regard to pensions.[62]

Southern unionists also raised economic concerns over partition when it emerged onto the policy agenda. A customs frontier between the two parts of Ireland would undoubtedly cause disruption. A report from Belfast

---

[58] Ibid., 266. The Guinness brewery alone was said to pay 'something like four millions to the revenue': ibid., 218. It was claimed in 1923 to pay in income tax and excise duties 'about ten millions a year to the revenues of the Free State Government' (*Roscommon Herald*, 1 December 1923).

[59] Philip Ollerenshaw, 'Businessmen and the Development of Ulster Unionism, 1886–1921'. *Journal of Imperial and Commonwealth History* 28, 1 (2000): 47.

[60] Buckland, *Irish Unionism 1: The Anglo-Irish and the New Ireland, 1885–1922*, 267.

[61] *Irish Times*, 20 April 1912.

[62] Erskine Childers, *The Framework of Home Rule* (London: Edward Arnold, 1911).

to London immediately prior to its establishment noted that 'Dublin sends large consignments of Guinness's stout and porter, as well as spirits, mineral waters, tobacco, matches, biscuits, confectionary and provisions into Northern Ireland.'[63] The southern linen supply chain was particularly vulnerable, as noted in a newspaper report from 1923, which pointed out that the linen trade in the South

> is almost entirely dependent on the North for its supplies. Goods are also sent backwards and forwards across the border for dyeing, bleaching, etc., and if these movements are to be made more difficult and expensive it will certainly mean that an already hard-hit industry cannot be carried on.[64]

The Dublin Chamber of Commerce had warned that partition would exacerbate the lack of economic expertise by depriving the prospective southern parliament 'of the steadying influence and business training of the men of Ulster.'[65] It also expressed concern at the costliness of the further duplication of administrative machinery that partition would entail.[66]

Business leaders proved, towards the end, to be among the more pragmatic within the southern unionist community. Midleton informed the British cabinet in 1921 that 'almost all the most influential businessmen and the largest landowners in the south' were now 'willing to concede their financial interest to an Irish parliament rather than face the continuance of the chaos of the last 15 years.'[67] Walter Guinness pronounced in parliament that the only alternative to the Treaty was chaos: 'In accepting it they might be embarking on a slippery slope, but a slippery slope was preferable to a precipice.'[68]

2.3 Vestiges of Pre-1922 Divisions in Irish Business Life

That the business establishment inherited by the new state had been predominantly unionist would constrain economic policymaking, particularly in the 1920s but also further into the future. It would take many more decades for

---

[63] Cited in Catherine Nash, Lorraine Dennis, and Brian Graham, 'Putting the Border in Place: Customs Regulation in the Making of the Irish Border, 1921–1945'. *Journal of Historical Geography* 36, 4 (2010): 421–31.

[64] *Irish Times*, 3 March 1923.

[65] *Irish Times*, 1 June 1920.

[66] Louis M. Cullen, *Princes & Pirates: The Dublin Chamber of Commerce, 1783–1983* (Dublin: Dublin Chamber of Commerce, 1983), 93.

[67] Buckland, *Irish Unionism 1: The Anglo-Irish and the New Ireland, 1885–1922*, 218.

[68] McDowell, *Crisis and Decline: The Fate of the Southern Unionists*, 112.

the sectarian divisions in Irish business life to be eroded. Though recruitment of a predominantly Catholic staff became inevitable in many companies due to the decline of the Protestant population south of the border, it has been suggested that 'until the 1960s at least, the Catholic and Protestant communities essentially lived apart [. . .] in a kind of mutually agreed apartheid'.[69] A survey of South Dublin Protestants conducted in the 1980s revealed that most who had entered the labour market prior to 1955 had found their first jobs in workplaces where the majority of their co-workers were Protestant.[70] When the *Irish Times* asked a group of several dozen young Protestants in 1965 if there was any discrimination that might influence their choice of career, no one could think of any. Their response had been that 'there are plenty of Protestant employers'.[71]

The extent to which this 'apartheid' was 'mutually agreed' can be exaggerated: the situation undoubtedly caused resentment. Businessman Michael Smurfit recalls in his autobiography that there were many companies, even in the 1960s, where Catholics could never join the management team, 'no matter how good they were at their job', while Catholic firms such as his found it difficult to make sales to Protestant companies.[72] Catholic blame was frequently directed towards the Masonic Order, which had seen an upsurge in membership in the 1920s. Though there were suspicions of discrimination on the Catholic side as well, the Knights of Columbanus, which had been established as a counterweight to the Freemasons and moved its headquarters south of the border in the 1920s, are not considered to have gained as much of a foothold in business life.

'Empire loyalists' continued to find favour in Guinness's recruitment to management positions, and oral history accounts of working life in Jacobs refer to a strong Masonic influence in recruitment and promotion.[73] Even in services sectors, which might have been expected to have been more sensitive to consumer sentiment, change was slow. Though the proportion of Catholics to Protestants among the directors of the Bank of Ireland is estimated to have increased from one-third in the late 1930s to approximately two-thirds some thirty years later, Catholics made up more than 95 per cent of the population of the state at the latter date.[74] Craig Gardner, the

[69] Terence Brown, *The Irish Times: 150 Years of Influence* (London: Bloomsbury, 2015), 293.

[70] Kurt Bowen, *Protestants in a Catholic State: Ireland's Privileged Minority* (Dublin: Gill and Macmillan, 1983), 95.

[71] *Irish Times*, 23 March 1965.

[72] Michael Smurfit, *A Life Worth Living: Michael Smurfit's Autobiography* (Dublin: Oak Tree Press, 2014), 79–80.

[73] On Guinness, see Finbarr Flood, *In Full Flood: A Memoir* (Dublin: Liberties Press, 2006), 74; W. & R. Jacob & Co. Oral History Collection, South Dublin Libraries.

[74] Francis Stewart Leland Lyons, 'Reflections on a Bicentenary', in *Bank of Ireland 1783–1983, Bicentenary Essays*, ed. Lyons, 207–208.

largest accountancy firm, appointed its first Catholic partner in 1944. The first appointment of a Catholic to the board of Easons came in 1947: economist and statistician R. C. Geary would later recall that he had been 'particularly struck by [the appointment of] a young Catholic graduate friend of mine to executive rank and later to a directorship [. . .] That would occasion no comment now. It did then.'[75] The last vestiges of these divisions disappeared with the opening up of the economy in the 1960s and 1970s, as will be discussed in a later chapter.

Appendix 2.1 Business Establishment Unionist Affiliations

It was suggested in the text that the political sympathies of most business leaders would have been well known. Table 2.3 provides evidence on the unionist affiliations of leading business proprietors.

Table 2.3 Selected sources on unionist affiliations

Source	Business leaders
Great Unionist Demonstration, Dublin (1887)	Lord Ardilaun, James Talbot Power, John Jameson, Sir John Arnott, T. P. Cairnes, Maurice Dockrell, Robert Tedcastle, Pim (various), Goodbody (various)[a]
Unionist Convention for the Provinces of Leinster, Munster and Connaught, Dublin (1892)	J. F. G. Bannatyne, Pim (various), T. P. Cairnes, Maurice E. Dockrell, George Pollexfen, Sir Richard Martin, Lord Ardilaun, Sir John Arnott, Goodbody (various), W. J. Goulding, Lord Iveagh, John Jameson, Whyte family of Balbriggan (various), Beamish (various), George Pollexfen, Sir John Power, F. H. Thompson, T. H. Cleeve, Sir Ralph Cusack[b]
Others listed as unionist in the 1890s	Sir Henry Cochrane[c], Frank Brooke[d], Michael Murphy[e], James Ogilvie[f] Howard Grubb[g]
Catholic Petition against Home Rule (1893)	Charles and Richard Martin, James and John Talbot Power, John Smithwick, Michael Murphy[h]
Irish Unionist Alliance (1913)	Sir John Arnott, Cairnes (various), Sir Maurice Dockrell, Sir Robert Gardner, Sir William Goulding, Goodbody (various), Guinness (various), William Hewat, G. N. Jacob, Jameson (various), F. V. Martin, J. Mooney, Sir John Nutting, Pim (various), J. F. Stokes, Fane Vernon[i]
South County Dublin Unionist Registration Association (1915)	Viscount Iveagh, Sir Maurice Dockrell, Sir Stanley Cochrane, Andrew Jameson, Frank V. Martin, Sir John Nutting, James Talbot Power[j]

Continued

[75] Cited in Cullen, *Eason & Son: A History*, 385.

Table 2.3 *Continued*

Source	Business leaders
Irish Unionist Alliance (1919–1920)	Sir John Arnott, Guinness (various), Odlum (various), W. P. Cairnes, C. E. Denny, George Shackleton,[k] Sharman Crawford[l]
Unionist Anti-Partition League (1919)	Sir John Arnott, John Good, Sir William Goulding, Guinness (various), Viscount Iveagh, Andrew Jameson, John Mooney, Sir Harold Nutting[m]

Note: In the vast majority of cases, these were delegates or officials rather than ordinary members of the various associations.
Source: author.
[a] *Irish Times*, 3 December 1887.
[b] Unionist Convention for Provinces of Leinster, Munster and Connaught. 'Report of Proceedings, Lists of Committees, Delegates', Irish Unionist Alliance, 1892.
[c] *Irish Times*, 18 June 1892.
[d] *Irish Times*, 18 April 1896.
[e] MacMahon, *A Most Respectable Meeting of Merchants, Dublin Chamber of Commerce: A History*, 139.
[f] *Freemans Journal*, 29 November 1897.
[g] *Irish Times*, 18 November 1893.
[h] *Irish Times*, 15 and 24 March 1893.
[i] *Irish Independent*, 17 November 1913.
[j] *Irish Independent*, 4 June 1915.
[k] *30th Annual Report, 1919–1920* (Dublin: Irish Unionist Alliance, 1920).
[l] *Irish Independent*, 22 January 1921.
[m] *Irish Times*, 28 January 1919.

3
Firms of Note in 1922

Though the Irish Free State was predominantly agricultural at its establishment in 1922, several local manufacturing firms had significant international reputations. The Guinness brewery at St James's Gate was reputed to be the largest in the world, and biscuit-maker W. & R. Jacob's Dublin factory remained far larger at the time than its recently established branch plant near Liverpool. Bacon curer Henry Denny and tobacco manufacturer P. J. Carroll also had substantial export trades, as did some of the country's textiles producers, distilleries, and other firms in particular niche areas. Very many more firms had significant reputations within the home market of course: manufactured goods (including processed foods) made up 50 per cent of the consumer price index of the 1920s, and in a number of sub-sectors the domestic market was dominated by local producers.

This chapter provides an outline of the histories of the notable manufacturing firms in operation in the Free State at independence, many of which appear in the pages of James Joyce's *Ulysses*, which is set in the Dublin of 1904. Those that employed a workforce of 500 or more at any stage through to 1972 will surface again in later chapters. Many other company names from the period survive as well-known brands down to the present day.

3.1 Food, Drink, and Tobacco

Almost all of the processed products tested for a series of articles in the British medical journal *The Lancet* in the 1850s had been found to have been adulterated. Notwithstanding the significant legislation that followed, the persistence of careless or fraudulent practices made brand names of particular importance in Food, drink, and tobacco. Irish sectors varied substantially in terms of the quality and consistency of their produce, the factors on which the value of their brands depended. Bacon brands were valuable and guarded jealously; Irish butter was largely unbranded and had a poor reputation. Guinness prosecuted those engaged in adulteration; Irish whiskey brands were less well protected.

Industry and Policy in Independent Ireland, 1922–1972. Frank Barry, Oxford University Press.
© Frank Barry (2023). DOI: 10.1093/oso/9780198878230.003.0003

Table 3.1 Free State Census of Industrial Production (CIP), 1926: Food, Drink, and Tobacco

Sector	Employment, 1926 (excluding out-workers)
Bacon curing	1,823
Butter, cheese, condensed milk, and margarine	3,261
Grain milling	3,012
Bread, biscuits, and flour confectionery	8,129
Sugar confectionery and jam making	2,174
Brewing	4,625
Malting	945
Distilling of spirits	429
Aerated waters, ciders, cordials, and cognate liquors	1,001
Tobacco	2,096

Source: author.

Table 3.1 shows the distribution of employment across the various subsectors of Food, drink, and tobacco in 1926, the first year for which the Free State Census of Industrial Production was produced. Though employment levels would have been somewhat different in 1922, the numbers provided give a sense of the extent to which the leading firms dominated within each sub-sector. Brewing and bacon curing were highly concentrated, flour milling and bread production much less so. In some industries, the same firms would remain dominant throughout the entire period to European Economic Community (EEC) accession. In others, such as flour milling and tobacco, the largest firms at the end of Cumann na nGaedheal's period in office had been established in the Free State only over the previous decade. The order in which sectors are discussed largely follows that of the census.

Bacon Curing

Bacon curing was concentrated primarily in the dairying regions of Munster, where pigs were raised on the milk that had been skimmed to extract butterfat. The hugely popular 'Limerick mild cure' dated from the 1880s.[1] Several firms, including the market leaders Henry Denny & Sons and O'Mara Bacon,

---

[1] Alexander Shaw, 'The Irish Bacon-Curing Industry', in *Ireland: Industrial and Agricultural*, ed. Department of Agriculture and Technical Instruction (Dublin: Brown and Nolan, 1902), 254.

held patents on aspects of the curing process and Irish produce—particularly of Limerick origin—sold at a premium on the London and US markets.

By the turn of the century, Limerick had overtaken Waterford as the centre of the bacon export trade. Waterford-based Denny had several plants in each of the cities as well as elsewhere in Munster. The other major Limerick operations—O'Maras, Mattersons, and Shaws—were run by local families. The acquisition by one of the O'Maras of the old Liberties firm Donnellys in 1907 gave them control of much of the Dublin trade. By the 1930s, the O'Maras—whose family firm would be renamed the Bacon Company of Ireland in 1938—also had plants in Claremorris and Letterkenny.

The two largest bacon curers identified in Table 3.2 were among the earliest Irish multinationals. Denny opened a factory in Chicago in 1882 and E. M. Denny—a sister company established by one of the founder's sons who had moved to England to oversee their London agency—later took ownership of the largest private bacon company in Denmark. The O'Maras bought the rights to the Russian Bacon Company in 1891 and ran the operation, located at a rail junction 400 kilometres southeast of Moscow, for more than a decade. In 1902, they invested in an enterprise in the Balkans to which they brought over several of their Limerick staff to train the local workers in how to produce the types of bacon most highly prized on the London market.[2]

The individual bacon factories typically employed in the region of 100–200 workers. Denny employed around 500 across its various plants in peacetime and perhaps substantially more during the First World War when E. M. Denny was official supplier to the war office. Control passed to the London sister company on the death of Charles Edward Denny in 1927. It would be among those derided as 'pseudo-Irish' by National Farmers' Association president Rikard Deasy in 1966.[3] Most of its operations had

Table 3.2 Employment in major bacon-curing firms

Henry Denny & Sons (1820)	500 (1900), 400 (1931), 500 (1935, 1960), 700 (1968), *c.* 400 (1972)
O'Maras (1839)/Bacon Company of Ireland (1938)	*c.* 400 (1920s–1930s), 500 (1960), 300 (1971)

Source: author.

[2] Patricia Lavelle, *James O'Mara: A Staunch Sinn Féiner, 1873–1948* (Dublin: Clonmore and Reynolds, 1961).

[3] *Irish Times*, 28 June 1966. Others included Lunham Bros, which had been sold to a UK concern in 1928, and the Castlebar Bacon Company, which was British-owned from its establishment in 1917.

transferred to Northern Ireland by then to avail of easier access to the British market.

While bacon curers and farmers battled over pig prices, there were instances of cooperation on product quality.[4] There were linkages, too, beyond the immediate sector. Daniel Denny, a younger brother of Henry, established a factory in Waterford to produce wrapping materials for the bacon trade, as J. & L.F. Goodbody also did at Clara. Gouldings opened plants in Waterford and Limerick to source dried blood from the bacon factories for use as an organic fertilizer.

By the time of EEC accession, many of the older firms had been acquired and newer, larger, more diversified food producers had come to dominate the sector. The oldest surviving bacon factory in the country, the Denny facility near Gracedieu in Waterford City, closed in 1972.

Dairy Products and Margarine

The highly variable quality of Irish farmhouse butter had caused it to be looked upon in Britain 'as only a very second-rate article'.[5] These problems persisted into the creamery era initiated by the invention of the mechanical separator by Swedish engineer Gustav de Laval in 1878. Denmark's cooperatives produced butter to a consistently high standard and almost all of it was marketed from the early 1900s under a national trade mark, the 'Lurbrand'. In Ireland, 'production methods were still primitive, and the marketing system, if such it could be called, was deplorable'.[6] Over the fifty years to 1910, Irish butter lost much of its share of the British market to Denmark.

At home, private and cooperative creameries battled for control of the sector. The 'war of attrition' began around 1900 when two-thirds of creameries were in private ownership, many of them branches of British enterprises.[7] By 1920, two-thirds were cooperatives.[8] The remaining privately owned monolith was the Condensed Milk Company of Ireland. At its collapse in the

---

[4] Edward J. Riordan, *Modern Irish Trade and Industry* (London, New York: Metheuen, E. P. Dutton, 1920), 80.

[5] *Strattens' Dublin, Cork and South of Ireland: A Literary, Commercial and Social Review, with a Description of Leading Mercantile Houses and Commercial Enterprises* (London: Stratten & Stratten, 1892), 152.

[6] Patrick Bolger, *The Irish Co-operative Movement: Its History and Development* (Dublin: Institute of Public Administration, 1977), 64.

[7] P. F. Fox and Proinnsias Breathnach, 'Proprietary Creameries in Ireland', in *Butter in Ireland: From Earliest Times to the 21st Century*, ed. Peter Foynes, Colin Rynne, and Chris Synnott (Cork: Cork Butter Museum, 2014), 67–70.

[8] Ibid.; William Jenkins, *Tipp Co-op: Origin and Development of Tipperary Co-operative Creamery Ltd* (Dublin: Geography Publications, 1999), 50.; Bolger, *The Irish Co-operative Movement*, 196–98.

early 1920s, it employed a workforce of 3,000 across Munster, including 500 at its Lansdowne headquarters in Limerick City.[9] The individual cooperatives were tiny by comparison. Even by the 1930s, Mitchelstown's workforce remained below 200. The majority employed fewer than ten people.

The history of the Condensed Milk Company serves as a microcosm of the political and economic conflicts of the era. It was owned by the Quebec-born Cleeve brothers, the eldest of whom had come to Limerick as a young man to work for his mother's family. Condensed milk had grown in popularity following its use as an army ration during the American civil war. The Cleeves began to manufacture the product at Lansdowne in 1883, along with the tin cans in which it was sold. The company earned massive profits from army contracts during the Boer War and other major conflicts. Condensed milk exports came to fully half the value of Irish brewery exports in 1918.[10] The Cleeves, meanwhile, had expanded into butter, cream, cheese, and toffee, and had established scores of creameries, separating stations, and other operations in Limerick, Tipperary, and adjoining counties. They were more successful than the cooperatives in their quality control processes. While most Irish cheese disappeared from British shelves with the re-emergence of foreign supplies from the end of the First World War in 1918, theirs continued to sell 'for the simple reason that [its quality] was able to challenge comparison with cheese made anywhere'.[11]

The war of attrition involved plants being located overly close to each other to capture local milk supplies. These could not then be operated to sufficient capacity during the winter months. Enemies of the Cleeves complained of their practice of 'sending carts miles away right into suppliers' doors for milk *and paying fancy prices*' (italics added).[12]

That the Cleeves were unionist did not spare their creameries from British military reprisals against the rural population during the war of independence.[13] Their large industrial labour force also rendered them vulnerable to the wave of 'soviet' or 'red flag' agitation that swept the country in the wake of the Russian Revolution. A major cause of the bitter industrial relations environment was the deflation of the years following the end of the First World War, to which businesses responded by attempting to impose wage cuts. For the Condensed Milk Company, the problem was even more acute: the large amounts of produce it held in stock had collapsed in value with the

[9] *Cork Examiner*, 13 May 1922.
[10] Riordan, *Modern Irish Trade and Industry*, 157, 91.
[11] Jenkins, *Tipp Co-op*, 68, 77.
[12] Cited in ibid., 33, 60.
[13] See e.g. *Freemans Journal*, 30 September 1920.

end of the agricultural boom in 1920. Ill will between workers and farmers led to the destruction of plant and equipment during the factory occupations, and further damage was inflicted by the Irregulars during the civil war.[14] The company's collapse in 1923 would lead eventually to the establishment of the Dairy Disposal Company, one of the first state-sponsored bodies of the Free State era.

Though milk distribution is not included in the Census of Industrial Production, the major Dublin distributors—Hughes Brothers of Rathfarnham, Merville Dairies of Finglas, and Tel-el-Kebir of Monkstown—began to pasteurize and bottle their milk supplies in the early 1920s.[15] The H. B. brand of ice cream first appeared on the market in 1926. By the 1960s, the milk distributors had become major employers. Premier Dairies—formed from the amalgamation of Merville, Tel-el-Kebir, and a later entrant, Dublin Dairies—had a workforce of 1,500 at its establishment in 1966. The largest milk distributors are included among the major dairy firms identified in Table 3.3.

There were also in the 1920s two well-known Irish margarine producers. Margarine had been developed by a French chemist in 1869 and Limerick butter merchants W. & C. McDonnell and Cork firm Dowdall, O'Mahoney & Co. had both entered the industry following study visits by the proprietors to Continental Europe. Employment at McDonnells peaked at 400 during the First World War. Its buy-out by the Dutch company Jürgens in 1918 is described in the Unilever archives as 'the first in a wave of post-war competitor acquisitions'.[16] Dowdall, O'Mahoney & Co. remained the smaller of the two. It would be acquired by US firm Kraft Foods in 1969.

Table 3.3 Employment in selected firms in the dairy sector

Condensed Milk Company of Ireland	2,000 (1898), 3,000 (1922)
Merville Dairies (pasteurization, bottling, distribution, ice cream production)	150 (1932), 540 (1960)
Hughes Brothers (as for Merville)	70 (1935), 110 (1941), 800 (1968)

Source: author.

---

[14] Jenkins, *Tipp Co-op*, 73–77.

[15] Tel-el-Kebir, which was founded in 1884, derived its exotic name from a battle in Egypt at which the firm's founder had saved the regimental colours: Pat Doyle and Louis P. F. Smith, *Milk to Market: A History of Dublin Milk Supply* (Dublin: Leinster Milk Producers' Association, 1989), 96–97. It was owned by the Sutton family, the only Catholic proprietors among the group. Merville was owned by the Craigie brothers.

[16] Unilever archives: Unilever Ireland (Holdings) Ltd and Subsidiary Companies: B1752.IRE/WM, 1858.

Bread, Grain Milling, and Flour Confectionery

Bread had displaced the potato as the staple of the Irish diet since the famine of the 1840s. It made up 6 per cent of the consumer price index in the 1920s (ten times its weight in the index for 2022) and an even higher share of wage expenditures.[17] The largest of the many hundreds of substantial bakery companies were the four industrial-scale producers mentioned in the previous chapter. Bolands and Johnston, Mooney & O'Brien also produced the bulk of their own flour: the former since its acquisition of Pim's Mills on Grand Canal Dock in 1873, the latter since its formation in 1889.

By the turn of the century, Bolands had added a further two huge establishments to its original premises on Capel Street: one was in Kingstown (Dun Laoghaire), the other was the massive City of Dublin bakery on Grand Canal Street that would serve as de Valera's headquarters in the 1916 Rising. By 1924, the third largest Dublin producer, Kennedys, had added a further five bakeries to its original establishment on Parnell Street.

Flour milling as a stand-alone activity was dominated by Bannatyne & Sons, with Odlums a distant second. Bannatyne controlled a number of mills in Limerick and elsewhere across Munster as well as the Goodbody mills in Clara. The earliest Odlum mills in Maryborough/Portlaoise dated from 1845. Others had been acquired or established across south Leinster over the following decades. By the 1970s, all of the major bread and flour producers were vertically integrated. Odlums and Kennedys had taken their first steps towards integration in 1924 when they participated in the establishment of the Dublin Port Milling Company, part of the milling complex that comprises the only surviving landmark of majesty in the Dublin docklands of today.

Other grain millers of note in the early Free State era included the Shackletons of County Kildare—extended family of the famous Antarctic explorer—and the Pollexfens of Sligo, maternal family of W. B. Yeats, of whom he wrote with great affection in his various memoirs and his 1914 poem 'Pardon, Old Fathers'. The Pollexfen mills were in Sligo, Mayo, and South Donegal. The Shackleton mills, the most significant of which—the Anna Liffey mill in Lucan—would remain in operation until the 1990s, were in Carlow, Kildare, and Dublin. Polar explorer Ernest Shackleton's branch of the family operated the Barrow Mills in Carlow. These were bankrupted in 1927 and resurrected as the Barrow Milling Company in 1935.

---

[17] *Irish Independent*, 12 May 1928.

'Fancy biscuits' had grown in popularity with the fall in prices that followed the application of steam power to the production process in the 1840s. Brothers William and Robert Jacob, whose family had been bakers of sea biscuits or 'hard tack' in Waterford, opened a substantial new 'steam biscuit factory' in Dublin in 1853 when their recent entry into the market for fancy biscuits proved a success. The British sector was dominated by Quaker firms, which the public regarded as trustworthy. The Jacobs too were Quakers, as were their future partners, the Bewleys.

The company's export trade took off in the 1880s with the launch of the cream cracker, which was developed following a visit by the proprietor to the United States to study the popularity of the American soda biscuit. Two of its other enduring varieties also date from the late Victorian era. Its 'Mikado' capitalized on the wave of orientalism that swept the United Kingdom at the time; its 'Kimberley' was named for the gemstone areas relieved from siege in 1900 during the second Boer War.

Space constraints at the Dublin factory necessitated the use of expensive night-time shift work, and it was reportedly for this reason that a decision was taken to begin construction of a branch plant near Liverpool in 1912. The new factory expanded rapidly due to the 'enormous demand of the army and navy canteens in every part of the world'.[18] Fear of punitive taxation led to the operations being split into separate companies in 1922. By 1932 the workforce at Aintree had grown to equal that of the Dublin plant and by 1954 had expanded to 5,000, more than twice the size of its former parent (Table 3.4). Though the Jacobs were regarded as paternalistic employers, this had not saved them from becoming centrally involved in the bitter Dublin industrial dispute of 1913.

Table 3.4 Employment in selected firms in bread, biscuits, and grain milling

Jacobs (biscuits)	3,000 (1911, 1928), 2,000 (1951), >2,000 (up to 1972)
Bolands (bread and flour)	800 (1888), 420 (1925), 500 (1935), 600 (1939), >500 (to 1972)
Johnston, Mooney & O'Brien (bread and flour)	450 (1936), 600 (1941), >500 (to 1972)
Kennedys (bread)	540 (1948), 400 (1971), closed 1971
Bannatyne/Goodbody (flour)	c. 500 (1900), c. 800 (1929); acquired by Ranks (1930)
Odlums (flour)	300 (1938, 1963), c. 500 (1972), Odlum Group >1,000 (1972)

Source: author.

[18] The Ambassador of Commerce: supplement to Liverpool Daily Post and Mercury, 7 July 1924, 57.

Sugar Confectionery

The structure of the sugar confectionery sector would change dramatically with the Cumann na nGaedheal tariffs of the 1920s. Dublin firm Williams & Woods was by far the largest producer of sweets and jams in the Free State in 1922. The other major jam producer was the Quaker firm Lamb Brothers, originators of the Fruitfield label (Table 3.5). Armagh-based Lambs had opened a factory in Inchicore in 1918 and would transfer its headquarters to Dublin in 1944.

Methodist-owned sweet maker Lemons had relocated to the Confectioners' Hall on Dublin's Sackville Street (now O'Connell Street) in the 1840s. Leopold Bloom, fictional hero of Joyce's *Ulysses*, muses on its signage as he gazes through the window on his wanderings:

> Lozenge and comfit manufacturer to His Majesty the King.
> God. Save. Our. Sitting on his throne sucking red jujubes white.

Lemons had a management relationship with Savoy Cocoa, another retailer-turned-manufacturer, and would take over a recently developed factory of Savoy's in Drumcondra when trade expanded with the tariffs of the mid-1920s. Toffee maker North Kerry Manufacturing (NKM) transferred production from Listowel to Dublin in 1921. NKM and Savoy Cocoa would both be taken over by major UK confectionery manufacturers within a year or so of the Cumann na nGaedheal tariffs coming into effect.

Table 3.5 Employment in selected firms in sugar confectionery

Williams & Woods (1856), Dublin	200 (1897), 477 (1924), >500 (from late 1920s)
Lambs (1918), Dublin	200 (1936), 375 (1960), 300 (1971)

Source: author.

Brewing, Bottling, and Malting

The Guinness brewery at St James's Gate was referred to in an 1889 guide to the breweries of the United Kingdom as 'without doubt the largest establishment of its kind in the world'.[19] A supplement to the *Manchester Guardian* in

---

[19] Alfred Barnard, *The Noted Breweries of Great Britain and Ireland*, Vol. 3 (London: Joseph Causton & Sons, 1889), 3, 6.

1923 noted that its output was considerably greater than the joint output of the next two largest breweries of the time.[20] From the 1820s, with the establishment of a steamer service to Liverpool and the expansion of the British railway network, its growth had been primarily export-driven. Indeed, it was, for a long time, better known in England than in parts of the west of Ireland.[21]

Having abandoned ale brewing at an early stage in its history, the company by the 1920s was producing three basic varieties of stout and porter. Its porter was sold only in Ireland at this stage and was typically consumed on draught. Its main product, Extra Stout, was sold across Britain and Ireland and bottled by specialist firms or by the publicans to whom it was delivered, while Foreign Extra Stout was produced for warmer climatic conditions and exported to more distant locations.[22] Product consistency had been achieved by 1821 by the adoption of a standard procedure for the production of Extra Stout (then known as Extra Superior).[23] Leaving bottling to others was cost-effective but raised the possibility of adulteration, which Guinness countered by appointing travelling investigators and a qualified chemist to support its pursuit of transgressors through the courts.

Employment at St James's Gate exceeded 1,000 by the mid-1800s and had reached 3,500 by the early twentieth century. All of the other Irish breweries were tiny by comparison. Those in operation in the Free State in 1922 are listed in Table 3.6.[24] Three had closed by 1926. Around half of the remainder had closed by 1972. Many of the others had changed hands over the previous two decades.[25]

The fortunes of the bottling and malting industries were closely related to those of Guinness and the distilleries. By 1892, E. & J. Burke had operations in New York and Liverpool as well as in Dublin, and was 'the largest shipper in the world of Guinness's extra foreign stout, and the most extensive exporter

---

[20] *Manchester Guardian Commercial*, 26 July 1923.

[21] Cormac Ó Gráda, 'Triocha bliain ag fás: Some Reflections on a Classic'. Contribution to a conference marking the thirtieth anniversary of the publication of J. J. Lee's *Ireland: Politics and Society*, Royal Irish Academy, 24 April 2019.

[22] Dublin Port and Docks Board, *Dublin Port Yearbook* (Dublin: Dublin Port and Docks Board, 1926), 53. Guinness began to brew draught stout in 1959. Porter production ceased in 1973.

[23] Patrick Lynch and John Vaizey, *Guinness's Brewery in the Irish Economy 1759–1876* (Cambridge: Cambridge University Press, 1960), 160.

[24] The table is compiled from a report in the *Freemans Journal* of 7 March 1917 and from Riordan, *Modern Irish Trade and Industry*, 159–60. A number of others mentioned in these sources had closed by 1922.

[25] Accurate dating is complicated by the fact that the breweries and the brewery companies that operated them are not synonymous. In the case of Watkins, Riordan provides a date of 1736, the company's advertisements referred to its 'celebrated beer and porter, best in 1789, best today', while the company name was adopted only in 1905 when Joseph Watson & Co. merged with Jameson & Pim. As in the case of Guinness, new breweries were frequently constructed on the foundations of existing ones. Beer is said to have been brewed at the Watkins site in Dublin's Liberties since before the dissolution of the monasteries: *Whitaker's Red Book of Commerce, or Who's Who in Business* (London: J. Whitaker and Sons, 1912).

Table 3.6 Free State breweries in operation in 1922

Company, location, and date of establishment	Developments to 1972	Selected employment
Arthur Guinness, St James's Gate, Dublin (1759)	Remains in operation	3,000 (1923), remains generally >3,000 up to 1972
Beamish & Crawford (1792)	Acquired by Canadian Breweries 1962	>100 (1907), 150 (1936), 170 (1962), 350 (1970)
Cairnes: (i) Castlebellingham, County Louth (early eighteenth century); (ii) Drogheda, County Louth (1825)	(i) Castlebellingham brewery closed 1923; (ii) Drogheda brewery acquired by Guinness 1959; closed 1961	(i) 53 (1923) (ii) 207 (1939)
Cherry Bros, Creywell Brewery, New Ross, County Wexford (c. 1830)	Acquired by Guinness 1952; brewery closed 1955 and production moved to Strangman in Waterford	60 (1936)
John D'Arcy and Son, Anchor Brewery, Usher Street, Dublin (1818)	Brewery closed 1926; production moved to Watkins, Jameson & Pim	–
Deasy and Co., Clonakilty, County Cork (1780)	Brewing ceased c. 1940.	30 (1941)
P. & H. Egan, Tullamore, County Offaly (1852)	Brewing ceased c. 1924.	–
Great Northern Brewery, Dundalk, County Louth (1897)	Acquired by Smithwicks 1953; sold to Guinness 1960; converted to production of Harp Lager	24 (1941, 1960), 130 (1971)
P. Kiely and Sons, St Stephen's Brewery, Waterford (1835)	Brewing ceased 1947	20 (1935)
George H. Lett, Mill Park Brewery, Enniscorthy, County Wexford (1810)	Brewing ceased 1956	–
Macardle, Moore and Co., Dundalk (1863)	Acquired by Irish Ale Breweries & Guinness, 1962	90 (1958), 150 (1968)
Mountjoy Brewery (Findlater's), Russell Street, Dublin (1852)	Closed 1956	60 (1935)
James J. Murphy and Co., Lady's Well Brewery, Cork (1856)	Acquired by Watney Mann 1967	216 (1914), 170 (1935), 200 (1960)
Thomas Murphy and Co., Clonmel, County Tipperary (1838)	Closed c. 1928	100 (1910s)

Continued

Table 3.6 *Continued*

Company, location, and date of establishment	Developments to 1972	Selected employment
Robert Perry and Sons, Rathdowney, County Laois (1831)	Acquired by Guinness 1957; closed 1966	80 (1935), 50 (1962), 40 (1966)
E. Smithwick and Sons, St Francis Abbey Brewery, Kilkenny (1710)	Acquired by Irish Ale Breweries & Guinness 1964	110 (1935), 200 (1960)
Strangman, Davis and Co., Waterford (1792)	Closed 1946; acquired and reopened by Guinness 1954	60 (1936)
Watkins, Jameson and Pim, Ardee Street, Dublin (1789)	Closed 1937	100 (1937)

Source: author.

of cased whiskey in Dublin.[26] Burke employed 150 at its bottling plant and bonded warehouses off Dublin's Bachelors Walk in 1913. The company also owned the Hibernian Glass Bottle Works in Ringsend.

The scores of malthouses dotted across the country represented the main source of demand for Irish barley. Though farmers railed against what they saw as Guinness's exploitation of its near-monopoly position, by 1913 the company was purchasing more than twice as much of the crop as it had done thirty years previously. In addition, thanks to the experimental programmes it conducted with maltsters John H. Bennett & Co., and with the Department of Agriculture and Technical Instruction, 'a much larger proportion of the crop was of malting quality, commanding a higher price'.[27] Other brewers, to the same end, imported selected seeds, which they supplied to farmers at cost price.

Minch Norton would become the largest stand-alone malt producer following the merger of the two Midlands-based family businesses in 1921. It employed 150 across its ten establishments in the 1930s. Beamish & Crawford produced much of its own malt, as did the Tullamore distillery of D. E. Williams, which had partner maltings in Banagher, Birr and other neighbouring areas.

---

[26] *Strattens' Dublin, Cork and South of Ireland: A Literary, Commercial and Social Review*, 36. The Liverpool house also bottled Bass for export across the world.

[27] Stanley R. Dennison and Oliver MacDonagh, *Guinness 1886–1939: From Incorporation to the Second World War* (Cork: Cork University Press, 1998), 102.

Distilling

Though Dublin had been 'the whiskey powerhouse of the world' for much of the nineteenth century, output of Scotch had grown to double that of Irish whiskey by the early 1900s.[28] The sector contracted further with the imposition of First World War restrictions and Prohibition in America. By 1926, Free State area spirit production had declined to one-fifth of its 1912 level.[29]

The Scottish and Irish distillers had responded differently to the major innovation of the age—the development of the 'patent' or 'Coffey' still (named for its inventor, Irishman Aeneas Coffey). The traditional pot still, whose use was largely retained in Ireland, produced pure malt whiskey from home-grown corn. The new type of still employed a different process to produce what was frequently referred to as 'silent spirit'. This could be made from cheaper imported cereals and blended with a small proportion of traditional pot-still whiskey to provide flavour.[30] The new method was substantially more economical and produced more malleable blends.

The Irish industry also lost out to its Scottish competitor in the market for traditional pot still whiskey however.[31] Irish whiskey

> was sold in barrels to publicans and merchants who bottled it, or more frequently blended it and sold it under their own label. [Many] bought whiskey blended by a merchant without any awareness of whether they were consumers of Power's, John Jameson or some other product. Ceding blending and bottling to outsiders also opened up possibilities for [mis-labelling] or dilution with inferior spirits.[32]

The structure of the Scottish industry was far more favourable to collective marketing and promotion. By 1922, the Distillers Company Ltd (DCL) owned all but one of the Scottish patent-still distilleries and had a close collaborative agreement with the remaining one, while also controlling most of the patent distilleries in England and Ireland.[33] This quasi-monopolistic structure facilitated development of the export trade.

---

[28] Brian Townsend, *The Lost Distilleries of Ireland* (Glasgow: Neil Wilson Publishing, 1997), 3; Andy Bielenberg, *Ireland and the Industrial Revolution: The Impact of the Industrial Revolution on Irish Industry, 1801-1922* (London, New York: Routledge, 2009), 97; see Table 5.2.

[29] Ibid, 97, Table 5.2.

[30] The Irish industry argued that use of the term 'whisky' or 'whiskey' should be restricted to the traditional product. A Royal Commission of 1909 determined otherwise: Robin J. C. Adams, 'The "Made in Ireland" Trademark and the Delineation of National Identity', in *National Brands and Global Markets: An Historical Perspective*, ed. David Higgins and Nikolas Glover (Abingdon: Routledge, 2023): 46–66.

[31] Cormac Ó Gráda, *Ireland: A New Economic History 1780-1939* (Oxford: Clarendon Press, 1994), 301; Bielenberg, *Ireland and the Industrial Revolution*, 94.

[32] Mary E. Daly, *Dublin: The Deposed Capital, 1860-1914* (Cork: Cork University Press, 1984), 29.

[33] Ron B. Weir, 'In and Out of Ireland: The Distillers Company Ltd. and the Irish Whiskey Trade 1900-39'. *Irish Economic and Social History* 7, 1 (1980): 52; Ron B. Weir, 'The Patent Still Distillers and

Table 3.7 provides a list of distilleries in operation in the Free State area in 1920. Around half of these closed over the following decade, while those that remained open ceased production for large parts of the year.[34]

Table 3.7 Free State area distilleries in operation in 1920

Distiller	Distillery	Distillery developments to *c.* 1972
John Jameson (1810)	Bow Street Distillery, Dublin (1780)	Closed 1971; production transferred to Powers and later to Midleton
John Power	John's Lane, Dublin (1791)	Closed 1974; production transferred to Midleton
Dublin Distillers (1889)	George Roe, Thomas Street (1757) William Jameson, Marrowbone Lane (1752) Dublin Whisky Distillery, Jones' Road (1872)	George Roe and William Jameson closed in 1923, Jones's Road in 1926
Cork Distilleries* (1867)	Murphy's, Midleton (1825)	Production transferred to new Irish Distillers complex 1975
	Wise's, North Mall, Cork City (1779)	Closed 1920
Distillers Company Ltd (DCL)	Phoenix Park, Dublin (1878) Dundalk, County Louth (pre-1800)	Closed early 1920s
Cassidy's	Monasterevin, County Kildare (1784)	Closed 1921
B. Daly/D. E. Williams	Tullamore, County Offaly (1829)	Closed 1954
John Locke	Kilbeggan, County Westmeath (1757)	Closed 1953; reopened in the 1990s
Allman & Co.	Bandon, County Cork (1825)	Closed 1930s
Glen Distillery	Kilnap, County Cork (1882)	Closed 1920s

Note: *CDC's Watercourse distillery was dormant in the 1920s but operated intermittently since then.
Source: author.

the Role of Competition', in *Comparative Aspects of Irish and Scottish Economic and Social Development, 1660–1900*, ed. Louis M. Cullen and T. Christopher Smout (Edinburgh: John Donald, 1975), 142.

[34] The same caveats as to the dates of establishment and decommissioning as discussed in the case of brewing apply. Dundalk distillery had been in operation as Malcolm Brown & Co. since the early 1800s but was acquired by Scottish DCL in 1912. Similarly, the distillery at Marrowbone Lane in Dublin pre-dated its acquisition by John Jameson's nephew, William.

Employment figures for the distilleries in the decade or so prior to 1922 suggest an aggregate workforce of around 1,500.[35] By 1926, the figure for distilling reported in the Census of Population stood at around 900, and that reported by the Census of Industrial Production at around 500, confirming the sharp contraction suggested by the data on spirit production.

Scotland's DCL closed its distilleries in Chapelizod and Dundalk in the early 1920s and all three of the companies that had merged to form the Dublin Distillers' Company in 1889 ceased production over the course of the decade.[36] The George Roe distillery had been the largest in Dublin in the Victorian era. Its directors identified the lack of brand recognition as the source of its failure. The Dublin firms with stronger brand recognition, Jameson and Powers, survived.[37] There was a further contraction in employment between 1926 and 1929, at which point the industry appeared to be on the verge of extinction.

Aerated Waters

There were two significant producers of soft drinks or 'aerated waters' in Dublin in the early twentieth century, with 'smaller ones to be found in nearly every fair-sized town throughout the country'.[38] A. & R. Thwaite, founded by a father-and-son team of apothecaries, had been producing soda water in Dublin since the late 1700s. Belfast firm Cantrell & Cochrane's Dublin factory was larger than Thwaite's, though it employed no more than a couple of hundred in 1929. It had been opened on Nassau Place at the rear of the Cochrane family townhouse on Kildare Street in 1868, where it would remain for the next 100 years.

The early success of Cantrell & Cochrane's ginger ale owed much to the temperance movement. It was described in advertisements as

> sparkling like champagne, agreeable to the taste as that much lauded and very costly wine, but not leaving [repentance] and self-reproach as a heritage of the morrow.[39]

---

[35] Jameson, Powers, and each of the establishments operated by Cork Distilleries and Scotland's DCL employed in the region of 150 to 300 people. Tullamore and the ailing Dublin Distillers Company each employed around 100, and the more localized distilleries employed fewer than 50.

[36] On the closure of the DCL distilleries, see Weir, 'In and Out of Ireland: The Distillers Company Ltd. and the Irish Whiskey Trade'.

[37] Townsend, *The Lost Distilleries of Ireland*, 95.

[38] Riordan, *Modern Irish Trade and Industry*, 164. Thirty-one of the soft-drinks producers from beyond Dublin are listed in an *Irish Times* article of 10 September 1928.

[39] Cited in Desmond S. Greer and James W. Nicolson, *The Factory Acts in Ireland, 1802–1914*, Vol. 12 (Dublin: Four Courts Press, 2003), 272.

Paradoxically, having concentrated its efforts on the export market, the company suffered a decline in sales when Prohibition led to the emergence of a large number of US competitors. From 1927, Thwaites, Cantrell & Cochrane and E. & J. Burke were linked through a complicated pattern of cross-ownership, which was reflected in the formation of a new company, Mineral Water Distributors. From the initial letters of the new company would emerge the soft drinks brand *MiWadi*.

Tobacco

Irish and British tobacco consumption were on a par in the early twentieth century, though pipe tobacco retained a stronger hold in Ireland. Prior to the establishment of a customs frontier in 1923, cigarette sales were dominated by imports. The market leader, as in Britain, was Bristol firm W. D. & H. O. Wills, whose 40 per cent share was largely accounted for by the low-priced and unfiltered Woodbine.[40]

The largest indigenous Free State area manufacturers were P. J. Carroll of Dundalk and T. P. & R. Goodbody of Dublin (Table 3.8). Goodbody had relocated to a site off the South Circular Road when its factory in Tullamore was destroyed by fire in the 1880s. Carrolls moved to a modern, purpose-built factory in 1912 when its original premises too were destroyed by fire. Half of its output in 1923 was sold in Britain and Northern Ireland.[41] Its dispatch of 30,000 Silk Cut cigarettes to soldiers fighting at the front in the opening phases of the First World War had elicited repeat orders numbering in the millions, and its 'Sweet Afton' brand, introduced in 1919, proved hugely popular in Scotland. It capitalized on the Dundalk connection with

Table 3.8 Largest tobacco manufacturers in the Free State in 1922

Firm	Location and period in operation	Employment
P. J. Carroll	Dundalk (1824–2008)	150 (1907), 400 (1934), ≥500 (from 1953)
T. P. & R. Goodbody	Dublin (1886–1929)	320 (1908), 200 (1929)

Source: author.

[40] Andy Bielenberg and David Johnson, 'The Production and Consumption of Tobacco in Ireland, 1800–1914'. *Irish Economic and Social History* 25, 1 (1998): 1–21; Riordan, *Modern Irish Trade and Industry*, 183.
[41] *Irish Times*, 3 March 1923.

Robert Burns, whose sister had lived in the town and was buried near the factory gates.

There were only 500 employed in tobacco manufacturing in the Free State prior to the erection of the customs frontier.[42] The structure of the industry changed considerably thereafter. Goodbodys would exit in 1929, and Carrolls would expand substantially over the following decades. Dublin, Cork, and Limerick also each hosted a number of smaller tobacco manufacturers.

3.2 Textiles, Clothing, Footwear, and Leather

A form of branding of relevance to textiles and clothing was the use of the Irish national trade mark *Déanta i nÉirinn*. In response to the growing manifestation of nationalist sentiment (particularly the 'Buy Irish' campaign initiated by the 'Irish Ireland' newspaper *The Leader*), some British manufacturers had begun to use Irish place names and terms such as Hibernian, Harp, Shamrock, and Gaelic in their branding. The passage of the Merchandise Marks Act of 1887 had made it a criminal offence to apply misleading descriptions as to where goods had been produced. The Irish national trade mark became legally enforceable in 1907 and by 1920 some 450 firms, mostly in the Free State area, had been licensed to use it.[43] Many of the legal actions taken or warnings issued in response to transgressions pertained to textiles and clothing (and also to flour).[44] Table 3.9 shows the composition of the textiles, clothing, and footwear sector in 1926.

Non-woollen Textiles

Limerick had been well-known for its lace in the past, as Dublin had been for its poplin, but both industries were on the verge of extinction by 1922.[45] Linen went into decline with the change in tastes and fashions of the First World War era, but production had been sustained over the war years by the demand for aeroplane cloth. Cork Spinning & Weaving closed in 1928. Greenmount Weaving of Harold's Cross in Dublin closed in 1922, though it reopened shortly afterwards upon being acquired by Boyne Weaving of

---

[42] *Saorstát Éireann: Irish Free State Official Handbook* (Dublin: Talbot Press, 1932), 142.
[43] Adams, 'The "Made in Ireland" Trademark and the Delineation of National Identity'.
[44] Riordan, *Modern Irish Trade and Industry*, Appendix VI.
[45] The only substantial factory-style lace operation, which was located in Limerick department store Cannocks, closed in the 1920s. The main surviving Dublin poplin maker was the 100-year-old Richard Atkinson & Co.

Table 3.9 Free State CIP, 1926: Textiles, clothing, and footwear

Sector	Employment, 1926: CIP, table 1 (excluding out-workers)
Linen, cotton, hemp, jute, and canvas	1,658
Woollen and worsted (including blanket making)	2,332
Clothing	4,001
Boots and shoes	967
Hosiery	849

Source: author.

Table 3.10 Leading firms in non-woollen textiles

Company name and location	Employment
Cork Spinning & Weaving (1889), Cork	1,000 (1919); closed 1928
Greenmount Weaving (1808), Harold's Cross, Dublin	550 (1922); merges into Greenmount & Boyne
Boyne Weaving (1865), Drogheda	900 (1910), 600 (1923); merges into Greenmount & Boyne
Greenmount & Boyne (1925), Dublin and Drogheda	590 (1929), 800 (1936), 800 (1960), 200 (1972)
J. & L. F. Goodbody (1865), Clara, County Offaly (and Waterford from the 1930s)	700 (1912), 800 (1920), remains >500 (up to 1972)

Source: author.

Drogheda. The merged firm, Greenmount & Boyne, would remain for many decades one of the leading manufacturers in the state. It remained primarily export-oriented in the 1920s. From the 1940s, it would begin to diversify into rayon and cotton.

Jute had become a popular sacking material when hemp supplies from Russia were disrupted by the Crimean War and cotton supplies from the southern United States were cut off by the American civil war of the following decade. The Clara factory of J. & L. F. Goodbody was one of the earliest jute plants in Europe outside the vast Dundee cluster. Established in 1865, it remained strongly export-oriented until well into the Free State era. It would remain a substantial employer through to 1972 (Table 3.10). By the time of EEC accession it had largely transitioned into polypropylene.[46]

---

[46] Though the implied size of these major non-woollen textiles firms alone exceeds the figure for total employment reported in the Census of Industrial Production, not all of their activities would necessarily have been allocated to the sector. The census notes for example that the cooperage departments of large breweries were included under timber rather than brewing.

Woollen and Worsted Textiles

By the late 1800s, Cork had emerged as the centre of the mechanized woollen industry in Ireland.[47] Proximity to the port was of importance as Irish wool is too coarse for the production of finer cloths. The area's main advantage according to Bielenberg however was the lead set by Martin Mahony & Brothers, whose technical and organizational innovations were copied by other local producers.[48] The family had been involved in the woollen industry since 1750 but the reputation of the firm dated largely from the opening of the Blarney Woollen Mills in 1824. It would remain the largest enterprise in the sector throughout the period to 1972 (Table 3.11).

The other major Cork mills were in nearby Douglas. The O'Brien Brothers' woollen mills, St Patrick's, dated from 1882. The Morrogh Brothers' Mills were established several years later with money made from the South African mining industry, where John Morrogh had been a director of De Beers. Other significant manufacturers included the Athlone Woollen Mills, F. & J. Clayton of Navan, Convoy in Donegal, the Providence Mills at Foxford in Mayo, Mulcahy, Redmond & Co. in Ardfinnan, County Tipperary, and Hill & Sons of Lucan. The Athlone Mills, the oldest of the group, had been set up in 1858 by an English-based Irish doctor at the prompting of his Lancashire industrialist brother-in-law. Providence, the most recent, had been established in 1892 by Sister Agnes Morrogh-Bernard of the Sisters of Charity to provide employment for the impoverished local population. Most of the woollen mills were in Catholic ownership. Hill & Sons was a Quaker enterprise.[49] Other than Blarney, even the largest of the others generally employed a maximum of 200–300 workers.

Table 3.11 Leading firm in woollens and worsteds: Blarney Woollen Mills

Firm, date of establishment, location	Employment
Blarney Woollen Mills (1824)/Martin Mahony & Brothers (1750), Blarney	750 (1892), 600 (1919), > 500 (up to 1972)

Source: author.

[47] Andy Bielenberg, *Cork's Industrial Revolution 1780–1880* (Cork: Cork University Press, 1991), 31, 39.
[48] Ibid., 40.
[49] The small Kilkenny Woollen Mill was established by the Countess of Desart and her brother-in-law in 1903. Lady Desart, upon her appointment to the senate in 1922, would be the first person of Jewish faith to serve in the parliament of the new state. The Kilkenny mill would be acquired in the 1920s by Business Party TD Andrew O'Shaughnessy, whose family also owned the Dripsey and Sallybrook Mills in County Cork.

The woollen and worsted sector had 'expanded at an unprecedented rate during the course of the 1914–18 War' but lost considerable ground thereafter.[50] From the 1920s, it would be protected by tariffs. The Navan and Athlone Mills closed in the 1960s, Morrogh in 1971, Ardfinnan in 1973. Convoy, Providence and Hill & Sons remained in operation beyond EEC accession, as did Blarney and St Patrick's.

Clothing, Hosiery, and Knitwear

The clothing sector, though sizeable, consisted for the most part of relatively small establishments. One of the few large employers was the Cork City firm Dwyer and Co. (Table 3.12). Established as a drapery and general-purpose wholesaler in the 1820s, by 1918 it was producing a broad range of clothing and footwear and had a workforce of 700, 70 of whom were employed in the firm's boot factory. Members of the extended Dwyer family would go on to establish Sunbeam and Seafield, two of the largest textiles companies of the protectionist era. The original Dwyer business traded largely under the Lee brand: by the 1960s, manufacturing accounted for only a small share of its activities.

The Limerick Clothing Factory had a particularly rich history. Founded by Scottish immigrant Peter Tait in 1850, it employed the recently invented mechanical sewing machine to produce ready-made clothing, particularly military uniforms, and was for a time the largest such concern in the world. It employed close to 2,000 at its peak in the nineteenth century. Tait went bankrupt when a consignment of Alabama cotton bartered for Confederate

Table 3.12 Leading firms in clothing, hosiery, and knitwear

		Employment
Dwyer & Co.	Cork	700 (1918), 800 (1939). Excluding footwear: 310 (1960), 450 (1972)
Limerick Clothing Factory	Limerick	800 (1899), 400 (1911), 600 (1919), 320 (1936), 350 (1962), 270 (1968)
Smyth & Co.	Balbriggan, County Dublin	Including out-workers: 460 (1898), 450 (1929), 470 (1936). Factory hands: 250 (1962)

Source: author.

[50] Committee on Industrial Organisation, *Report on Survey of the Woollen and Worsted Industry* (Dublin: Stationery Office, 1965), 44.

army uniforms was seized by Union forces during the American civil war and the company was bought out by a conglomerate of Limerick business-men. Employment stood at 600 in 1919 but declined to below 500 by 1929 at the latest. It would be acquired by UK company Aquascutum in 1969 and closed in 1974.

The largest and most famous hosiery firm in 1922 was Smyth & Co. of Bal-briggan, which dated from 1768. Many of its employees up to the 1950s were out-workers. The Oxford English Dictionary records that 'Balbriggan' came to be used in the late nineteenth century as a term for a knitted cotton fab-ric, used for stockings and underwear, 'named after the town of Balbriggan in Ireland where it was originally made'. The company survived until 1980. The Templecrone Co-operative Society in Donegal reduced its reliance on outworkers with the opening of its 'machine knitting factory' in Dungloe in 1919.[51] This factory too remained in operation into the EEC era.

Department Stores

Though not included in the Census of Industrial Production, the department stores of the period were significant producers of clothing, furniture, and fur-nishings. The emergence of the 'monster houses' in the mid-1800s had been vigorously opposed by smaller traders who argued that their importation of 'slop productions' from Britain was ruining entire classes of Irish tradespeo-ple.[52] By the turn of the century, in-house production of a range of the items sold on their premises had become standard.

There were seven major department stores in Dublin at the foundation of the state as well as several in Cork, Limerick, and Waterford.[53] Owner-ship of many passed through the hands of the same group of businesspeople. These included Limerickman Michael J. Clery and Scottish expatriates John Arnott, George Cannock, and William Todd. By the 1930s, Pim Brothers had been surpassed in size by several of the other Dublin stores. Table 3.13 tracks the evolution of employment in the major Dublin stores up to the 1930s and 1940s, beyond which their relative significance as manufacturers declined.

[51] *Irish Independent*, 31 October 1919.

[52] Stephanie Rains, 'Here Be Monsters: The Irish Industrial Exhibition of 1853 and the Growth of Dublin Department Stores'. *Irish Studies Review* 16, 4 (2008): 493.

[53] Frank Barry, 'The Life and Death of Protestant Businesses in Independent Ireland', in *Protestant and Irish: The Minority's Accommodation with Independent Ireland*, ed. Ian d'Alton and Ida Milne (Cork: Cork University Press, 2019), 155–70.

Table 3.13 Selected Dublin department stores in operation in 1922

Department store	Employment, selected years
Todd, Burns & Co., Mary Street	400–500 (1905), 620 (1935), 725 (1941)
Clery's, O'Connell Street	600 (1941)
Arnott's, Henry Street	200 (*c.* 1900), 400–450 (1918), 500 (1931)
Switzers, Grafton Street	250 (*c.* 1900), 425 (1935), 300–400 (1947)
Pim Brothers, South Great George's Street	600 (1894), 300 (1934)

Source: author.

Footwear and Leather

By the late 1880s, more than 80 per cent of the footwear sold in Ireland was imported, and the Irish sector was largely specialized in the less-skilled agricultural boot segment.[54] The five footwear firms in operation in 1924 supplied only 6 per cent of the state's requirements, and most of the 359 workers in the industry were employed on a part-time basis.[55] Leather production too was moribund. Riordan estimated that there were only around 500 employed across all of the twelve tanneries in operation in 1920, of which the largest by far was O'Callaghan's City Tannery in Limerick.[56] Its workforce over the entire period up to its demise in 1967 did not rise much above the 160 employed there during the First World War.

The oldest of the footwear firms still in operation in 1922 was James Winstanley of Dublin, which dated from 1852. Though Hilliard & Sons of Killarney and Lee Boot of Cork would both expand with the introduction of protection, neither would attain the scale of the UK firms that entered as a consequence of the tariffs. Hilliard would team up with a British partner to become Hilliard & Palmer in 1936 and would become a subsidiary of UK firm G. B. Britton in 1965. Lee Boot was a Dwyer family company. Its survival, Bielenberg notes, was due to its ability to update the plant periodically and to keep abreast of technological and organizational changes in England, which may have been a result of the resources available to it from within the Dwyer group.[57]

---

[54] Bielenberg, *Cork's Industrial Revolution 1780–1880*, 83.

[55] Tariff Commission, 'Report on the Application for a Tariff on Leather'. Report no. 11 (Dublin: Stationery Office, 1931), 22; D. J. Dwyer, 'The Leather Industries of the Irish Republic, 1922–55: A Study in Industrial Development and Location'. *Irish Geography* 4, 3 (1961): 175–89.

[56] Riordan, *Modern Irish Trade and Industry*, 178.

[57] Bielenberg, *Cork's Industrial Revolution 1780–1880*, 84.

3.3 Other Manufacturing Industries

Sectors other than the ones surveyed above made up the remaining one-third of manufacturing employment in 1926. They are grouped here into broader categories than those employed in the Census of Industrial Production. Certain industrial segments were included in a separate 'miscellaneous' category in order to maintain the confidentiality of the firm-level data submitted to the census authorities. In the 1926 Census of Industrial Production, these included poplin, leather, brush making, ship and boat building, tobacco pipes, and roofing felt.[58]

Metals and Engineering

The metals and engineering sector of the 1920s consisted of agricultural machinery and transport equipment fabrication and the diverse activities of the numerous general foundries then still in existence. Transport companies were treated separately in the census so the many thousands employed in the railway engineering yards where many of the state's mechanical craft workers served their apprenticeships are not included in Table 3.14. The largest of the railyards were the Inchicore and Dundalk engineering works of the Great Southern & Western and Great Northern railway companies (Table 3.15).

Most of the Dublin engineering work would transfer to Inchicore with the railway amalgamations of the mid-1920s and the formation of Great Southern Rail (GSR). Latterly part of the state transport company CIÉ, these works would remain a major employer through to 1972 and beyond. The liquidation of the Great Northern in the mid-1950s would put the livelihoods of the more than 1,000 then employed in Dundalk at risk. The Industrial Engineering Company would be established by the state to provide employment for the displaced workers. Its fortunes are discussed in a later chapter.

The other rail yards in operation in 1922 were at Broadstone, headquarters of the Midland Great Western, and the much smaller ones at Grand Canal Street, close to the Westland Row terminus of the Dublin & South Eastern Railway Company. Some rail work continued at Broadstone until it was decommissioned as a terminus in the 1930s. Most of the bus fabrication work then being conducted at the site transferred to the bus and tram facility of the Dublin United Transport Company (DUTC) when the latter merged with the

---

[58] The major brush maker was I. S. Varian & Co., which dated from 1798. The most significant producer of tobacco pipes was Kapp & Peterson, which was established in the mid-1890s. The leading firms in the other miscellaneous segments are mentioned elsewhere in the text.

Table 3.14 Free State CIP, 1926: Other manufacturing industries

Sector	Employment, 1926: Irish Free State CIP, table 1 (excluding out-workers)
Metals and engineering	
Coach, wagon, and motor body building and construction of motor vehicles	1,447
Metals (excluding engineering)	1,276
Engineering and implements	1,081
Other	
Bricks, glass, and monumental masonry	782
Timber	2,776
Wood furniture and upholstery	1,555
Paper making and manufactured stationery	611
Printing, publishing, bookbinding, and engraving	5,128
Soap and candles	410
Fertilizers, chemicals, drugs, and paints	1,102
Miscellaneous industries (sugar, polishes, brush making, ship and boat building, poplin, leather, vegetable oils, smoking pipes, roofing felt, other miscellaneous)	3,065

Source: CIP.

Table 3.15 Railway engineering works

Facility	Company	Employment (year)
Inchicore Railway Works, Dublin	Great Southern & Western/Great Southern Railways/CIÉ	1,600 (1917), 1,500 (1922), 1,400 (1954), 1,420 (1964), 2,000 (1975)
Dundalk Rail Yards	Great Northern Rail	1,000 (1914), 800 (1925), 700 (1934), 1,100 (1956)
Broadstone Rail Yards, Dublin	Midland Great Western	600 (1917)

Note: Not included under manufacturing in the CIP for 1926.
Source: author.

Great Southern to form CIÉ in 1945. Some 300–400 people were employed at the former DUTC facility in Inchicore up to 1972. The Grand Canal Street railyards, where the first locomotive engine manufactured in Ireland had been built, closed in 1925.

Shipbuilding and ship repair went into sharp decline in the years following the end of the First World War. The British Admiralty shipyards at

Table 3.16 Ship and boat building and repair

Facility	Location	Employment
British Admiralty Yard, Haulbowline	Cork	3,000 (1917), 1,000 (1921), 89 (1928)
Rushbrooke	Cork	800 (1917), 600 (1923), 400 (1946), 200 (1955), Verolme from 1959
Dublin Dockyard Company/Liffey Dockyard	Dublin	450–500 (1912), 750–1,000 (1920), 300 (1930), 550 (1936), 500 (1943), 450 (1952), 600 (1960), 250 (1968)

Source: author.

Haulbowline had employed 3,000 in 1917, and 1,000 were still on the books when it was announced in 1921 that they were to close. By the end of the decade, only a skeleton staff remained. The nearby shipyards at Rushbrooke and Passage West suffered collateral damage from the reduction in naval traffic. Owned at the time by UK company Furness & Withy, they closed in 1930. Rushbrooke would be reopened in 1941 and would be taken over by the Dutch company Verolme in 1959.

The Dublin Dockyard Company also employed around 1,000 in the years immediately prior to its closure in the early 1920s. The dockyard was reopened by UK company Vickers in 1924 but remained paralysed by industrial conflict throughout the 1920s. Its ownership changed several times over subsequent decades, with employment fluctuating between 250 and 600 depending on the state of the order book (Table 3.16).

Struck by the poverty of the country during a brief visit in 1912, American industrialist Henry Ford had resolved to build a tractor plant in Cork—the county of his father's birth—as a contribution to Ireland's industrial development. Production of cars and trucks would be most efficiently located close to major clusters of consumer demand; for tractors, for which the market was dispersed, a peripheral location would be less disadvantageous. Construction of the 'Fordson' tractor plant commenced in 1917. The project began as a private family venture but would be integrated into the Ford Motor Company in the early 1920s. At its peak later in the decade, it would be by far the largest manufacturing employer in the state.

The tractor market collapsed with the international agricultural depression of the early 1920s however and the Cork foundry was put to use producing car parts for the Ford assembly plant in Manchester. Plans to build an integrated production facility in Britain would come to fruition with the opening of the Dagenham plant in 1931. The Cork factory would be repurposed several years later to assemble primarily for the protected local market. It would remain a significant employer until its closure in 1984.[59]

Ireland's general foundries had become increasingly vulnerable to specialist machinery imports from Britain over the course of the nineteenth century. Those that survived, apart from Philip Pierce & Co. in Wexford, tended to concentrate on 'less sophisticated iron and wrought-iron goods like manhole covers, gates, street lamps, bollards, pumps, railings and other street furniture'.[60] Though most had passed their peak by the time of independence, their legacy remains apparent on the urban streetscapes of today. The Drogheda Iron Works had, in its time, built ships, bridges, barges, and steam locomotives as well as the diving bell that now stands as a remnant of industrial archaeology on the south bank of the Liffey in Dublin. Established by Thomas Grendon in 1835, it survived until 1970. The Dundalk Iron Works, which dated from 1788, would be liquidated in 1928. The Hive Iron Works and Merrick Engineering in Cork also survived in a much diminished state into the Free State era. The former closed in the 1930s; the latter struggled on into the 1960s. Two of the three surviving Limerick foundries closed in the 1920s. The Shannon Foundry survived beyond 1972.

From its establishment in the mid-1800s, Pierce & Co. of Wexford had developed a significant reputation as a producer of agricultural machinery. It was also in the 1920s one of only a handful of bicycle manufacturers in the state.[61] It remained in operation until 1980. Wexford town, which benefited from good transport links and proximity to the crop-growing regions of the country, hosted three foundries in total. The Selskar Ironworks closed in the 1930s. The Wexford Engineering Company would be converted in the 1960s into an assembly plant for Renault cars.

Dublin's size afforded the best opportunities for survival, though four foundries had disappeared from the vicinity of Hammond Lane within living memory when the foundry of that name was revived by Scotsman David Frame in 1902. Hammond Holdings would become a major industrial group,

---

[59] Much of the material on Ford comes from Thomas Grimes, 'Starting Ireland on the Road to Industry: Henry Ford in Cork'. Unpublished Ph.D. thesis, National University of Ireland, Maynooth, 2008.

[60] Bielenberg, *Cork's Industrial Revolution 1780–1880*, 113.

[61] The Fiscal Inquiry Committee of 1923 reported that 100 of its 350 workers of the time were engaged in the manufacture of bicycles: Fiscal Inquiry Committee, Final Report (Dublin: Stationery Office, 1923), 21.

Table 3.17 Metals and engineering other than rail, ships, and boats

Ford, Cork city (1919)	1,429 (1920), 1,800 (1923), major employer through to 1972
Philip Pierce & Co., Wexford (1839)	450 (1914), 350 (1923), 220 (1926), 500 (1941), 450 (1960), 260 (1969), 200 (1974)
Hammond Lane Foundry, Dublin (1902)	Foundry only: 150 (1913), 200 (1947), 230 (1962), 160 (1971), Hammond Holdings >500 (from 1930s)
Newcomen Ironworks (Smith & Pearson), Dublin (1901)	200 (1922), 300 (1939), 370 (1960), 420 (1966)

Source: author.

and Frame would go on to establish Irish Steel. The foundry itself, which moved in 1911 to Great Brunswick Street/Pearse Street, employed a similar workforce to the Smith & Pearson ironworks in East Wall. The foundry of former shipbuilders Ross & Walpole of North Wall closed in the 1920s; William Spence & Son of Cork St. closed in 1930; Sharkeys of Church Street closed in the 1940s. Art metalworkers J. & C. McGloughlin would merge with Tonge & Taggart to form the TMG Group in 1954. Other than the diversified Hammond Lane Group, the foundry companies only rarely employed a workforce of 500 or more (Table 3.17).

Building Materials, Glass, and Furniture

Builders' providers are not tracked closely through to the 1970s as only a segment of their activities fall within the definition of manufacturing. The major enterprises in the sector at independence included Dublin firms Brooks Thomas, Dockrells, and T. & C. Martin; Francis Spaight and James McMahon of Limerick; Robert McCowen of Tralee; Haughtons of Cork; and Graves & Co. of Waterford and New Ross (Table 3.18). Brooks Thomas remained the largest employer in 1972, followed by Dockrells, Concrete Products of Ireland (Chadwicks), and Heitons, which had transitioned from its earlier incarnation as a coal importer and distributor.

T. & C. Martin, Spaight, and McMahon were primarily engaged in the timber trade. Graves & Co., like Spaight, had originated as a shipping company. It encountered the fire-resistant roofing materials it would later produce at New Ross while engaged in business in Denmark in the 1870s. Its Waterford operation dealt primarily in timber. Graves & Co. would merge with Dockrells in 1971. Haughtons would merge with Brooks Thomas in 1969.

Table 3.18 Selected building materials firms

Firm	Employment
Brooks Thomas (1865), Dublin	200 (1933), 750 (1968), 1,180 (1972)
Thomas Dockrell (1822), Dublin	'Several hundred' (1912), 500 (1960), 670 (1972)

Source: author.

Though 70–80 per cent of the furniture sold in the 1920s was produced domestically, furniture establishments employed an average of only fifteen workers.[62] Among the largest of the furniture firms was the mattress, furniture, and furnishings manufacturer Michael O'Dea of Dublin. O'Dea's workforce would expand to 250–300 in the 1920s with the imposition of a tariff on furniture. It would be acquired by UK company Bond Worth in 1969.

Glass bottle production had been concentrated in Ringsend since the late eighteenth century when it was banished from inner-city Dublin for environmental reasons. All three of the Ringsend bottle works collapsed in the 1910s and 1920s in the face of competition from the recently automated British industry. The Irish Glass Bottle Company would be resurrected under tariff protection in the early 1930s and would remain a significant employer in 1972.

Paper, Print, and Packaging

Paper making had largely died out in Ireland, other than in Dublin, by the mid-1800s.[63] By 1920, even the five paper mills on the rivers west of the city were inactive for long periods of time. There were only forty-one employed in the sector in 1928. Paper making, too, would be resurrected under tariff protection. Printing and production of stationery and packaging materials, by contrast, were shielded from import competition by the requirements for customized service, and these segments hosted around a dozen firms with workforces of 200–300 at the foundation of the state. The largest employers were the Dublin firms Alexander Thom & Co. and Helys (Table 3.19), both of which feature in Joyce's *Ulysses* as former employers of Leopold Bloom. Thom & Co. had been established by a young Scottish immigrant in 1825 and had been appointed official government printer for Ireland in 1876. Helys

[62] The proportion of sales produced domestically in 1926, 1929, and 1931 is reported in the 1931 Census of Industrial Production, xiv.
[63] Bielenberg, *Cork's Industrial Revolution 1780–1880*, 79.

Table 3.19 Selected printing, stationery, and packaging firms

Firm	Employment	Firm	Employment
Helys (1896)	500 (1916), 400–500 (1933), 450 (1960)	*Freeman's Journal* (1763)	300 (1924)
Alexander Thom (1825)	500 (1912) 700 (1916), 400 (1921), 500 (1948, 1960)	*Irish Independent* (1905)	300 (1911), 500 (1926), 600 (1935), 800 (1950), 900 (1960), 1,200 (1966)

Source: author.

operated a substantial retail premises on Dame Street and a large printing plant, the Acme Works, on nearby Dame Court.

Most of the firms in the sector were Protestant-owned, though Browne & Nolan had expanded by catering to the captive market for Catholic and nationalist publications.[64] Unusually, Cahill & Co., a large-scale printer of popular paperbacks, produced primarily for the export market.[65] By 1972, many of the firms had been acquired as part of the decade-long battle between the Smurfit and Clondalkin Paper Groups for control of the sector.

The largest national newspapers also each employed around 300 in the lead-up to independence. The *Freeman's Journal* had been the most prominent Catholic/nationalist paper in the late nineteenth century but was rapidly eclipsed by William Martin Murphy's *Irish Independent* from its launch in 1905. By 1921, the *Independent* had a circulation of 134,000 copies a day.[66] The *Journal*'s circulation had remained stagnant at around 35,000.[67] Until the 1980s, the *Independent*'s masthead proclaimed its incorporation of its former rival, which it acquired upon the latter's demise in 1924. Its workforce would double to 600 over the following decade and would double again by 1966. It would remain the largest-circulation Irish newspaper in 1972.

Chemicals

The chemicals sector of the early Free State era was dominated by fertilizers, of which the most significant producer by far was W. & H. M. Goulding

---

[64] Daly, *Dublin: The Deposed Capital, 1860–1914*, 46.
[65] *Irish Times*, 16 September 1927.
[66] Ian Kenneally, 'Nationalist in the Broadest Sense: The Irish Independent and the Irish Revolution', in *Independent Newspapers A History*, ed. Mark O'Brien and ; Kevin Rafter (Dublin: Four Courts Press, 2012): 39–51.
[67] Felix M. Larkin, '"A Great Daily Organ": The Freeman's Journal, 1763–1924'. *History Ireland* (2006): 44–49.

(Table 3.20). Established in Cork in 1856, Gouldings held a number of scientific patents and was another of the country's earliest indigenous multinationals, though both of its foreign operations – in France and the United States – were short-lived.[68] By 1922, it had plants in Dublin, Cork and Waterford, and a further three in Northern Ireland. It also owned or controlled three other Free State firms, including the Dublin docklands company Morgan Mooney & Co.

Though there were firms of note in both soap and candle making, there were only 230 employed in these sectors prior to the introduction of tariffs in the 1920s. The Rathbornes had been producing candles in Dublin since 1488. The family firm, John G. Rathborne, was taken over by the Dublin Quaker soap manufacturer John Barrington & Sons in 1914. Barringtons was acquired by Lever Brothers several years earlier. Lever would dispose of its candle-making interests to Shell in 1923 and would build a major new soap factory on Dublin's Sheriff Street in 1927. The largest producer of paints and varnishes was the Shandon Chemical Works, established by Stanley (later Sir Stanley) Harrington and his brothers in 1885. It merged with its main British supplier to become Harrington-Goodlass Wall in 1922. The new firm would be awarded the contract to supply the Free State Post Office with paint of 'Saorstát green' and would later, in collaboration with ICI, act as paint supplier to Ford.

One further chemicals firm of note was the phosphorescent match producer Paterson, whose factory at Hammond Lane was acquired by the Liverpool firm Maguire & Miller in 1919. The principal of the latter, Alexander Maguire, was of Liverpool-Irish stock and had been knighted for his promotion of a safer form of phosphorus than the variety then in common usage. He would later also be honoured by the Pope for his sponsorship of the Catholic Social Action movement. The Dublin enterprise was renamed Maguire & Paterson in 1922. It employed a workforce of 200–300 throughout the period to 1972.

Table 3.20 Leading chemicals firm: Goulding Fertilizers

Gouldings (1856)	Fertilizers	800–1,000 (1912), major employer through to 1972

Source: author.

---

[68] It had opened a plant in France in the 1870s to source raw materials for the local market, and established a factory in Florida in the 1890s to economize on shipping costs from Ireland. Both operations closed within a few years.

4

The Irish Free State of the 1920s

Official data on industrial conditions in the Irish Free State are available only from 1926. Analyses that take this as their starting point are likely to understate significantly the expansion that occurred over the first decade of independence. The economy was in the midst of a severe downturn in 1922. The UK recession of the previous two years had been the worst in living memory and the agricultural boom of the First World War period, which had been of particular significance to rural Ireland, had just collapsed. Industry too was under severe pressure. Wartime demand for Irish manufacturing output had been sustained by the absence of competing imports on the British market as well as in Ireland. Import competition had rebounded to intense levels by the early 1920s.[1]

These difficulties were compounded by the bitter industrial relations environment of the time and the death, destruction, and economic disruption of the eleven-month civil war which broke out in mid-1922.[2] The number of days lost through industrial disputes over the four years 1922–1925 would not be reached again until the late 1960s.[3] The civil war resulted in several thousand deaths, with destruction of property and infrastructure estimated to have amounted to some 30 per cent of national income.[4] The costs of the disruption to trade and economic activity have not been quantified.

Free State industry, and the economy more generally, is likely have been in recovery by 1926.[5] The earliest of the Cumann na nGaedheal tariffs were also beginning to have an effect. The economic rebound was facilitated by the successful management of the Free State public finances, which contrasted

---

[1] David Johnson, *The Interwar Economy in Ireland* (Dundalk: Dundalgan Press, 1989), 3–5; Edward J. Riordan, *Modern Irish Trade and Industry* (London, New York: Metheuen, E. P. Dutton, 1920).

[2] The civil war was fought over the acceptability of the constitutional limitations on independence upon which Britain had insisted, given the potential for a more widespread unravelling of the bonds of empire. Under the terms of the Anglo-Irish Treaty of 1921 the Irish Free State was established as a Commonwealth dominion with a status equivalent specifically to that of Canada.

[3] Teresa Brannick, Francis Devine, and Aidan Kelly, 'Social Statistics for Labour Historians: Strike Statistics, 1922–99'. *Saothar* 25 (2000): 114–20.

[4] Seán Kenny and Eoin McLaughlin, 'The Political Economy of Secession: Lessons from the Early Years of the Irish Free State'. *National Institute Economic Review* 261, 1 (2022): 48–78.

[5] R. C. Geary, 'Irish Economic Development since the Treaty'. *Studies: An Irish Quarterly Review* 40, 160 (1951): 404. The trough across Europe generally was reached in 1925: Sidney Pollard, *Peaceful Conquest: The Industrialization of Europe, 1760–1970* (Oxford: Oxford University Press, 1981), 278.

Industry and Policy in Independent Ireland, 1922–1972. Frank Barry, Oxford University Press.
© Frank Barry (2023). DOI: 10.1093/oso/9780198878230.003.0004

with the early experiences of the newly established states on Europe's eastern peripheries. Unable to raise revenues by conventional means, these other new states were forced into extreme measures 'to cope with relief and reconstruction and to ease the pressure of political and social disorders'.[6] The inflationary and currency chaos that ensued would adversely impact on their policy choices into the future.[7]

4.1 Establishment of the State

The first proclamation issued by the Provisional Government in January 1922 directed that all law courts, civil and public servants, and others hitherto under the authority of the British government 'shall continue to carry out their functions unless and until otherwise ordered by us'.[8] The legal system was largely maintained intact. The case of the civil service was more complicated.

Nationalists had been bitterly hostile to the 'Dublin Castle' bureaucracy that had administered the country in conjunction with Whitehall under British rule. An underground civil service had been created during the war of independence, but the split over the terms of the Treaty meant that the loyalty of the body in its entirety could not be relied upon. Plans to construct a completely new apparatus were abandoned and 'the civil service of the Dáil was assimilated into the old Castle administration rather than the other way round'.[9] From 1924, all new civil servants would be recruited by open competitive examinations.

The large-scale transfer of officials from the previous administration would leave a legacy of mistrust of the new civil service which, though particularly prevalent on the anti-Treaty side, was evident across all political parties. Suspicions pertained particularly to the Department of Finance and its two most senior figures, Joseph Brennan and J. J. McElligott. Claims that they were 'unalterably and fanatically attached to the English interest' were definitively without foundation.[10] Brennan had served in a variety of administrative

---

[6] Derek H. Aldcroft, *Europe's Third World: The European Periphery in the Interwar Years* (Aldershot: Ashgate, 2006).

[7] Barry Eichengreen and Douglas A Irwin, 'The Slide to Protectionism in the Great Depression: Who Succumbed and Why?' *Journal of Economic History* 70, 4 (2010): 871–97.

[8] Martin Maguire, *The Civil Service and the Revolution in Ireland, 1912–38: 'Shaking the Blood-Stained Hand of Mr. Collins'* (Manchester: Manchester University Press, 2013), 128.

[9] Ibid., 138.

[10] The claim was made by Seán McEntee, cited in ibid., 207. De Valera appears to have been more fair-minded: Anna Devlin and Frank Barry, 'Protection versus Free Trade in the Free State Era: The Finance Attitude'. *Irish Economic and Social History* 46, 1 (2019): 3–21: fn 118; Maguire, *The Civil Service and the Revolution in Ireland'*, 220.

positions since 1912 but—as he would reveal for the first time more than fifty years later—had provided detailed financial advice to Collins and the Treaty negotiating team on strict condition of anonymity and at great personal risk.[11] McElligott too had served in the Crown service but had been dismissed and jailed for his participation in the 1916 Rising. He was recruited by Brennan from London, where he had risen to become managing editor of the British financial weekly, the *Statist*.

Suspicions of Brennan and McElligott reflected a mix of frustration at the British Treasury system in which they had been schooled—and which was adopted at their behest—and at their adherence to Treasury thinking on the benefits of free trade and the importance of balanced budgets and low taxation. Their personal histories contrasted with those of some of the senior officials of the new Department of Industry and Commerce, whose promotion of a more interventionist agenda appears to have inured them from suspicion. The appointment of Gordon Campbell, son of Lord Glenavy, as Secretary of Industry and Commerce was said to have delighted Irish unionists.[12] Campbell too had been a member of the Crown bureaucracy, as had R. C. Ferguson, an Ulster Presbyterian who would become Assistant Secretary of the department in 1927.

The failure of the new state to live up to the economic expectations of the nationalist movement has been blamed, even by many modern historians, on the conservative principles that the senior figures in the Department of Finance espoused. An alternative perspective is provided by Seán Cromien, who served as Secretary of the Department in the 1980s and 1990s. 'It was very important', Cromien asserts, 'that the new state should proceed prudently in its budgetary and financial affairs':

> The fact that it soon established a reputation for being a well-run country where British and other businessmen and investors could do business was largely the result of the policy advice of Brennan and McElligott. [This served as] a useful corrective to the unreasonable expectations of the young and inexperienced politicians who took office in 1922 and those who succeeded them in 1932.[13]

The Treasury system that generated such hostility accorded the Department of Finance a central role in controlling the expenditure of other government departments. As T. K. Whitaker would explain to a sceptical audience

---

[11] Leon O'Broin, 'Joseph Brennan, Civil Servant Extraordinary'. *Studies: An Irish Quarterly Review* 66, 261 (1977): 25–37.

[12] Pauric J. Dempsey, 'Campbell, Charles Gordon', in *Dictionary of Irish Biography*, https://www.dib.ie/ (Cambridge: Cambridge University Press, 2009).

[13] Seán Cromien, 'Brennan, Joseph', in *Dictionary of Irish Biography* https://www.dib.ie/ (Cambridge: Cambridge University Press, 2009).

of senior officials of these other departments in 1953, the Department of Finance position 'must inevitably be conditioned not only by the merits of the proposals themselves—not always as apparent to others as to the sponsors—but also by their implications, in conjunction with everything else, for the national finances and the national economy'.[14] The resilience of the system is reflected in the fact that it remains in operation to this day.

That Whitaker too was a proponent of free trade and low taxation demonstrates the strong line of continuity in Department of Finance thinking over the decades. The stance of the Department of Industry and Commerce has frequently been portrayed as 'developmentalist', while that of the Department of Finance has been criticized as negative and obstructionist.[15] There was a similar continuity in the Industry and Commerce position advanced by Campbell and his successors John Leydon and J. C. B. McCarthy, with whom Whitaker would cross swords in the 1950s. Though Leydon had served in the Department of Finance from 1923, he would become a trusted advisor to Lemass upon becoming Secretary of Industry and Commerce in 1932 and would remain so even after his retirement from the civil service in 1955.[16]

The Department of Finance, even under Cumann na nGaedheal, did not win every significant policy battle between the two departments. Neither would prove to have a monopoly of wisdom on economic and industrial development strategy. Whitaker would point out in 2005 that the Department of Finance approach forced others 'to punch hard to get their point across', to which Garret FitzGerald responded: 'It is a very important role and it's not always as negative as it seems.'[17]

4.2 Economic Policy

In the other newly established states of the interwar period, which stretched from Finland in the north to Yugoslavia in the south,

Lack of self-determination and the impossibility of an independent economic policy were considered to be the main reasons for previous failures [. . .] The

---

[14] Cited in Devlin and Barry, 'Protection versus Free Trade in the Free State Era: The Finance Attitude'.

[15] John Joseph Lee, *Ireland 1912–1985: Politics and Society* (Cambridge: Cambridge University Press, 1989); Brian Girvin, *Between Two Worlds: Politics and Economy in Independent Ireland* (Dublin: Rowman & Littlefield, 1989); Gary Murphy, *In Search of the Promised Land: The Politics of Post-War Ireland* (Cork: Mercier Press, 2009).

[16] Leydon had been offered the position of Secretary of Industry and Commerce upon Campbell's succession to his father's title just before the 1932 general election but delayed accepting the offer until it had been approved by the new government.

[17] T. K. Whitaker, 'Opening Up to the International Economy: Ireland in the 1950s'. Witness seminar, Centre for Contemporary Irish History, Trinity College Dublin, 19 January 2005.

new Zeitgeist of surging nationalism which equated independence with economic self-sufficiency became the cradle of a new modernization philosophy.[18]

It had been presumed that an independent Ireland too would rapidly turn protectionist. The long-established trade relationships of the other new states had been severed however by the collapse of the empires of which they had been a part, while the Irish Free State retained free access to the massive export market on its doorstep. The social and political pressures that it faced to create new jobs were also far weaker: land redistribution in Ireland was much further advanced, there were substantially fewer landless labourers, and emigration options remained more easily accessible.[19] Even the livelihoods of the close-to-subsistence farmers of the west of Ireland who would prove the bedrock of early Fianna Fáil support were dependent on international trade. They were exporters of pigs and eggs and net consumers of wheat, the main agricultural product on which protectionists proposed to impose tariffs. The price of the young cattle that they sold on to the 'ranchers' of the midlands and east was determined by the price these cattle would ultimately sell for on the British market.[20] The constellation of political pressures that determined Irish trade policy – and the trade policies of other states across the world – would change with the onset of the Great Depression.

The Cumann na nGaedheal governments of the first decade of independence were pragmatists rather than ideologues. Though they did not adhere as closely to laissez-faire principles as is generally imagined, they prioritized stability:

> They had before their eyes the example of financial collapse in many countries. In such circumstance they were naturally reluctant to make experiments. The difficulties of managing a system to which they were unaccustomed in a period of instability both at home and abroad was great enough; to overhaul that system was out of the question.[21]

The fiscal position of the state in its early years was extremely precarious. Compensation for property losses and expenditure on the army absorbed

[18] Ivan T. Berend, 'The Failure of Economic Nationalism: Central and Eastern Europe before World War II'. *Revue économique* 51, 2 (2000): 315–22.

[19] The Common Travel Area Agreement between Ireland and Britain allowed mutual freedom of travel, residence, and work. (Northern Ireland would introduce an employment permit system in 1947.) The US restrictions on immigration introduced in 1924 were also relatively generous to Ireland.

[20] Department of Agriculture, *Committee of Inquiry on Post-Emergency Agricultural Policy* (Dublin: Stationery Office, 1945), 49.

[21] Simon Kepple, 'A Survey of Taxation and Government Expenditure in the Irish Free State, 1922–36'. MA thesis, University College Cork, 1938, 74. (I am grateful to Peter Clarke for bringing this document to my attention.)

almost three-quarters of government revenue in 1924.[22] The share of the UK national debt for which the state was potentially liable under the terms of the Treaty amounted to 80 per cent of national income: this would be written off only as part of the Boundary Commission settlement of 1925.[23]

The pensions issue had been central to earlier discussions of the economics of independence. As a share of national income, Irish pension expenditures were the highest in Europe.[24] To bring them into line with the United Kingdom by this measure would have required a rate cut of between 30 and 50 per cent. The one-shilling cut imposed by Finance Minister Ernest Blythe amounted to a reduction of 10 per cent and was announced as the government prepared for the launch of the first national loan, when establishing the creditworthiness of the state was a key priority.[25] Though the 10-shilling rate had been restored by 1928 (subject to a tighter means test), the decision is widely agreed to have been a factor in the governing party's loss of popularity and eventual loss of power.

As for the alternative of raising income tax, here too the government was constrained. Not only had nationalists long argued that Ireland had been overtaxed, but it was also believed that if economics lay at the core of the North–South divide, then low taxation might make a united Ireland more attractive to northern unionists.[26] Of most immediate concern was the prospect of further capital flight. 'Some of those who paid large amounts in income tax were out of sympathy with the new regime and transferred their domicile to Great Britain.'[27] It was not that large-scale migration would ensue but that adverse changes in relative income tax rates could have serious consequences for the Exchequer, and for the business environment more generally.[28]

---

[22] John FitzGerald and Seán Kenny, '"Till Debt Do Us Part": Financial Implications of the Divorce of the Irish Free State from the United Kingdom, 1922–1926'. *European Review of Economic History* 24, 4 (2020): 818–42.

[23] Ibid.

[24] Peter H. Lindert, 'The Rise of Social Spending, 1880–1930'. *Explorations in Economic History* 31, 1 (1994): 12: table 1C.

[25] Even in the years following the rate cut, pension payments accounted for more than 10 per cent of government spending: Cormac Ó Gráda, '"The Greatest Blessing of All": The Old Age Pension in Ireland'. *Past & Present* 175, 1 (2002): 124–61.

[26] John M. Regan, *The Irish Counter-Revolution, 1921–1936: Treatyite Politics and Settlement in Independent Ireland* (Dublin: Gill and Macmillan, 2001), 254; Kevin O'Higgins, cited in Mel Farrell, '"Few Supporters and No Organisation"? Cumann na nGaedheal Organisation and Policy, 1923–33'. Ph.D. thesis, National University of Ireland Maynooth, 2011, 103.

[27] James Meenan, *The Irish Economy since 1922* (Liverpool: Liverpool University Press, 1970), 246.

[28] Lord Iveagh, the main shareholder in Guinness, had five residences in England and three in the Free State at his death in the 1920s. In a court battle over where taxes were to be paid, his estate claimed England as his permanent domicile (*Irish Times*, 20 October 1928). That relative tax rates were a factor in Anglo-Irish calculations is explicitly mentioned by Nora Robertson, *Crowned Harp: Memories of the Last Years of the Crown in Ireland* (Dublin: Allen Figgis and Co., 1960), 145.

The double taxation agreement signed with the United Kingdom in 1926 was based on a model advocated by the League of Nations. It necessitated responding even more closely to developments in British taxation and it became customary for this reason to delay the Irish budget until several weeks after the British budget had been announced.[29] From 1927, the income tax rate had been brought below that in the United Kingdom and did not subsequently exceed it, even under the more radical administrations of the 1930s.[30] Criticism of Cumann na nGaedheal's reliance on indirect taxation overlooks the fact that the much more extensive tariffs of the 1930s and beyond had exactly the same effect on consumer prices.[31]

Currency policy was another area of controversy in the early Free State. The new currencies launched in the eastern periphery states had depreciated sharply, with severe inflationary—and sometimes hyperinflationary—consequences. Decisions on currency were less pressing in Ireland. Though there was, for the first number of years, 'no legal tender in circulation identifiable as such', British currency notes and coins continued to circulate freely and Irish private bank notes remained fully payable in sterling.[32] The deflation resulting from Britain's desire to restore the currency to its pre-war Gold Standard exchange rate was dramatically disruptive of industrial peace but was largely over by the time the Free State was established.[33] From the early 1920s, 'hostility towards inflation became the *leitmotif* of economic policy across Europe'.[34]

A new Irish pound, linked one-to-one with sterling and fully backed by a reserve of sterling and sterling securities, was eventually introduced in 1928. The arrangement ensured that developments in Irish retail prices and interest rates paralleled those in the United Kingdom.[35] It also tightly constrained fiscal policy, which could otherwise erode confidence in the currency link.[36]

---

[29] The effect of the agreement was that persons resident in the Free State and not in the United Kingdom paid only Irish income tax on their income deriving from both jurisdictions (and vice versa): *Saorstát Éireann: Irish Free State Official Handbook* (Dublin: Talbot Press, 1932), 91.

[30] These data are charted in Kenny and McLaughlin, 'The Political Economy of Secession: Lessons from the Early Years of the Irish Free State'.

[31] Joseph Johnston, 'An Outlook on Irish Agriculture'. *Studies: An Irish Quarterly Review* 28, 110 (1939): 195–209. Edward Nevin, 'The Irish Price Level: A Comparative Study', Economic Research Institute Paper No. 9, 1962.

[32] Maurice Moynihan, *Currency and Central Banking in Ireland, 1922–1960* (Dublin: Gill and Macmillan and Central Bank of Ireland, 1975), 20.

[33] Ryland Thomas and Nicholas Dimsdale. 'A Millennium of Macroeconomic Data for the UK'. *Bank of England's Historical Macroeconomic and Financial Statistics: Version* 3 (2017): Sheet A47.

[34] Patricia Clavin, *The Great Depression in Europe, 1929–1939* (New York: Macmillan, 2000), 31–33.

[35] Membership of the sterling bloc has been found to have facilitated lower borrowing costs during the troubled interwar period: FitzGerald and Kenny, '"Till Debt Do Us Part": Financial Implications of the Divorce of the Irish Free State from the United Kingdom, 1922–1926'.

[36] Patrick Honohan, 'Currency Board or Central Bank? Lessons from the Irish Pound's Link with Sterling, 1928–79'. *Banca Nazionale del Lavoro Quarterly Review* 50, 200 (1997): 39–67.

By mutual agreement, the cost of exchanging the currencies was set at zero. The decision was warmly welcomed by the commercial and banking communities. Though the opposition gave the impression of being less than fully convinced of its merits, Fianna Fáil, once in power, would prove no more keen than Cumann na nGaedheal had been to change the arrangement.

It has been suggested that Keynes may have had the Free State in mind when discussing the merits of such a 'currency board' system:

> For countries which are small compared with their neighbours, or do not contain independent financial centres of international importance, an Exchange Standard may be ideal. But it does undoubtedly involve some measure of dependence on the country whose money is chosen as the basis of the Exchange Standard, which may be hurtful to the national pride.[37]

The hurt to national pride notwithstanding, Irish economists have been strongly supportive of the policy. Honohan writes that the temptation to abandon sterling for political reasons was resisted 'and the consequences must overall be considered a success'.[38] To Ó Gráda, 'the logic of maintaining the link with sterling in the interwar period was compelling'.[39]

Southern unionist concerns that a nationalist government would be fiscally profligate proved unfounded. The annual fiscal deficit rarely exceeded 2 per cent of national income until the 1950s.[40] The informal partnership established between William Martin Murphy, Presbyterian Charles Eason, and Quaker George Jacob during the bitter Dublin lock-out of 1913 had helped to stabilize business sentiment.[41] So too did the appointment of a number of business leaders to the new Free State Senate. These included the banker and distiller Andrew Jameson; Arthur Jackson, the head of Pollexfen grain millers; Benjamin Haughton, principal of the Cork Timber and Iron Company; and members of the Guinness and Goodbody families. Catholic nationalist appointees included margarine manufacturer James Charles Dowdall, who would later join Fianna Fáil. Four members of a loose Business Party

[37] Cited in Moynihan, *Currency and Central Banking in Ireland, 1922–1960*, 109.

[38] Honohan, 'Currency Board or Central Bank?

[39] Cormac Ó Gráda, 'Money and Banking in the Irish Free State 1921–1939', in *Banking, Currency and Finance in Europe between the Wars*, ed. Charles H. Feinstein (Oxford: Clarendon Press, 1995), 414–33.

[40] John FitzGerald and Seán Kenny, 'Managing a Century of Debt'. *Journal of the Statistical and Social Inquiry Society of Ireland* 48 (2018): 1–40.

[41] Louis M. Cullen, *Princes & Pirates: The Dublin Chamber of Commerce, 1783–1983* (Dublin: Dublin Chamber of Commerce, 1983), 92.

alliance were elected to the lower chamber in 1923. Three of them—building contractor John Good, coal distributor William Hewat, and brewer Richard Beamish—were former unionists. The fourth was the creamery owner and textile manufacturer Andrew O'Shaughnessy. Eager for stability and encouraged by the cautious financial policies of the new government, most business interests threw their support behind the pro-Treaty party.

The old elite did not have everything its own way, however. The land settlement up to this point had 'involved the transfer of ownership from ten thousand or so landed proprietors, mainly Protestant and Unionist, to half a million or so mainly Catholic and Nationalist landholders'.[42] Thirty per cent of agricultural land still remained in the hands of the landlord class. These were 'the hard knots that it had been impossible to disentangle under the system of voluntary purchase'.[43] Upon being informed that there were multitudes of landless men prepared to enforce their claims 'with the gun and the torch', William T. Cosgrave advocated that negotiations be concluded rapidly to discourage landlords from making exorbitant demands.[44] The vast bulk of the remaining estates had been bought out by the end of the Cumann na nGaedheal era.[45]

Sir John Keane, a Senator and director of the Bank of Ireland, was sharply critical of what he referred to as the policy of land 'nationalisation'.[46] Criticism of the 'nationalisation' of electricity generation and distribution was led by ex-unionist parliamentarians and the *Irish Times*. Parliamentary criticism of the decision not to follow the United Kingdom in abolishing corporation profits tax in 1924 was led by the ex-unionist John Good TD.[47] Hewat and Good were among the principal opponents of the state-led amalgamation of the railways.[48]

Relations with the financial community had been strained by the Bank of Ireland's unwillingness to participate in the first national loan without a guarantee from the British, which was not forthcoming. The refusal of the

---

[42] Cormac Ó Gráda, 'Irish Agriculture after the Land War', in *Land Rights, Ethno-nationality and Sovereignty in History*, ed. Stanley Engerman and Jacob Metzer (London: Routledge, 2004), 131–52.

[43] Elizabeth R. Hooker, *Readjustments of Agricultural Tenure in Ireland* (Chapel Hill, NC: University of North Carolina Press, 1938), 103.

[44] Cited in Mary E. Daly, *The First Department: A History of the Department of Agriculture* (Dublin: Institute of Public Administration, 2002), 114.

[45] Hooker, *Readjustments of Agricultural Tenure in Ireland*. Land distribution remained hugely divisive into the Fianna Fáil era. The decline in smaller land holdings would ultimately be driven primarily by emigration: Cathal O'Donoghue, 'A Century of Irish Agriculture: A Policy Driven Sector'. *Journal of the Statistical and Social Inquiry Society of Ireland* 51 (2022): 86–127.

[46] Maurice Manning and Moore McDowell, *Electricity Supply in Ireland: The History of the ESB* (Dublin: Gill and Macmillan, 1984), 37.

[47] Dominic de Cogan, 'The Wartime Origins of the Irish Corporation Tax'. *Irish Journal of Legal Studies* 3, 2 (2013): 15–32.

[48] *Weekly Irish Times*, 17 May 1924.

banks to underwrite the loan without a substantial commission incensed the Department of Finance since it meant 'that [they] declined to make any subscription whatever to the Loan on the terms on which it will be issued to the general public'.[49] Their practice of depositing their excess liquidity in London would remain a matter of controversy for decades.

Though the 1926 Banking Commission rejected the long-held nationalist view that this deprived the economy of investment capital, it recommended the establishment of a state bank of sorts to meet the credit requirements of smaller farmers and co-operative societies. The problem it identified pertained specifically to agriculture. The unwillingness of local communities to tolerate foreclosures meant that land could not serve as a reliable form of collateral.[50] An Agricultural Credit Corporation was duly established in 1927. The Trade Loans (Guarantee) Schemes of the 1920s were a precursor of sorts to the Industrial Credit Company which would be established under Fianna Fáil in 1933.[51] Only in the late 1960s, when the stability of sterling had come increasingly into question, were the external assets of the Associated Banks 'repatriated' to the Central Bank.

The ex-unionist accounting monopoly was tackled more aggressively. Craig Gardner and Stokes Brothers & Pim between them audited the majority of companies quoted on the Stock Exchange. The flow of official business directed to these firms under both Cumann na nGaedheal and subsequent administrations was disproportionately small. The auditing contracts for the first state commercial enterprises established in 1927—the Agricultural Credit Corporation, the Electricity Supply Board, and the Dairy Disposal Company—went to emerging Catholic firms.[52]

Even those strongly critical of Cumann na nGaedheal's performance in office recognize the significance of its achievements in the fields of electricity generation and distribution, which were decried as 'socialist' and 'confiscatory' in conservative quarters at the time. Of the 160 electricity undertakings in operation in the Free State area prior to the establishment of the Shannon hydro-electric plant, most—apart from those in the hands of local

---

[49] Joseph Brennan, cited in Ronan Fanning, *The Irish Department of Finance, 1922–58* (Dublin: Institute of Public Administration, 1978), 97.

[50] Banking Commission, *Second, Third and Fourth Interim Reports* (Dublin: Banking Commission, 1926).

[51] Mary E. Daly, 'Government Finance for Industry in the Irish Free State: The Trade Loans (Guarantee) Acts'. *Irish Economic and Social History* 11, 1 (1984): 73–93.

[52] Tony Farmar, *The Versatile Profession: A History of Accountancy in Ireland since 1850* (Dublin: Chartered Accountants Ireland, 2013), 70.

authorities—were tiny. Guinness and a number of other manufacturers produced their own electricity. Industrial concerns outside the major urban areas still largely depended on water, steam power, or internal combustion engines. Electricity consumption per capita was among the lowest in Europe.[53]

Germany had begun to invest in its hydro-electric resources following the loss of some of its major coal-mining regions in the wake of Versailles. The proposals for a similar scheme at Shannon were developed by an Irish engineer, T. A. McLaughlin, who had been working with Siemens-Schuckert in Germany. McLaughlin had presented his ideas to Patrick McGilligan, the Irish High Commissioner in London, and McGilligan, having developed a mastery of the technical issues involved, promoted the scheme assiduously upon his appointment as Minister for Industry and Commerce in 1924.[54] Private-sector interests favoured a smaller hydro-electric station on the Liffey. Shannon, however, was seen as a project of major national significance. It was understood that widespread provision of electricity would raise living standards, enhance industrial and agricultural productivity, facilitate regional development, and reduce the country's dependence on imported coal. The Department of Finance was side-lined to a large extent in the discussions. Brennan was concerned over the massive cost of the scheme though public finance pressures had eased by the time the bulk of the funds had to be raised. McElligott and Finance Minister Ernst Blythe were more favourably disposed to the entire undertaking.[55] The ex-unionist establishment was critical of the awarding of the contract to Siemens rather than to a British firm.[56]

Work on the hydro-electric plant had already begun before the question of how the power was to be distributed was settled. The low population density of the country made it difficult to attract private-sector interest, and it was eventually decided that a single company, the Electricity Supply Board (ESB), would be granted responsibility for both production and distribution on a not-for-profit basis—the first such integrated state scheme outside the Soviet Union. Existing electricity undertakings were acquired by compulsory order. Private owners were compensated according to a fixed formula while municipally owned undertakings—many of them in the former unionist strongholds of South Dublin—were acquired without compensation.

---

[53] R. F. Browne, 'The Electricity Supply Board'. *Journal of the Statistical and Social Inquiry Society of Ireland* 18 (1947): 564.

[54] Lothar Schoen, 'The Irish Free State and the Electricity Industry, 1922–1927', in *The Shannon Scheme and the Electrification of the Irish Free State*, ed. Andy Bielenberg (Dublin: Lilliput Press, 2002), 28–47.

[55] Cromien, 'Brennan, Joseph'; Daly, 'Government Finance for Industry in the Irish Free State: The Trade Loans (Guarantee) Acts'.

[56] Schoen, 'The Irish Free State and the Electricity Industry, 1922–1927', 41.

Sir John Keane was sharply critical of the plan to subject electricity to the same 'poisonous virus' that he had railed against in the case of land pur-chase.[57] Business Party TD William Hewat referred to the ESB's remit as signalling the 'complete elimination of private enterprise'.[58] The *Irish Times* too saw it as part of a pattern of growing state intervention, reflected also in the industrial tariffs then being adopted, and in transport policy, where 'railways and canals passed to the safe keeping of a government department'.[59]

The establishment of the Dairy Disposal Company (DDC) was another departure from laissez-faire principles. It emerged as a consequence of the collapse of the massive Condensed Milk Company of Ireland. The origi-nal company was liquidated in October 1923 with debts totalling half a million pounds. Its assets were bought out by a group of investors led by Andrew O'Shaughnessy and re-established as the Condensed Milk Company of Ireland (1924). British wholesaler Lovell and Christmas became the major shareholder, into which O'Shaughnessy's Newmarket Dairy Company was absorbed.

The long war of attrition with the proprietary creameries had depleted the cooperative movement of most of its cash and credit. Having been warned by O'Shaughnessy that Lovell and Christmas had sufficient resources to crush the cooperatives, the government was notified that it was prepared to sell the Condensed Milk Company to the cooperative body, the Irish Agricultural Organisation Society (IAOS). The offer, however, was 'an indirect approach to the government, since the company must have been aware that the IAOS lacked the necessary capital'.[60]

There were 580 creameries and separating stations in the Free State at the time, 400 of which were owned cooperatively. The Condensed Milk Com-pany owned 113 of the remaining private concerns. The government seized the opportunity to end the war of attrition. The offer was accepted and the Dairy Disposal Company was established to purchase the Condensed Milk Company and the other proprietary creameries. Over the following years, it closed large numbers of redundant plants, transferred dozens more to new cooperative societies, and developed the creamery industry extensively in West Kerry and County Clare.[61] The economies of scale that had allowed the original company to successfully engage in marketing and distribution were

[57] Manning and McDowell, *Electricity Supply in Ireland: The History of the ESB*, 37.
[58] Ibid., 68.
[59] *Irish Times*, 5 and 6 April 1927.
[60] Daly, *The First Department: A History of the Department of Agriculture*, 129.
[61] Mícheál Ó Fathartaigh, *Irish Agriculture Nationalised: The Dairy Disposal Company and the Making of the Modern Irish Dairy Industry* (Dublin: Institute of Public Administrations, 2014).

lost however.[62] Marketing problems would continue to blight the sector for most of the next half-century. Though clearly intended as an interim solution, the Dairy Disposal Company would be wound up only in the years following Ireland's accession to the European Economic Community.[63]

Other agri-food developments of significance included the establishment of the Irish Sugar Manufacturing Company and the rigorous systems of agricultural inspection and control introduced by Minister for Agriculture Patrick Hogan. The acts introduced by Hogan, though considered draconian at the time, enabled Irish produce to recover from the poor reputation it had earned during the First World War. The margin separating the price of Irish and Danish butter on the British market fell by half between 1924 and 1929.[64]

Sugar beet production had been subsidized in Britain since 1924. An agreement was reached with a consortium of Belgian and Czechoslovak interests to develop the industry in Ireland and a sugar beet factory was opened in Carlow in 1926. The subsidies paid both to the company and to growers were more generous than those on offer in Britain, and the response of Irish growers was substantially stronger than expected. The large profits that accrued to the company proved embarrassing to the government.

By 1931, the factory was supplying one-quarter of national requirements and employing 40–50 workers year-round and up to 600 during the three-month busy season. The operation ran into difficulties with the Depression-era collapse in international sugar prices and the strong resistance by growers to the tapered reduction in the subsidy (which had been announced at the initiation of the project). A proposal by the Department of Industry and Commerce in 1931 to build additional factories emphasized that they should be Irish owned and controlled, though the capital cost involved was regarded as beyond the means of Irish investors.[65] The Carlow factory would be bought out by the new Fianna Fáil government in 1933.

[62] P. F. Fox and Proinnsias Breathnach, 'Proprietary Creameries in Ireland', in *Butter in Ireland: From Earliest Times to the 21st Century*, ed. Peter Foynes, Colin Rynne, and Chris Synnott (Cork: Cork Butter Museum, 2014), 96.

[63] It has not been possible to determine exact employment numbers for the Dairy Disposal Company prior to 1964. The estimates provided for earlier decades are based on the assertion by Smith and Quinn, among others, that it had handled over 20 per cent of manufacturing milk since its establishment: Louis P. F. Smith and Gerard Quinn, *A Study of the Evolution of Concentration in the Irish Food Industry 1968–1973* (Brussels: EU Commission, 1975), 16.

[64] T. K. Daniel, 'Griffith on His Noble Head: The Determinants of Cumann na nGaedheal Economic Policy, 1922–32'. *Irish Economic and Social History* 3, 1 (1976): 55–65.

[65] Mary E. Daly, *Industrial Development and Irish National Identity, 1922–1939* (New York: Syracuse University Press, 1992), 97–98.

4.3 Trade Policy Debate

Tariff policy was the subject of impassioned debate from the foundation of the state. Supporters of free trade included the major exporting firms and sectors such as transport, banking, and trade, which were closely integrated into the British economy. In the case of agriculture, as Meenan notes,

> Farmers could be prosperous only if they were able to export. But precisely because the British market was open to the world, the Irish farmer could compete only if his products were of good quality and capable of being sold at a competitive price. Tariffs, rates and taxes had to be kept as low as possible.[66]

Following some dissension within the ranks of smaller Irish manufacturers, the Dublin Industrial Development Association had joined the Federation of Irish Industries in endorsing protection in 1924.[67] The republican parties—Sinn Féin and later Fianna Fáil—were strongly supportive, while Cumann na nGaedheal, as an alliance born solely of acceptance of the Treaty, was divided on the issue, as the Irish Parliamentary Party had been.[68]

A Fiscal Inquiry Committee was appointed by the Executive Council in June 1923 to report on the effects of existing or proposed trade restrictions.[69] Four of its five members were university economists. It heard evidence from interested parties in over forty sessions held between July and September 1923, though few of the larger export-oriented firms made submissions. In its final report, the Committee concluded that the volume of industry keen to obtain a protective tariff was small. Most of the industries seeking protection were described as 'debilitated' rather than of the infant-industry type that underlay the analysis of German economist Friedrich List, who had been a major influence on Arthur Griffith.[70] It also pointed to the adverse impact it would have on consumers and on the cost base of exporting industries. Presciently, it also warned that the new vested interests that protectionism would create would make it difficult to reverse course later.[71]

In his subsequent discussions with Ernest Blythe, the Minister for Finance, McElligott argued:

---

[66] James Meenan, 'From Free Trade to Self-Sufficiency', in *The Years of the Great Test 1926–39*, ed. Francis MacManus (Cork: Mercier Press, 1967), 69–79.

[67] Daly, *Industrial Development and Irish National Identity*, 22–23.

[68] James McConnell, *The Irish Parliamentary Party and the Third Home Rule Crisis* (Dublin: Four Courts Press, 2013), ch. 10.

[69] *PDDE*, 15 June 1923.

[70] Fiscal Inquiry Committee, Final Report (Dublin: Stationery Office, 1923), para. 96; Daniel, 'Griffith on His Noble Head: The Determinants of Cumann na nGaedheal Economic Policy, 1922–32'.

[71] Fiscal Inquiry Committee, Final Report para. 124.

The largest element in costs is wages and wages depend largely on the cost of living, which is always high in protected countries. The best way we can help [manufacturers] is to bring down, say, charges for transport and power [. . .] Better organisation, better marketing etc., are matters independent of protection and the incentive to them is often removed by protection.[72]

The protectionist voice diminished within the pro-Treaty camp over the course of the decade. Two supporters of the Griffith approach—Defence Minister Richard Mulcahy and Minister for Industry and Commerce Joseph McGrath—left the cabinet in the aftermath of the Army Mutiny of 1924, though Mulcahy returned in 1927. A memo from Gordon Campbell suggesting fifteen industries that could be protected without impacting on the cost of living was withdrawn on the resignation of McGrath.[73] J. J. Walsh, the Minister for Posts and Telegraphs, complained of the government's pandering to 'ranchers and importers'. He publicly supported Fianna Fáil in the 1932 general election.[74] Seán Milroy, a founder of the Irish Protectionist League, resigned from the party along with McGrath, accusing ministers of relying on civil servants whose loyalties, if not pro-British, were controlled by the Freemasons.[75] The standing committee of the party agreed, branding those in the Department of Finance as 'alien and anti-Irish'.[76]

The conclusions of the Fiscal Inquiry Committee were not accepted in their entirety by government however. W. T. Cosgrave, President of the Executive Council, had stated at the outset that 'the Committee is not expected to advocate policy. That will be a matter for the people and the government when they have the facts before them.'[77] Blythe announced in the Dáil in 1924:

[While not prepared] to recommend anything approaching a general tariff with the substantial rise in the cost of living which would inevitably follow [. . .] neither are we prepared to let the industrial drift continue, and content themselves with preaching efficiency and the virtues.

[72] Memorandum from McElligott to Blythe, September 1923, cited in Devlin and Barry, 'Protection versus Free Trade in the Free State Era: The Finance Attitude'.

[73] Campbell to McElligott, 3 March 1924, cited in Girvin, *Between Two Worlds: Politics and Economy in Independent Ireland*, 33.

[74] Patrick Maume, 'Walsh, James Joseph', in *Dictionary of Irish Biography* (Cambridge: Cambridge University Press, 2009).

[75] John M. Regan, 'The Politics of Utopia: Party Organisation, Executive Autonomy and the New Administration', in *Ireland: the Politics of Independence* ed. Mike Cronin and John M Regan (New York: St Martin's Press, 2000), 40.

[76] Ibid., 47–49.

[77] PDDE, 15 June 1923.

It was decided to 'impose certain duties which will give us a limited but sufficient experiment in the use of a tariff for the stimulation of Irish industry'.[78]

Tariffs were imposed in the Finance Act of 1924 on a range of items including boots and shoes, soap and candles, sugar confectionary, cocoa preparations, and glass bottles. The duty on tea was reduced in order to counteract the impact on the cost of living.[79] Duties on tea, coffee, and cocoa were abolished completely in 1925 in conjunction with the announcement of further tariffs on apparel, woollen textiles, and furniture. University College Dublin economist George O'Brien, who had served on the Fiscal Inquiry Committee, noted that 'protection is a costly process but [. . .] the result may be worth the cost [. . .] The mischief begins when people deceive themselves into the belief that protection is a method of getting something for nothing.'[80]

Though the Department of Agriculture remained solidly anti-protectionist, farmers joined the campaign for protection in 1926 as agricultural prices fell and bad weather persisted.[81] An experimental duty on oatmeal was imposed in 1926, and a Tariff Commission was established later that year. Presumably to avoid being directly importuned by those seeking protection, Industry and Commerce accepted that the Minister for Finance be granted sole power to refer applications to the Commission and to nominate both the secretary and chairman. McElligott considered that it was 'the duty of the Department of Finance to see that the time of the Tariff Commission is not wasted in examining a particular proposal unless there appears, *prima facie*, to be a case that is worthy of consideration.'[82]

From August 1927, when they entered the Dáil, Fianna Fáil subjected the Commission to constant criticism. Lemass complained about the time taken to prepare its reports and the waste of time and money in making submissions to a body that he suggested was likely to prove doctrinaire in its opposition. In providing a forum for opposition to tariffs to be voiced, the Commission adopted a more holistic view than similar bodies in Britain and the Commonwealth.[83] Its reports are described by Meenan as 'models of clarity' and commended for their awareness of 'the many links that bind even the most dissimilar industries to one another'.[84] Of the fourteen reports issued by

---

[78] *PDDE*, 25 April 1924.
[79] Ibid.
[80] George O'Brien, 'The Budget'. *Studies: An Irish Quarterly Review* 14, 54 (1925).
[81] Daly, *Industrial Development and Irish National Identity*, 27.
[82] McElligott to Blythe, 22 October 1926, cited in Girvin, *Between Two Worlds: Politics and Economy in Independent Ireland*, 37–38.
[83] Louden Ryan, 'The Nature and Effects of Protective Policy in Ireland, 1922–1939'. Ph.D. thesis, Trinity College Dublin, 1949, 42–50.
[84] James Meenan, 'Irish Industry and Industrial Policy 1921–1943'. *Studies: An Irish Quarterly Review* (1943): 209–18.

the Commission between its establishment and the general election of 1932, ten nevertheless adjudicated in favour of tariffs.[85] The government, meanwhile, sought to remove some of the disabilities of Irish industry through the provision of electric power and by means of low taxation.

From 1930, with the onset of the Great Depression, the potential for import substitution began to be looked at more closely. Agriculture's opposition weakened as export volumes and output prices fell and other agricultural exporters began to target the UK market more aggressively.[86] The global downturn prompted Cosgrave to announce the establishment of a permanent Tariff Commission in late 1930. All five of the reports of the reconstituted Commission—on butter, bacon, oats, linen goods, and certain categories of leather—granted protection within months of the applications for tariffs being submitted.[87]

In November 1931, following the election of a protectionist government in Britain, the Executive Council took powers under the Customs Duties (Provisional Imposition) Act to impose such duties as it might decide were 'immediately necessary to prevent an expected dumping of goods or other threatened industrial injury'. The first batch of duties was imposed in late November.[88] This Act, similar to those adopted elsewhere around this time, was seen as a response to temporary abnormal circumstances and was intended to operate only for nine months. It was used sparingly during the remainder of Cumann na nGaedheal's period in office. The political environment would change dramatically with the formation of the first Fianna Fáil government in 1932.

4.4 Sectoral and Firm-Level Consequences of Selective Protection

The first Irish tariffs, which came into effect with the establishment of a customs frontier in April 1923, duplicated those of Britain. The most significant of these in the Irish case were the duties on manufactured tobacco and on motor vehicles and parts. Employment in tobacco manufacturing quadrupled over the next three years. Though tariff announcements were generally followed by a rush to import stocks, the experimental tariffs introduced in 1924

[85] Ryan, 'The Nature and Effects of Protective Policy in Ireland', 41–42. Daly notes that the number of applications is likely to have far exceeded the number of reports issued: Daly, *Industrial Development and Irish National Identity*, 39–41.

[86] Ibid., 56.

[87] Ibid., 46.

[88] *PDDE*, 4 November 1931.

and 1925 also had an immediate impact on output and employment, as is evident from contemporary newspaper reports. By 1930, there had been a marked decline in imports of most of the tariffed items other than footwear, and more than 100 new factories had been opened in the newly protected sectors.[89]

The first Census of Industrial Production (CIP) was produced for 1926. The data in Table 4.1 suggest that some 9,000 jobs had already been created in sectors that had been tariffed by that date. Though partly a consequence of recovery (rather than solely of protection), this was a far from inconsiderable achievement.[90] By 1930, a further 4,000 jobs had been added in these sectors.[91]

By contrast, only 400 jobs had been added by 1930 in the sectors that had been tariffed *since* 1926, suggesting that the lowest-hanging fruit had been picked first.[92] The most effective of the tariffs were those on consumer products. The 1924 tariff on glass bottles was set at too low a level to resuscitate the industry as it had met with strong resistance from the drinks producers, jam makers and chemists for whom bottles represented a significant cost. The 1929 tariff on woollen and worsted textiles was vigorously opposed by clothing producers.

An issue that had yet to be resolved concerned the policy to be adopted towards British firms that established operations behind the tariff wall. Most of the substantial UK firms that commenced production in the Free State in the 1920s and 1930s already had experience of operating 'tariff factories' in other Commonwealth countries.[93] Within a year of the establishment of the customs frontier, three constituent firms of the Imperial Tobacco Company—Players, Wills, and pipe tobacco and snuff producer William Clarke & Son—had opened factories in Dublin. As the same tariff was automatically levied on goods shipped in the opposite direction, indigenous tobacco manufacturer P. J. Carroll & Co. opened a plant in Liverpool to protect its British and cross-border sales. Two Northern Irish tobacco firms,

---

[89] *Saorstát Éireann: Irish Free State Official Handbook*, 143.

[90] A figure of 9,000 new jobs was reported in the *Irish Times* of 11 December 1926, though the total has been calculated on a somewhat different basis here.

[91] The CIP reports that manufacturing employment increased by 6,000 between 1926 and 1929, with job gains in tariffed sectors thought to have exceeded job losses in other areas (Daly, *Industrial Development and Irish National Identity*, 77). While coverage of the CIP may have improved over these years, the scope of the 1929 census actually narrowed. The preliminary figures for 1926 reported in the *Irish Trade Journal* were revised in line with those for 1929 when the censuses were published jointly in 1933 (CIP, 1926 and 1929, vi).

[92] *Saorstát Éireann: Irish Free State Official Handbook*, 142.

[93] These included Imperial Tobacco (which operated as British American Tobacco beyond the former UK), Rowntree, Cadbury, and Dunlop, as well as less prominent firms such as Wilson and McBrinn.

Table 4.1 Employment in 1926 and 1930 in sectors tariffed by 1926

Industry	Date of tariff	Full-time employment equivalent at date of tariff	Employment in September/ October 1926	Employment on 1 September 1930
Manufactured tobacco	1 April 1923	500†	2,096†††	2,081†
Footwear	1 April 1924	250†	967†††	1,227†
Glass bottles	1 April 1924	25†	127††	193†
Soap and candles	1 April 1924	230†	410†††	620†
Confectionery, jams, and biscuits*	1 April 1924	3,400†	5,051††	5,367†
Wholesale clothing: men's and boy's factory-made clothing, hats, caps, ties, and umbrellas	1 April 1925	805†	2,290††	3,733†
Shirt making	1 April 1925	410†	1,572††	1,844†
Hosiery	1 April 1925	500†	849†††	1,354†
Blanket making	1 April 1925	130†	548††	462†
Furniture, including brush making and metallic bedsteads	1 April 1925	444†	1,274††	2,010†
Corset making	1 April 1925	–††	83††	n.a.
Oatmeal	1 April 1926	250†	500††	544†
Total employment		**6,944**	**15,767**	**19,435**

Sources: †*Saorstát Eireann Irish Free State Official Handbook* (Dublin: Talbot Press, 1932), 142; ††'Protection in Free State', *Irish Times*, 11 December 1926 (based on results reported in various issues of the *Irish Trade Journal*); †††CIP, 1926; *: the numbers provided for the confectionary sector differ from those reported in the CIP as biscuits were also included (*Irish Trade Journal*, August 1928, 139).

Murray & Sons and Gallahers, would also commence operations in Dublin over the next several years.

Government minister J. J. Walsh was particularly vocal in his opposition to the entry of external firms because of the detrimental impact this would have on their domestic competitors.[94] Goodbody Tobacco had taken on an extra 100 workers in 1923. It ceased production in 1929. Fianna Fáil would seek to

---

[94] *Irish Times*, 12 May 1923; Daly, *Industrial Development and Irish National Identity*, 35–36.

address the issue through the Control of Manufactures Acts of 1932 and 1934. Gallahers would close its plant in 1932 when the new Fianna Fáil government imposed a discriminatory duty on raw tobacco imports by firms established since 1922. (The government claimed that the aim of the policy was to protect small firms rather than specifically indigenous enterprises.) Three hundred workers – many of them former Goodbody employees – lost their jobs with the closure of the Gallaher plant, which caused the first serious rift between the new Fianna Fáil administration and its Labour Party allies.[95] As the main domestic rival to Players–Wills, Carrolls would expand significantly over the following decades. Its workforce increased to 400 by 1934 and would exceed 500 from the early 1950s.

The other major tariff that came into effect automatically with the establishment of a customs frontier was on motor vehicles and parts. This raised a dilemma for government. Ford has ceased tractor production with the collapse of the agricultural boom in 1920, and the Cork plant had been repurposed to produce parts for the company's vehicle assembly plant in Manchester. Ford's trade with the United Kingdom would now be subject to tariffs. It appeared likely that an agreement could be secured to have the charges on trade between the jurisdictions waived. Ford's refusal to commit to remaining in Cork however meant that the loss in tariff revenue on imported cars dominated government considerations and the potential agreement was not pursued. Employment at the Cork plant fluctuated massively over the decade. It reached a high of 7,000 in 1929 when tractor production resumed, but 6,000 were laid off the following year as a consequence of the Great Depression.[96] A decision by the company to close the Cork plant was reversed when the new Fianna Fáil government banned the importation of fully assembled vehicles.

Details of some of the firm-level developments in tobacco and other sectors impacted by the tariffs of the early Cumann na nGaedheal years are provided in Table 4.2. The tariff on confectionery products introduced in 1924 was regarded by the Cosgrave administration as the most successful of its protectionist experiments. Its introduction has been credited to the influence of Joseph Milroy, proprietor of the recently established Dublin Confectionery Works and brother of one of the TDs who had resigned from Cumann na nGaedheal over the government's reluctance to introduce more thoroughgoing protectionist policies. Within a year of the tariff, Williams & Woods, the largest confectionery firm, had taken on 'from 400 to 500

---

[95] *Irish Times*, June 11, 1932.

[96] *Irish Times*, 7 March 1929; Thomas Grimes, 'Starting Ireland on the Road to Industry: Henry Ford in Cork'. Unpublished Ph.D. thesis, National University of Ireland, Maynooth, 2008, 125.

Table 4.2 Selected firms established/acquired as a result of the tariffs of 1923–1926

Sector	Firm and date of establishment or acquisition	Nationality	Employment
Tobacco	Imperial Tobacco (1923)	UK	1,500 (1928), major employer (to 1972)
	Murray and Co. (1925)	UK	c. 100
	Gallaher Tobacco (1931)	UK	300 (1932)
Confectionery	Williams & Woods (acquired by Crosse & Blackwell, 1928)	UK from 1928	477 (1924), 900 (1926), remains ≥500 (to 1972)
	Savoy Cocoa (Rowntree from 1926)	UK from 1926	150 (1923), > 500 (from 1932)
	NKM (Mackintosh from 1925)	UK from 1925	100 (1922), 200–300 from mid-1920s; in partnership with Rowntree from 1931
	Clarnico–Murray (1926)	UK	200–300
	R. & W. Scott (1927)	UK	200–300
	Urney Chocolates (1924)	Irish	250 (1929, 1939), >500 (from 1960)
	Blue Badge Cream Toffee (Devlin's) (1924)	Irish	100–200; acquired by Urney (1960)
	Oatfield Sweets (McKinney's) (1927)	Irish	c. 100
Clothing	Wilson & McBrinn (1926)	UK	200 (1927), 250 (1932), 300 (1939), 400 (1960, 1966)
	Montague Burton (1927)	UK	c. 300
	Taylor & Co. (1925)	UK	150 (1936), 200 (1953)
Corsets	Leethem and Co. (1925)	UK	66 (1926), 100 (1929), 300 (1936), 225 (1966)
Hosiery	Sunbeam (1928)	Irish	200 (1931), 250 (1933), >500 (from 1935)
	W. P. McCarter & Co. (1931)	Irish	200 (1937), 300 (1958)
Soap and candles	Castle Forbes Soap Factory (Lever Bros) (1927)	UK	300 (1929), 350 (1935), 400 (1961), 500 (1971)
Footwear	Halliday (1928)	UK	100 (1928), 200 (1933), 300 (1934), 360 (1941), >500 (from 1946)
	Hanover Shoes (Dwyer family) (1925)	Irish	150 (1926), 200 (1962)

Source: author.

extra hands'.[97] It was acquired by UK firm Crosse & Blackwell in 1928. Williams & Woods would remain a major employer through to 1972. Other British firms to establish behind the tariff barrier included Mackintosh, which acquired NKM in 1925, and Rowntree, which acquired Savoy Cocoa the following year. The firms would operate in partnership in Ireland under the aegis of Associated Chocolate and Confectionery from 1931. Clarnico-Murray opened a factory in Dublin in 1926. Scottish jam maker R. & W. Scott followed in 1927.

New indigenous firms established in the wake of the tariff included Liam Devlin's Blue Badge Cream Toffee in Dublin and Oatfield Sweets in Letterkenny, County Donegal. Urney Chocolates—named for the parish in West Tyrone where the business was started in 1917—shifted production to Tallaght in 1924 following a fire at its Northern Ireland factory. Urney would become a major employer and would acquire Devlins and a number of other smaller firms before itself being acquired by US firm W. R. Grace & Co. in 1963. Employment at the Shannon Confectionery Works expanded from 30 to 120 over the next few years. Inchicore jam producer Lambs diversified into sweets. Lemons opened a new factory in Drumcondra.

There were rapid employment increases also in ready-made clothing, shirt making, and furniture. Of the sixteen new ready-made tailoring factories established in 1925 and 1926, the most significant were Lee Clothing in Cork (part of the Dwyer family group), Belfast firm Wilson and McBrinn in Drogheda, and two Leeds firms: Montague Burton in Dublin and Taylor & Co. in Dundalk.

Sixteen new shirt factories opened over this two-year period, the majority of them in Donegal. Most were Northern Ireland firms. These included the Foyle Shirt and Collar factory in Lifford, Tillie & Henderson (Éire) in Carndonagh, and A. B. Grant and McCloskey and Co. in Buncrana. Some Northern Ireland shirtmakers outsourced work to Derry firm Porter and Co., which was already in operation in Castlefin. The Donegal factories generally employed a workforce of 100 or so. Shirt making remained concentrated in Dublin, where much of the work was conducted in-house in Pim Brothers, Todd, Burns and Co., and other department stores.[98]

The major development in soap products was the opening by Lever Bros of the Castle Forbes works on Dublin's Sheriff Street in 1927, into which the old Dublin soap manufacturer Barringtons was integrated.[99] New hosiery firms

[97] *Irish Times*, 17 April 1925.
[98] *Irish Trade Journal*, January 1927, 57.
[99] Unilever archives: GB1752.IRE—Unilever Ireland (Holdings) Ltd and Subsidiary Companies (GB1752.IRE/JB); *Irish Independent*, 8 July 1927, 9.

included Sunbeam in Cork and W. P. McCarter & Co. in Buncrana. Sunbeam would go on to become a massive employer throughout the period to EEC accession. McCarter would rise to prominence in the 1980s as producer of the US brand 'Fruit of the Loom'. Martin Mahony built a new hosiery factory in Blarney. Greenmount and Boyne expanded into blouses and lingerie. The corset maker alluded to in the sectoral statistics was British firm Leethem and Co., which established in Dublin in 1925.

There were also substantial developments in footwear. Within a year of the tariff, employment at Lee Boot, one of the Dwyer family companies, expanded from 200 working primarily part-time to 300 working full-time.[100] The Dwyers also established a new women's footwear firm, Hanover Shoes. Within a year of its opening in 1925, it had a workforce of 150. The firms would merge to form Lee Footwear in 1965. The Dwyers had been strong lobbyists for protection and all of their various operations—in clothing, shirt making, and footwear—expanded as a consequence of the policies adopted. Hosiery and knitwear producer Sunbeam was established by a younger generation of the family.

Leeds firm Halliday, which specialized in heavy agricultural boots, transferred production to Dundalk in 1928. It would enter into an agreement to produce for Clarks Shoes in 1938, when the market for its boots contracted with the growing popularity of rubber wellingtons. The agreement formed part of Clark's efforts to circumvent the restrictions imposed by the Control of Manufactures Acts that Fianna Fáil would introduce in the 1930s.[101]

The final major episode of foreign direct investment of the Cumann na nGaedheal era was the acquisition of the Bannatyne–Goodbody milling group by UK firm Ranks in 1930. Proposals for a tariff on flour had been rejected on the grounds that it might induce Jacobs to shift further production to the United Kingdom.[102] It was clear however that some form of intervention was in the offing. The acquisition proved timely as British and Irish millers responded to overcapacity by forming a cartel in 1931, which gave Irish-based producers a disproportionate share of the market. Imports of flour other than under licence would be banned in 1933.[103] Resolutions objecting to the industry passing into foreign hands were passed by a number of local authorities.[104]

The extent of 'tariff jumping' by British firms was stronger than anticipated, and the Department of Industry and Commerce shared some of the con-

---

[100] *Irish Times*, 17 April 1925.
[101] Jon Press, *The Footwear Industry in Ireland, 1922–1973* (Dublin: Irish Academic Press, 1989), 70.
[102] *Manchester Guardian*, 12 May 1928.
[103] Daly, *Industrial Development and Irish National Identity*, 49, 50, 94.
[104] *Irish Times*, 7 March 1930.

cerns expressed by the Cumann na nGaedheal Minister J. J. Walsh and by the opposition Fianna Fáil party at these developments. An analysis prepared by the department in October 1928 noted how, by the sale of domestic firms in protected sectors, 'the owners turned into cash for their own pocket the concession which they, in common with other firms in the industry, were given by the state on national grounds'.[105] Departmental officials recommended that the minister be empowered to prohibit such transfers or to approve them only after the increased value had been surrendered to the state. Though the report expressed doubt 'that the economic penetration which had followed on the wake of protection here had yet attained the dimension of a national evil', it was feared that foreign staff might retain the key positions within such companies and that further tariff-driven industrial expansion might see 'effective control in the new industrial enterprises [. . .] pass to outside concerns'.[106]

Seán Lemass, who was shortly to become Minister for Industry and Commerce in the new Fianna Fáil administration, had stated in 1927 that 'unless we can ensure that the benefits derived from the imposition of protection are reserved for the Irish manufacturers as well as the consumers it is a dangerous policy to embark on protection'.[107] Given Fianna Fáil's commitment to import substitution, it is no surprise that legislation to control foreign ownership would be among the first matters to be addressed by the department under the new dispensation.

Another unanticipated consequence of the tariffs of the 1920s and beyond was the share of the resulting jobs that went to women.[108] This aroused disquiet among politicians and male trade union leaders and clauses would be introduced in the 1936 Conditions of Employment Act granting the Minister (Lemass) the power to ban women from certain areas of employment and to impose gender quotas on industries. Mary Daly characterizes the act as 'otherwise a progressive piece of legislation guaranteeing workers holidays with pay and regulating overtime, shift-work and night-work'. Noting that there is no evidence of efforts being made to enforce the clauses relating to women, she suggests that their inclusion may have been 'a cynical political response to popular pressure'.[109]

---

[105] Cited in Girvin, *Between Two Worlds: Politics and Economy in Independent Ireland*, 67.
[106] Cited in ibid., 68.
[107] Cited in Mary E. Daly, 'An Irish-Ireland for Business?: The Control of Manufactures Acts, 1932 and 1934'. *Irish Historical Studies* 24, 94 (1984): 252.
[108] Daly, *Industrial Development and Irish National Identity*, 123–126.
[109] Mary E. Daly, 'Women in the Irish Free State, 1922–39: The Interaction between Economics and Ideology', *Journal of Women's History* 7, 1 (1995), 99–116.

4.5 Largest Manufacturing Employers of 1929

The CIP reveals that – excluding the railway engineering works – there were nine manufacturing establishments employing 500 workers or more in 1929.[110] There were, in addition, at least a further six multi-establishment firms employing a workforce of this size. These firms, along with a number of others employing close to this figure, are listed in Table 4.3.

Even by 1929, four of the five largest firms were foreign-owned. These included Guinness, whose registered office had been in London since 1886, though the daily management of the company was overseen in Dublin. Players–Wills and Crosse & Blackwell were tariff-jumping operations. The takeover by Ranks of Bannatyne and Co. in 1930 might be considered an example of 'precautionary' tariff jumping. Among the firms with workforces of 500 or more, around half of the jobs were in foreign-owned companies. It is known both from the international evidence and from later Irish data that foreign companies are strongly over-represented in the larger firm-size and establishment-size categories. An educated guess as to the foreign share across all of industry in 1929 might be in the region of 20 per cent.

The foreign share would have been lower in 1926 when Ford employed a substantially smaller workforce and Williams & Woods had not yet been acquired. The share would have been lower still in 1922, prior to the opening of the British-owned tobacco factories in Dublin. Guinness and Ford, along with Furness & Withy (UK owners of Rushbrooke Dockyard), were the sole foreign-owned enterprises employing workforces of 500 or more at independence.[111] This might suggest a foreign share of perhaps 15 per cent at the time, slightly higher than the 10 per cent suggested as an upper bound in previous research.[112]

---

[110] Players–Wills was a multi-establishment firm but is included in the single-establishment category in Table 4.3 as the South Circular Road factory employed well in excess of 500 by this time. Wills had moved from Marrowbone Lane to the William Clarke site when the firms integrated in 1928. Players would remain in Glasnevin until the 1960s when it too moved to the South Circular Road site. The figure in the table includes employment at all of these establishments.

[111] On the basis of the data in Chapter 3, these three companies employed around 5,000 in the Free State in 1922. The denominator for 1922 is unknown but, on a CIP basis, may have been somewhere in the region of 50,000.

[112] Frank Barry, Linda Barry, and Aisling Menton, 'Tariff-Jumping Foreign Direct Investment in Protectionist Era Ireland'. *Economic History Review* 69, 4 (2016): 1285–308.

Table 4.3 Firms employing *c.* 400 or more in 1929

Firm name	Sector/products	Employment *c.* 1929	Ownership
Single-establishment firms			
Ford	Tractors and motor vehicle parts	3,800	US
Guinness	Brewing	3,210	UK
Jacobs	Biscuits	3,000	Irish
Players–Wills	Tobacco	1,500	UK
Williams and Woods/Crosse & Blackwell	Sugar confectionary and jams	900	UK
Goodbody (Jute)	Non-woollen textiles	800	Irish
Martin Mahony & Bros	Woollen textiles	600	Irish
Irish Independent	Printing and publishing	600	Irish
Bolands	Bread and flour	500	Irish
Multi-establishment firms			
Dwyer and Co.	Clothing and footwear	800	Irish
Bannatyne & Sons (Ranks from 1930)	Flour and grain milling	800	Irish (UK from 1930)
Gouldings	Fertilizers	700	Irish
Dairy Disposal Company	Dairy products	*c.* 600	Semi-state company
Greenmount & Boyne	Non-woollen textiles	590	Irish
Johnston, Mooney and O'Brien	Bread and flour	500	Irish
Firms with close to 500 employees			
Philip Pierce & Co.	Agricultural machinery and bicycles	250–450	Irish
Denny	Bacon	*c.* 400	Irish/UK
Limerick Clothing Factory	Clothing	*c.* 300–400	Irish
Alexander Thom & Co.	Printing and publishing	400	Irish
Helys	Printing, publishing, stationery	*c.* 300–450	Irish
Carrolls	Tobacco	*c.* 400	Irish

Source: author.

5

From the Great Depression to the End of the Emergency

The Great Depression began in 1929 and reached its trough in the Free State—as across most of the rest of Western Europe—in 1932–1933. The decades between the beginning of the depression and the formation of the first Inter-Party government in 1948 can be roughly divided into the four sub-periods for which the data are presented in Table 5.1. Firms employing 500 or more in or around 1948 are listed towards the end of the chapter.

Irish industry was only modestly impacted by the global depression even prior to the change in policy that followed Fianna Fáil's election victory in early 1932. UK manufacturing employment fell by 13 per cent between 1929 and 1931.[1] The decline in the Irish case—because of the very different structure of the two economies—was of the order of 2 per cent.

The second sub-period stretches from the last year of the Cumann na nGaedheal administration to the settlement of the land annuities dispute with Britain. While agriculture suffered severely as a consequence of the economic war, manufacturing boomed with the shift to full protection.[2] Employment increased by a dramatic 60 per cent over the years to 1938, three times the rate recorded in the United Kingdom. Productivity developments however would store up problems for the future. British labour productivity improved as industry recovered; Irish labour productivity declined as entirely new industries were conjured into being.[3]

Industrial expansion came to a halt with the onset of the Emergency, as the Second World War era was referred to in neutral Ireland. Production was constrained by shortages of fuel, raw materials, parts, and equipment.

---

[1] Ryland Thomas and Nicholas Dimsdale, 'A Millennium of Macroeconomic Data for the UK'. *Bank of England's Historical Macroeconomic and Financial Statistics: Version* 3 (2017): table A53.

[2] Daly refutes the claim that much of the recorded employment increase might have been a consequence of a gradual improvement in the coverage of the Census of Industrial Production: Mary E. Daly, 'The Employment Gains from Industrial Protection in the Irish Free State during the 1930s: A Note'. *Irish Economic and Social History* 15, 1 (1988): 71–75.

[3] Irish manufacturing output grew by 50 per cent over the period, UK output by 45 per cent, and UK employment by 23 per cent (UK output data from Stephen N. Broadberry, 'Manufacturing and the Convergence Hypothesis: What the Long-Run Data Show'. *Journal of Economic History* 53, 4 (1993): appendix 1).

Industry and Policy in Independent Ireland, 1922–1972. Frank Barry, Oxford University Press.
© Frank Barry (2023). DOI: 10.1093/oso/9780198878230.003.0005

Table 5.1 Developments in manufacturing
employment, selected sub-periods, 1929–1948

	Employment change	Percentage change (rounded)
1929–1931	−1,496	−2
1931–1938	36,342	60
1938–1945	148	≈ 0
1945–1948	22,229	23

Source: Census of Industrial Production; Statistical
Abstract (1952).

Though agriculture fared better, there was no bonanza for farmers as there had been during the First World War. British prices were strictly controlled and 'an inadequate supply of fertilisers, feedstuffs, and machinery depressed crop and milk yields'.[4] Manufacturing fell sharply up to 1942/43 but began to recover with the pick-up in trade from the time of the Normandy landings, and by 1945 the pre-war level of employment had been restored.

The vigorous rebound of the immediate post-war years paralleled developments elsewhere across Western Europe. The boom in the war-ravaged economies however was driven by reconstruction; the Irish boom owed more to the release of pent-up consumer demand.

The existential challenge posed by the deterioration in the balance of payments and the austerity policies that it triggered would be met with the transformative policy responses of the mid-to-late 1950s.

5.1 From the Great Depression to the Eve of the Emergency

Though Free State exports declined with the onset of the Great Depression, the terms of trade (the ratio of export to import prices) improved up to the outbreak of the economic war in July 1932. The collapse in global grain prices benefited Ireland's beef and dairy export sectors. It also reduced the cost of feeding pigs and poultry, which were staple products on smaller land holdings, and of bread and maize meal, which were particularly

---

[4] Cormac Ó Gráda and Kevin O'Rourke, 'Irish Economic Growth, 1945–88', in *Economic Growth in Europe Since 1945*, ed. Nicholas Crafts and Gianni Toniolo (Cambridge: Cambridge University Press, 1996), 388–426.

significant items in the diets of poorer households.[5] The lack of heavy industry served to protect the economy from the collapse in manufacturing trade.[6] As University College Cork (UCC) Professor of Economics John Busteed expressed it in 1931, 'you cannot "fire" a small farmer in the same way as you can "fire" 5,000 Ford workers'.[7] The decline in manufacturing between 1929 and 1931 corresponded closely to developments in the vehicle construction sector in which Ford was the dominant presence (Table 5.2). That Ireland entered the depression with low government debt and substantial external assets offered further significant benefits. There were no Irish banking failures.

Given the prevailing currency board arrangement, the Irish pound had fallen in value along with sterling when Britain left the gold standard in 1931. Depreciation served to cushion the depression and the United Kingdom became the first major country to surpass its pre-depression level of industrial production in 1934.[8] The benefits to Ireland were limited by the fact that most of its agricultural competitors on the UK market also devalued. Though Seán MacEntee, who would succeed Blythe as Finance Minister in the new Fianna Fáil administration, described sterling 'as a millstone round the necks of the people', he did not push the analogy further.[9] Devaluing against sterling would have forfeited the savings in transactions costs and other advantages of the interchangeability of the currencies. Blythe warned that few governments

Table 5.2 Employment in manufacturing and motor vehicle construction, 1929 and 1931

	1929	1931
Manufacturing	62,439	60,943
Coach, wagon, and motor body building and construction of motor vehicles (including tractors)	4,355	1,996

Source: CIP.

[5] Mary E. Daly, 'The Irish Free State and the Great Depression of the 1930s: The Interaction of the Global and the Local'. *Irish Economic and Social History* 38 (2011): 19–36.

[6] Commission of Inquiry into Banking, Currency and Credit, *Reports* (Dublin: Stationery Office, 1938), 53–73.

[7] Cited in Frank Barry and Mary Daly, 'Irish Perceptions of the Great Depression', in *The Great Depression in Europe: Economic Thought and Policy in a National Context*, ed. Michael Psalidopoulos (Athens: Alpha Bank Historical Archives, 2012), 395–424. The massive fluctuations in employment at the Ford plant associated with the on-again, off-again nature of tractor production occurred between the census dates reported in Table 5.2.

[8] Barry Eichengreen and Jeffrey Sachs, 'Exchange Rates and Economic Recovery in the 1930s'. *Journal of Economic History* 45, 4 (1985): 925–46.

[9] Cited in Barry and Daly, 'Irish Perceptions of the Great Depression'.

with adjustable exchange rates 'could withstand the temptation to get out of their difficulties by putting the printing presses to work'.[10]

Though clearly dramatic in the Irish context, and viewed with grave disquiet in the United Kingdom, the regime change that followed Fianna Fáil's accession to power in 1932 was moderate by international standards. Most of the fledgling democracies of the other new inter-war states had collapsed into autocracy. De Valera would suggest in later life that the founders of Fianna Fáil might perhaps with some justification have been described as 'socialists'.[11] The social welfare innovations and expansion in government spending over which the party presided were modest however in comparison to Roosevelt's 'New Deal' in America.[12] In his St Patrick's Day broadcast to the United States in 1934, de Valera likened Roosevelt's task to 'a major surgical operation' while Fianna Fáil's 'was more that of the physician patiently restoring a much-weakened but otherwise healthy body to full life and vigour'.[13] The default on land annuity payments was one of many episodes of sovereign default across Europe over the period.

The shift from 'selective' to 'full protection' was also part of a broader international trend. The United States had raised its tariffs in 1930. Britain, long the leading proponent of free trade, had turned protectionist in 1931. Many others had followed suit in the wake of the competitive devaluations triggered by the United Kingdom's abandonment of the Gold Standard earlier that year. The depression eroded belief in the benefits of free trade and minimal government intervention. The support that the United Kingdom began to offer its farming sector would have disadvantaged Irish agriculture regardless of the economic war. Other UK trading partners intervened to protect their farmers much as Ireland did. Agriculture's veto on industrial protection was weakened.[14]

---

[10] Cited in Daly, 'The Irish Free State and the Great Depression of the 1930s: The Interaction of the Global and the Local'.

[11] *Irish Times*, 19 May 1976.

[12] Data on Irish government spending are provided in the data appendix to John FitzGerald and Seán Kenny, 'Managing a Century of Debt'. *Journal of the Statistical and Social Inquiry Society of Ireland* 48 (2018): 1–40. US federal spending is charted in Price Fishback, 'US Monetary and Fiscal Policy in the 1930s'. *Oxford Review of Economic Policy* 26, 3 (2010): 402, figure 3. Though MacEntee, the first Fianna Fáil Minister for Finance, would suggest many years later that his 'was the very first Keynesian budget in this island' (*Irish Times*, 24 July 1974), the increase in spending in both Ireland and the United States was largely financed by taxation rather than by borrowing.

[13] 'De Valera's New Deal', *Round Table, A Quarterly Review of the Politics of the British Commonwealth* 95 (June 1934): 579.

[14] *Weekly Irish Times*, 22 March 1930.

Nor was the pre-1922 business establishment as hostile to state intervention as had been the case a decade earlier. For J. & L.F. Goodbody, expansion
of the domestic sugar and peat industries would provide it with a new source
of demand for its output of sacks, bags, and twine. It welcomed the protection
it received against imports from Calcutta in the lighter types of jute it would
soon produce in Waterford. Linen firms, which had been threatened by the
erection of a customs frontier with Northern Ireland in 1923, now too lobbied
for protection in the goods in which they were in competition with Northern
Ireland and which the United Kingdom had recently protected. One rep-
resentative of the industry stated that 'he did not want to see an Ireland of
thirty-two counties, as twenty-six were quite enough for him and the others
engaged in the linen trade'.[15]

The department stores expanded their manufacturing businesses behind
the tariff wall: Arnotts 'thanked God and the government's economic nationalism of the 1930s for the development of new knitting and making-up
industries which became vital during the period of the Emergency and were
very useful for years afterwards'.[16] The sharp decline in emigration resulting
from the global contraction increased the pressure on government to adopt
new job-creation policies. Timber firms and other builders' providers benefited from the expansion in house construction that ensued. The free trade
lobby was further weakened by developments at Ford and Guinness. With
excess capacity at its massive new plant in Dagenham and the collapse in the
global tractor market, Ford had made the decision to cease production in
Cork.[17] Guinness's plans to establish a brewery at Old Trafford near Manchester had been shelved at the outbreak of the First World War. It retained
ownership of the site but would open at Park Royal in London in 1936 instead.

Though Cumann na nGaedheal's 1932 election handbook denied that it
was a free-trade party, its more cautious economic approach was out of step
with the mood of the times. It also shared with other incumbent governments
the difficulty of securing re-election during a severe economic downturn.
From its foundation, Fianna Fáil had been ideologically committed not only
to protection but also to as high a degree of self-sufficiency as possible. Its
1932 manifesto committed to 'make ourselves as independent of foreign
imports as possible'.[18] Friedrich List, the German economist who had been a
major influence on Arthur Griffith, had been explicit that his 'infant-industry

[15] *Irish Times*, 23 February 1933.
[16] Ronald Nesbitt, *At Arnotts of Dublin, 1843–1993* (Dublin: A. & A. Farmar, 1993), 112.
[17] Thomas Grimes, 'Starting Ireland on the Road to Industry: Henry Ford in Cork'. Unpublished Ph.D.
thesis, National University of Ireland, Maynooth, 2008, 168.
[18] *Irish Press*, 11 February 1932.

argument' did not extend to agriculture. Fianna Fáil's agricultural policy was influenced by a separate stand of nineteenth-century thought in the person of Young Irelander James Fintan Lawlor, who had blamed the expansion of cattle at the expense of tillage for the depopulation of the country. Fianna Fáil policy would seek to reverse the process whereby, in de Valera's phrase, 'the bullock replaced the human being'.[19] The Fianna Fáil-aligned minority report of the 1928 Select Committee on Wheat Growing had asserted that since bread had become the staple of the Irish diet, 'there is therefore a presumption in favour of the opinion that the first function of farming in [the state] should be the production of wheat'.[20]

Nor was Fianna Fáil's advocacy of industrial protection confined to industries that would be expected to become internationally competitive, as List had advocated. The Banking Commission would conclude from its discussions with Leydon, Secretary of Industry & Commerce under Lemass, that there were 'scant prospects of paying for imports by the export of the products of the new industries'.[21] There was a difference in logic, too, between the import-substituting industrialization of primary producers and the 'defensive' industrial protection of the more advanced industrial economies.[22] Industry emerged *de novo* in the Free State as it did across much of Latin America, which also turned strongly protectionist at this time. Ireland's average tariff level in 1937 was the third highest of the twelve European countries and fifth highest of the twenty countries in total for which Ryan provides data.[23]

Though Keynes and others were arguing strongly for 'schemes of National Development' in the United Kingdom, Fianna Fáil showed no great enthusiasm for increased government spending in the lead-up to the 1932 general election. Retention of the land annuities, it was suggested, could be used to de-rate agricultural land, with the remainder 'available for the relief of

---

[19] *Irish Times*, 19 March 1934.

[20] James Meenan, *The Irish Economy since 1922* (Liverpool: Liverpool University Press, 1970), 96.

[21] Commission of Inquiry into Banking, Currency and Credit, *Reports*, 68.

[22] Heinrich Liepmann, *Tariff Levels and the Economic Unity of Europe: An Examination of Tariff Policy, Export Movements and the Economic Integration of Europe, 1913–1931* (London: George Allen and Unwin, 1938).

[23] Louden Ryan, 'Measurement of Tariff Levels for Ireland, for 1931, 1936, 1938'. *Journal of the Statistical and Social Inquiry Society of Ireland* 18 (1947): 109–32. Though O'Rourke shows that Ireland was not an outlier in terms of the quantitative restrictions it imposed, countries that devalued early along with Britain tended to adopt lower protectionist barriers. Ireland *was* an outlier in this regard: Kevin O'Rourke, 'Independent Ireland in Comparative Perspective'. *Irish Economic and Social History* 44, 1 (2017): 19–45; Barry Eichengreen and Douglas A Irwin, 'The Slide to Protectionism in the Great Depression: Who Succumbed and Why?' *Journal of Economic History* 70, 4 (2010): 871–97.

taxation, or for such purposes as the Dáil may determine'.[24] The party's economic programme included a promise to 'eliminate waste and extravagance in public administration' and to reduce the salaries of senior civil servants. Its job creation proposals focused on industrial protection and the expansion of tillage.

The first Fianna Fáil government, however, was reliant on the votes of the Labour Party, whose preconditions for support included a major housing programme, widows' and orphans' pensions, and measures to provide work or maintenance for the 85,000 men believed to be unemployed at the time.[25] While Fianna Fáil considered that Irish unemployment was only marginally related to the global depression, Labour's demands strengthened the hand of the left wing of the party.[26]

The first Fianna Fáil budget was a major break with the parsimony of the past. The control of the Department of Finance had been diminished by the appointment of a Cabinet Committee to adjudicate on budgetary matters.[27] Expenditure grew sharply both in absolute terms and as a share of national income.[28] Orthodox views on balanced budgets continued to be respected however, as was also the case under Roosevelt in the United States. That British income tax rates were significantly higher than they had been over the previous decade allowed the Irish government to follow suit. The basic rate of income tax was raised from three shillings and sixpence to five shillings in the pound in May 1932. The British rate had been raised to five shillings the previous September.

Registered unemployment in the early phases of the depression remained low. The announcement in May 1932 of a public works programme that would recruit workers off the live register resulted in the number *on* the register more than doubling between April and June. By December 1932, it had reached 103,000. A 'farmers' dole' was introduced in 1933. By the late 1930s, an average of 78,000 people were in receipt of assistance.[29] A new housing programme was initiated by the Department of Local Government.[30] Of the

[24] *Irish Press*, 11 February 1932. De Valera had asserted in 1928 that 'the country had already been taxed beyond its capacity': Irish Times, 11 July 1928.

[25] Daly, 'The Irish Free State and the Great Depression of the 1930s: The Interaction of the Global and the Local'.

[26] Barry and Daly, 'Irish Perceptions of the Great Depression'.

[27] Daly, 'The Irish Free State and the Great Depression of the 1930s: The Interaction of the Global and the Local'.

[28] FitzGerald and Kenny, 'Managing a Century of Debt'.

[29] Daly, 'The Irish Free State and the Great Depression of the 1930s: The Interaction of the Global and the Local'.

[30] Lemass, PDDE, Vol. 41, 20 April 1932, col 289; Mary E. Daly, *The Buffer State: Historical Roots of the Department of the Environment* (Dublin: Institute of Public Administration, 1997).

almost 91,000 houses built between 1923 and 1938, over 65,000 were built after 1932.[31]

The first major batch of new import duties was announced in April 1932 under legislation inherited from the previous administration. MacEntee's budget speech in May increased or imposed new tariffs on scores of manufactured items. The Cumann na nGaedheal legislation was superseded later in the year by a new act which expanded the scope for the imposition of duties by ministerial order. Freed from the oversight of the Department of Finance and the Oireachtas, trade and industry policy from this point 'became largely discretionary decisions determined by ministers and officials'.[32] The Banking Commission would complain that this 'necessarily introduces an element of uncertainty into the business life of the country, which is aggravated when full publicity is not given to the decisions taken'.[33] The Tariff Commission fell into abeyance. McElligott, Secretary of Finance, protested that 'the functions of this Department are being reduced to those of a Post Office'. Another senior Department of Finance official suggested dryly that the process of imposing duties by executive authority should be extended to cover all taxes.[34]

There is little evidence that the measures adopted by the new government were evaluated on the basis of any considered cost–benefit analysis, as had been the case under the Tariff Commission. As Lemass put it, he 'preferred to take the risk of making mistakes in proceeding in the way we are proceeding than to take the risk of producing the same results that the late Government had produced by inactivity'.[35] Protection was imposed across almost all sectors of industry.[36] The imposition of tariffs on intermediate inputs necessitated even higher tariffs on final output. In a study of the effective protection afforded Irish industry in the mid-1960s, McAleese suggested that the disparities found across industries—with those at the top of the scale afforded four times the protection accorded those at the bottom—'appear to reflect the rather haphazard method of awarding tariffs since the 1930s'.[37] At the end of 1931, fifty-nine articles had been covered by protective tariffs. By the

[31] J. Peter Neary and Cormac Ó Gráda, 'Protection, Economic War and Structural Change: The 1930s in Ireland'. *Irish Historical Studies* 27, 107 (1991): 250–66.

[32] Mary E. Daly, *Industrial Development and Irish National Identity, 1922–1939* (New York: Syracuse University Press, 1992), 178.

[33] Commission of Inquiry into Banking, Currency and Credit, *Reports*, 53–73.

[34] Anna Devlin and Frank Barry, 'Protection versus Free Trade in the Free State Era: The Finance Attitude'. *Irish Economic and Social History* 46, 1 (2019): 3–21.

[35] *PDDE*, 8 June 1932.

[36] Commission of Inquiry into Banking, Currency and Credit, *Reports*, 53–73.

[37] Dermot McAleese, 'Effective Tariffs and the Structure of Industrial Protection in Ireland'. Economic and Social Research Institute (ESRI) Research Series, 1971, 6.

end of 1937, almost 2,000 articles were subject to duties or to quantitative restrictions.[38]

Superimposed on the new government's protectionist agenda was the economic war with Britain which broke out in July 1932. Agrarian unrest in the late nineteenth century had induced the British Treasury to provide cheap loans to Irish tenant farmers to finance the massive land redistribution process then underway. The bonds issued to finance the Free State's 1923 Land Act had also been guaranteed by the British. The Cosgrave government, as part of the deal, had agreed to collect and maintain the flow of land annuity payments to London. These negotiations had been conducted in secrecy however and the agreement had not been ratified by the Dáil. De Valera's legal advisors suggested that it need not therefore be regarded as binding.[39] Fianna Fáil had adopted republican socialist Peadar O'Donnell's campaign against repaying the annuities in 1930 and, once in power, refused to forward them to London.

Britain retaliated with a range of punitive tariffs on Irish agricultural exports, to which the Free State responded by providing subsidies or bounties to many of the adversely affected sectors.[40] It also responded with punitive tariffs of its own. There were disagreements within the Cabinet on how aggressively the dispute should be pursued, but a general election in January 1933 saw Fianna Fáil returned to office with an overall majority. Annuity obligations on farmers were reduced by half, as had been promised in advance of the election, and the funds that had been retained in a suspense account pending resolution of the dispute were paid into the Irish exchequer, representing a substantial new source of funding for government.

The fortunes of industry and agriculture diverged sharply over the period of the dispute. There was a massive drop in rural living standards, with livestock farmers particularly adversely affected. Smaller farmers, who lived much closer to the margins of existence, benefited more from the reduction in annuity obligations and the introduction of the means-tested 'farmers' dole'.[41] The main driver of industry, by contrast, was the shift to full protection. The real wages of industrial workers improved, at least in Dublin, for which the only data are available.[42] While Britain's retaliatory duties targeted Free State

---

[38] Meenan, *The Irish Economy since 1922*, 142.

[39] Ronan Fanning, *The Irish Department of Finance, 1922–58* (Dublin: Institute of Public Administration, 1978), 280.

[40] The tariffs on pig products were marginally higher than the export subsidies. The opposite applied in the case of butter. The brunt of the tariffs was borne by live cattle exports: Cathal O'Donoghue, 'A Century of Irish Agriculture: A Policy Driven Sector'. *Journal of the Statistical and Social Inquiry Society of Ireland*, LI, (2022): 86–127.

[41] Cormac Ó Gráda, *Ireland: A New Economic History 1780–1939* (Oxford: Clarendon Press, 1994), 416.

[42] Commission of Inquiry into Banking, Currency and Credit, *Reports*, 62, 78, 109.

agriculture, Guinness's decision to open a brewery in the United Kingdom was reportedly triggered by a warning from the British authorities that a tariff might otherwise be imposed.[43] Brewing was among the few manufacturing sectors to record a decline in employment over the period.

The economic war declined in intensity with the coal–cattle pacts of the mid-1930s and was comprehensively settled in 1938. The British government had assumed that trade sanctions would be sufficient to unseat de Valera. By 1938, Fianna Fáil was electorally secure, Cosgrave was now too in favour of retaining the annuities, and British attention was increasingly focussed on developments in continental Europe. The terms of the settlement were such that Ireland is considered to have 'won' the economic war.[44] The 'Treaty ports' which had been retained by the British in 1922 were handed over, and a capitalized land-annuity liability of £80–100 million was written off in exchange for a lump-sum payment of £10 million (the maximum that the British estimated that the Irish state could afford). Trade would henceforth be conducted under the terms of the Ottawa Accords, which governed UK–Commonwealth economic relations. Most Irish industrial goods could enter the United Kingdom tariff-free (though numerous quantitative restrictions continued to apply), while British imports would be eligible for a preferential tariff rate—generally between one-half and three-quarters of the full rate—in Ireland.

The 1938 Agreement also committed the Irish government to have existing import restrictions replaced by duties that would offer 'adequate protection' to Irish industries while affording UK manufacturers the 'full opportunity of reasonable competition.'[45] Though this aspect of the settlement raised fears among some that extensive import competition from Britain might now resume, the outbreak of the Second World War and the vagueness of the language employed meant that little change of consequence occurred.[46] As one trade union organizer wryly remarked, 'if you can give reasonable protection and reasonable competition, well, it is wonderful.'[47]

The total area under tillage had barely changed over the course of the decade. Tillage farmers had simply switched from unsubsidized to subsidized crops. Sugar manufacturing expanded alongside sugar beet

[43] Stanley R. Dennison and Oliver MacDonagh, *Guinness 1886–1939: From incorporation to the Second World War* (Cork: Cork University Press, 1998), 249–57.

[44] Kevin O'Rourke, 'Burn Everything British But Their Coal: The Anglo-Irish Economic War of the 1930s'. *Journal of Economic History* 51, 2 (1991): 357–66.

[45] Louden Ryan, 'Protection and the Efficiency of Irish Industry'. *Studies: An Irish Quarterly Review* 43, 171 (1954): 317–26.

[46] Daly, *Industrial Development and Irish National Identity, 1922–1939*, ch. 8; Ryan, 'Protection and the Efficiency of Irish Industry', 319.

[47] Cited in Neary and Ó Gráda, 'Protection, Economic War and Structural Change: The 1930s in Ireland'.

production. Other spillovers from agriculture were relatively minor. Tobacco manufacturers and flour producers were required to use a certain proportion of home-grown product in their mix, though in neither case did consumers find the taste appealing. There were reports of instances of the home-grown product being dumped or sold onward at a loss. The area under tillage would rise by compulsory order during the Second World War, when the difficulty of sourcing imports provided industries with little choice but to conform to the mixing requirements.[48]

The 1938 Agreement marked the end of Fianna Fáil radicalism in the agricultural sphere. The primacy of the beef and dairy export trades was reinstated and a new equilibrium established that balanced the forces of export-oriented agriculture and protected industries.[49] This equilibrium would come under pressure in the mid-to-late 1950s through a combination of internal and external developments: balance-of-payments-induced crises on the one hand, and pan-European trade liberalization on the other.

Another component of Fianna Fáil's nationalist economic agenda pertained to the ownership of industry. By the end of the Cumann na nGaedheal era, most of the largest firms in the newly tariffed sectors were British-owned. Among the concerns expressed at the time were that foreign-owned subsidiaries would be unlikely to develop an export trade, that higher executive positions would tend to be filled by foreign staff, that branch plants would disappear rapidly in a downturn, and that foreign-owned companies might come to exercise monopoly positions in the market. Some suggested that foreign firms would impose 'appalling conditions'; others suggested the opposite—that they would pay wages that native firms could not afford.[50]

The Control of Manufactures Acts of 1932 and 1934 were designed to concentrate control of newly established firms in the hands of Irish citizens. The Dáil resisted some of Lemass's more interventionist tendencies, including suggestions that control might also apply to domestic undertakings and to foreign businesses established before the measures were enacted. Companies not fulfilling the criteria could apply for a licence to manufacture, but this could entail burdensome restrictions on location, domestic content, product mix, and the like. Paradoxically, some external firms with strong bargaining power were able to negotiate monopoly positions for themselves in the Irish market.

---

[48] Meenan, *The Irish Economy since 1922*, 117.
[49] Daly, *Industrial Development and Irish National Identity, 1922–1939*, 169.
[50] Frank Barry, 'Foreign Investment and the Politics of Export Profits Tax Relief 1956'. *Irish Economic and Social History* 38 (2011): 54–73.

As frequently occurred elsewhere however, restrictions on foreign ownership—which pertained to share capital, voting rights, and directorships—were largely left to languish on the statute books.[51] With the assistance of local law firms, foreign companies found ways of avoiding the necessity of having to apply for a licence. In many cases, 'finance, and hence control, was derived from loans or extended credit, or by means of an overdraft guaranteed by the English parent company'.[52] Trademarks and patents were frequently assigned such that effective control remained with the foreign partner.

The consequences of the acts, furthermore, sat somewhat uneasily with another element of government policy. The establishment by the state of the Industrial Credit Company (ICC) in 1933 'was rendered necessary by the inadequate financial facilities available for new industrial undertakings'.[53] It was, in part, a response to nationalist concerns that Irish industry had been starved of capital.[54] Ironically, according to the 1938 Banking Commission, the ICC presided in its early years over a net export of capital as ownership of some UK subsidiaries was transferred into the hands of Irish citizens.[55]

That the acts were not rigorously policed was indicative of a belated recognition by government of the value of the employment and expertise that foreign firms could provide. With the passage of time, the authorities came to prefer schemes that did not require licences as applications could lead to objections from local businesses.[56] The acts clearly provided the government with some leverage however. They were not fully repealed even with the major shift in policy on foreign direct investment in the 1950s.

5.2 Sectoral and Firm-Level Developments from 1931

Employment grew across almost all manufacturing sub-sectors over the sub-period 1931–1938, as shown in Table 5.3. The sectoral groupings that were subject to the least protection—Foods Other than Sugar and Sugar Confectionery (Group I) and Drink and Tobacco (Group III)—expanded

---

[51] Frank Barry, Linda Barry, and Aisling Menton, 'Tariff-Jumping Foreign Direct Investment in Protectionist Era Ireland'. *Economic History Review* 69, 4 (2016): 1285–308.

[52] Mary E. Daly, 'An Irish-Ireland for Business?: The Control of Manufactures Acts, 1932 and 1934'. *Irish Historical Studies* 24, 94 (1984): 263.

[53] John O'Donovan, 'State Enterprises'. *Journal of the Statistical and Social Inquiry Society of Ireland* 18 (1947): 332.

[54] On the scarcity of capital debate, see Ó Gráda, *Ireland: A New Economic History 1780–1939*, ch. 14.

[55] Commission of Inquiry into Banking, Currency and Credit, *Reports*, 56.

[56] Daly, 'An Irish-Ireland for Business?: The Control of Manufactures Acts, 1932 and 1934', 267.

Table 5.3 Sectoral developments, 1931–1948

Group	Sector	Employment, 1931	Employment, 1938	Employment change, 1931–1938 (%)	Memo item: Employment, 1948
I	Foods Other Than Sugar and Sugar Confectionery (bacon, butter, grain, bread, biscuits, etc.)	16,694	18,416	10	19,833
II	Sugar and Sugar Confectionery	2,577	4,926	91	7,025
III	Drink and Tobacco	8,736	8,331	−5	9,932
IV	Clay, Glass and Cement	676	3,028	348	3,708
V	Timber, Furniture etc.	4,368	6,854	57	7,346
VI	Motor Vehicles	1,996	3,921	96	6,318
VII	Other Metals, Engineering and Implements	2,665	7,605	185	9,025
VIII	Textiles and Clothing	10,970	21,417	95	27,354
IX	Footwear and Leather	1,195	6,547	448	8,046
X	Paper and Printing	6,399	9,315	46	10,939
XI	Chemicals and Miscellaneous	4,667	6,925	48	10,136
	Total	60,943	97,285	60	119,662

Source: CIP.

least. The decline in Drink and Tobacco was concentrated in brewing and was associated with the establishment of the new Guinness brewery in London.[57]

Within Group 1, there was little change in the various segments other than grain milling. Butter and bacon had been accorded some protection towards the end of the Cumann na nGaedheal administration. These measures were defensive. The tariff enabled some of the bacon producers that had been on

---

[57] The decline in beer exports between 1935 and 1938 closely matched the output of the new Guinness brewery which came into operation in 1936: Kieran Kennedy, Thomas Giblin, and Deirdre McHugh, *The Economic Development of Ireland in the Twentieth Century* (London: Routledge, 1988), 47.

the verge of liquidation to return to profitability.[58] Mitchelstown was granted a monopoly on processed cheese production. Restrictions on flour imports allowed Irish-based producers to form a cartel and divide the local market among themselves: as prices were set at levels that allowed the smaller operators to remain in business, the largest—Ranks and Odlums—earned substantial profits.[59] Employment in grain milling expanded by around 1,000.

The main growth in food processing was in Sugar and Sugar Confectionery (Group II), as had also been the case under Cumann na nGaedheal. A large component of the expansion reflected the establishment of the state-owned Irish Sugar Company (Comhlucht Siúcra Éireann) in 1933. Lemass had accepted, in a statement in the Dáil, that 'beet sugar cannot possibly compete with cane sugar if we are to regard everything from the accountant's point of view' but pointed to the spillover effects which had led other European countries, including Britain, to support the production of sugar beet.[60]

Though Daly estimates that the subsidy was a multiple of the amount that Lemass posited in his Dáil statement ('a cost to the community of an additional halfpenny a pound'), it nevertheless compared favourably to what had been paid in the 1920s.[61] The industry's establishment under state ownership, she suggests, was a reaction to the embarrassment to government that the experience of the 1920s had caused.[62] The Belgian-owned Carlow plant was purchased by compulsory order and three new sugar factories were established at Mallow, Tuam, and Thurles. There were five times as many employed across the four plants at the height of the sugar campaign in 1937 as there had been at the Carlow factory in 1931. By 1948, Irish Sugar was one of the largest manufacturing employers in the state.

Rowntree and Cadbury were the major British producers of chocolate confectionery. Rowntree had initiated operations in Dublin in the 1920s (as had Mackintosh, with whom it would shortly enter into partnership). When news emerged that a higher tariff on confectionery was in the offing, Cadbury, which was already losing money on its Irish exports, followed suit. The first Fry–Cadbury plant opened in East Wall in 1933. A second would be opened several years later in the recently vacated Gallaher Tobacco premises. Employment at the firm would remain modest until the 1950s however

---

[58] Edward Whelan, *Ranks Mills: The Industrial Heart of Limerick City* (Limerick: Limerick City Council, 2012), 49.

[59] Daly, *Industrial Development and Irish National Identity, 1922–1939*, 95; Stephen Odlum, *Flour Power, the Story of the Odlum Flour Milling Families* (Dublin: Zest Publications, 2015), 6.

[60] *PDDE*, 25 July 1933.

[61] Daly, *Industrial Development and Irish National Identity, 1922–1939*, 98.

[62] Ibid.

as a significant share of production was outsourced to Clarnico-Murray in Terenure. Fry–Cadbury's Dublin workforce of 200–300 in 1948 was similar to that of Urney, the major indigenous producer, and less than half that of Rowntree–Mackintosh. By 1971, Cadbury Ireland (as the Irish venture had been renamed) had become a major exporter of confectionery as well as chocolate crumb (the latter from its plant in County Kerry, which dated from the post-war era) and was another of the largest manufacturing employers in the state.

Three major new firms emerged in the Clay, Glass and Cement sector (Group IV). Several previous attempts to resurrect the Irish Glass Bottle Company had failed. It was successfully revived in 1932 by an Irish–Belgian consortium led by the former Cumann na nGaedheal minister Joseph McGrath. It diversified into sheet glass with the opening of a second Ringsend factory in 1936. Arklow Pottery opened in 1934, with early-stage training provided by several dozen workers brought in from Staffordshire Potteries. Cement Limited was established in conjunction with an Anglo-Danish concern attracted by the monopoly the firm had been granted for the production and importation of cement. Cement factories were opened in Drogheda and Limerick in 1938. All three of these firms employed workforces of 400 or so by the end of the decade. Employment at Irish Cement would exceed 500 by 1948. It would merge with Roadstone decades later to form Cement Roadstone Holdings (CRH), one of the major indigenous multinationals of the present era.

The imposition of quantitative restrictions on imports of fully built-up (FBU) vehicles led Ford to reverse its decision to close its Irish plant, though the employment levels at the height of tractor production in the late 1920s would never again be attained. The factory was now repurposed to assemble primarily for the domestic market. Around a dozen other firms also initiated assembly operations. Ford held at least a half-share of the Irish market in the 1930s and would continue to outsell any of its rivals up to 1972. Morris and Austin, the next most popular marques, were assembled by Dublin car dealerships G. A. Brittain and Lincoln & Nolan.[63]

Some 3,000–4,000 cars had been imported annually prior to the imposition of restrictions in 1933. Eight-and-a-half thousand were assembled in 1938. By 1950, the figure had grown to 17,000, while imports of FBU units had declined to just over 100.[64] Ireland was not the only jurisdiction to restrict FBU imports. Some car manufacturers were already producing completely

---

[63] Bob Montgomery, *Motor Assembly in Ireland* (Dublin: Dreoilin Publications, 2018), 212–30.
[64] Ibid., 11–16; Committee on Industrial Organisation, *Report on the Motor Vehicle Assembly Industry* (Dublin: Committee on Industrial Organisation, 1962), 24.

knocked-down (CKD) kits for assembly elsewhere. In other cases, particularly in the early phase of the new regime, 'fully built cars were dismantled, put into crates and shipped to Ireland where they were put back together again'.[65] US army jeeps purchased at the end of the war were dismantled in the United Kingdom by one particular Irish firm, Motor Distributors Ltd, before being imported to Ireland and reassembled by the same firm.[66] These cases bear echoes of Keynes's provocative Depression-era suggestion that unemployment could be eradicated were the Treasury to fill old bottles with banknotes, bury them in disused coalmines, and leave it to private enterprise to dig them out. As he went on to point out however, building houses would probably be more sensible.[67]

The requirement that the assemblers use certain locally produced components provided part of the motivation for tyre producer Dunlop to establish a plant in Ireland. Its first factory, established in the late Victorian era, had been in Dublin, but the company had relocated to Coventry by the turn of the century and was by now a major British multinational. It was warned by the Irish government in 1933 that if it failed to establish a local operation one of its competitors would be granted a monopoly of the tyre business in the state. Having secured a guarantee that imports would only be allowed in the types of tyres that it did not itself manufacture, it opened a plant on the grounds of the Ford factory in Cork.[68] Other early suppliers to the Ford assembly operation included Bray light-bulb producer Solus Teoranta, paint manufacturer Harrington Goodlass-Wall, and Irish Sewing Cotton in Westport.[69]

Irish Dunlop was the largest employer in the Chemicals and Miscellaneous segment (Group XI). Besides tyres, it also produced rainwear, wellington boots, and a range of other rubber items. By the late 1930s, it had a workforce of around 800, roughly equal to that of Ford. The two plants would close within a year of each other in the mid-1980s.

The largest employer in Group VII, 'Other Metals, Engineering and Implements', was the Hammond Lane Foundry Company, by then a holding company for the dozen or so firms in the Hammond Lane group. Irish Steel was established by the same proprietor, David Frame, in 1938. Though he had planned to locate the new company at the former Kynochs site in Arklow, he was prevailed upon by Lemass to establish at Haulbowline, which, as the

[65] Montgomery, *Motor Assembly in Ireland*, 142.

[66] Ibid., 202.

[67] John Maynard Keynes, *The General Theory of Employment, Interest and Money* (London: Macmillan, 1936), 129.

[68] Geoffrey Jones, 'The Growth and Performance of British Multinational Firms before 1939: The Case of Dunlop'. *Economic History Review* 37, 1 (1984): 35–53.

[69] Display advertisement for Ford, *Irish Times*, 3 January 1938.

Irish Times suggested, 'should go far to compensate Cobh [. . .] for the losses sustained by the departure of naval and military establishments from Queenstown Harbour'.[70] With the outbreak of war and the ensuing shortages of coal and other vital raw materials however, the company went into receivership in 1942. It struggled on during the war years and would eventually be rescued by the state.[71]

The largest employment increase was in textiles and clothing. Cork hosiery and knitwear producer Sunbeam, Greenmount & Boyne, Convoy Woollen Mills, and Northern Ireland company Abbey Clothing (which had a long-established factory on Dublin's Abbey Street) all expanded significantly in the 1930s. Sunbeam employed a workforce of 900 by the end of the decade.[72] Some 200 new textiles and clothing factories also opened over the seven years to 1938. UK company Polikoff (Ireland) would be, for much of its existence, the largest clothing manufacturer in the state.[73] It opened in Dublin in 1933. Salts, a subsidiary of a Yorkshire worsted spinning company, opened in Tullamore in 1937. The workforce at both firms would reach 500 within a few years of their establishment. J. & L. F. Goodbody opened a new jute factory in Waterford in 1936. Cotton fabric producer General Textiles opened in Athlone, also in 1936.[74] Dublin department store Arnotts established a number of manufacturing subsidiaries to cater to its in-store needs.

Halliday had been the only significant British footwear producer to establish in the Free State in the 1920s. Higher duties were now applied and imports other than under licence were prohibited shortly afterwards.[75] Twenty-one new boot and shoe factories opened between 1931 and 1938 and employment in the industry expanded by 4,000. Northern Ireland firm Edward Donaghy transferred its operation to Drogheda in 1932. Heavy boot manufacturer J. H. Woodington of Bristol also established in Drogheda. John Rawson and Co. of Leicester set up in Dundalk. Another British producer of high-quality shoes, Padmore & Barnes, established in Kilkenny. Rawson had a workforce in excess of 500 by 1935.[76] By the end of the decade, half of the

---

[70] *Irish Times*, 25 August 1939.

[71] Frank Barry and Joe Durkan, 'Team Aer Lingus and Irish Steel: An Application of the Declining High-Wage Industries Literature'. *IBAR—Irish Business and Administrative Research* 17 (1996): 58–72.

[72] UK company Wolsey's stake in Sunbeam, which had been acquired in 1933, had been bought out by the Dwyer family three years later, though the name Sunbeam–Wolsey was retained. A son-in-law of the Dwyers, having worked for Sunbeam, set up Seafield Fabrics in 1946 to produce synthetic fibres from rayon. A clothing subsidiary, Blackwater Cottons, was established several years later.

[73] It would be acquired by Abbey Clothing in 1963 and renamed Kilmaine Clothing.

[74] Established by a consortium of Irish and Belgian interests, its long-term managing director—the founder of the Lenihan family political dynasty—left the civil service at Lemass's instigation to become company secretary in 1937.

[75] These paragraphs draw on Jon Press, 'Protectionism and the Irish Footwear Industry, 1932–39'. *Irish Economic and Social History* 13, 1 (1986): 74–89.

[76] Ibid., 85, fn. 47.

workers in the sector were employed in UK firms, and many indigenous companies had entered into agreements with British manufacturers to produce the latter's brands for the Irish market.

The Cumann na nGaedheal government had hoped that incentivizing footwear production would be sufficient to revive the shoe leather industry.[77] The extension of protection to shoe leather led to the creation of a further 1,000 new jobs, though the price of the home-produced product was 20 per cent higher than its imported counterpart.[78] Irish Tanners opened a major plant at Portlaw and a subsidiary operation in New Ross in 1935. Tanneries were opened in Dungarven and Gorey in 1936, the latter in association with British footwear manufacturer J. H. Woodington. The Hitschmann family, whose businesses in the Sudetenland had been expropriated by the Nazis, opened a tannery in Carrick-on-Suir in 1938 under the name Plunder & Pollak (Ireland).

The major development in Paper and Printing (Group X) was the reopening of the Clondalkin paper mills. Some of the other smaller Dublin paper mills were also revived. Employment at Clondalkin expanded from 200 in the late 1930s to 500 a decade later. Today's vast Smurfit packaging business began life as a box-making factory in 1934. The factory was fully acquired in 1938 and renamed Jefferson Smurfit & Sons in 1942. The company would remain a minor employer until the 1960s. The Fianna Fáil newspaper, the *Irish Press*, had been established in 1931. It employed more than 300 in 1948; Smurfit employed fewer than 200.

Among the functions performed by the ICC were those which, in the case of public issues of established industries, 'would normally be discharged by private underwriters and would not be attended by undue risk'.[79] The Department of Industry and Commerce viewed the body as excessively risk-averse and overly constrained by Department of Finance orthodoxy.[80] Many of the firms discussed above, including a number of British subsidiaries, were among its most significant clients. Ranks (Ireland) was, next to Irish Sugar, the largest stock issue underwritten in its first year of operation. Irish Dunlop

---

[77] D. J. Dwyer, 'The Leather Industries of the Irish Republic, 1922–55: A Study in Industrial Development and Location'. *Irish Geography* 4, 3 (1961): 176.

[78] Press, 'Protectionism and the Irish Footwear Industry, 1932–39', 87, fn. 54. The leather sector had not been included in the CIP for 1931 as employment had been minimal at the time. Employment over subsequent decades would not increase much beyond the 2,000 or so recorded in 1948.

[79] O'Donovan, 'State Enterprises', 332.

[80] Mary E. Daly, 'Government Finance for Industry in the Irish Free State: The Trade Loans (Guarantee) Acts'. *Irish Economic and Social History* 11, 1 (1984): 92.

was one of the largest in 1935. Salts (Ireland) and Polikoff (Ireland) were the largest in 1937.[81] The former Cumann na nGaedheal minister J. J. Walsh was sharply critical of Fianna Fáil policy in this regard, writing in 1944:

> Not only did the enemy of their country get almost everything worth taking but the native taxpayer was compelled in many cases to supply him with the necessary finance to do so, through the Industrial Credit Company.[82]

5.3 The Emergency and Immediate Post-War Recovery

The industrial expansion of the post-1932 period came to a halt with the outbreak of war in 1939. Around 9,000 manufacturing jobs were lost over the following three years. Output fell more substantially than employment as production processes became more labour-intensive and efforts were made to keep people in work.[83] There was a decline also in the quality of the products available, as referred to earlier in the cases of flour and tobacco. The era can be seen as an enforced example of what has come to be referred to today as 'the circular economy'. Goods were repaired and reused in ways that remain familiar across much of the developing world. Dunlop harvested scrap rubber, Irish Steel harvested scrap metal, paper was made from straw and rags, and blankets were made from the clippings formerly discarded by clothing manufacturers.

The most significant contraction over the war years was in vehicle construction. Petrol became unavailable to most private motorists in January 1941. The Ford factory was reduced to operating at 4 per cent capacity. Used car parts were reconditioned, axle parts were made from old tram axles purchased from the railway companies, salvaged packing crates were used to produce clogs and other wooden items, and the nails removed from the crates were straightened for reuse. The Ford foundry was put to use producing cast-iron lavatory cisterns, gutters, and drainpipes. Some of the company's employees farmed the factory land; others harvested turf.[84]

The employment gains in the 'miscellaneous industries' category in the Census of Industrial Production (CIP) more than offset the job losses in

---

[81] Industrial Credit Company Ltd, *Twenty-One Years of Industrial Financing, 1933 to 1954* (Dublin: Industrial Credit Company Ltd, 1954), 17–22.

[82] Cited in Daly, *Industrial Development and Irish National Identity, 1922–1939*, 128.

[83] R. C. Geary, 'Irish Economic Development since the Treaty'. *Studies: An Irish Quarterly Review* 40, 160 (1951): 399–418.

[84] Grimes, 'Starting Ireland on the Road to Industry: Henry Ford in Cork', 212–14; Montgomery, *Motor Assembly in Ireland*, 80.

vehicle construction however. Employment numbers were not reported for individual sub-sectors, but among those which grew strongly in volume and value terms were coal and peat briquettes, 'canned goods, meat extract, etc.' and ship and boat building and repair. Though the many thousands employed in turf cutting were not included in the CIP, those employed in briquette production were. The tonnage of briquettes produced grew tenfold. The Turf Development Board produced peat briquettes at a factory adjacent to the Lullymore bog in County Kildare, which was accessed by the Grand Canal, and Great Southern Railways (GSR) produced coal briquettes at Inchicore, Broadstone, and Cork. The GSR briquettes, made from low-quality coal mixed with pitch, produced an unexpectedly satisfactory fuel. Within months of their appearance in 1942, 'the crisis in train punctuality ended'.[85]

Beef canning was initiated by processors Clover Meats and Roscrea Meat Products. Canned beef exports grew more than twenty-fold in value over the war years.[86] Clover also did a significant trade in 'erinox cubes', which were marketed as a tasty and nutritional substitute for tea, which was in extremely short supply. Employment at both Clover and Roscrea increased from pre-war levels of around 100 to wartime levels of around 350. Clover would be the second largest meat processor in the state at European Economic Community (EEC) accession.

The Liffey dockyard reopened under private ownership in 1940. Rushbrooke in Cork reopened the following year under the auspices of the state company Irish Shipping, which had been established to assist in the importation of essential commodities. Both dockyards employed workforces of 450–500 throughout the remainder of the war. There are indications from the UK archives that Irish ships chartered to the British authorities may have been serviced at the Dublin dockyard in exchange for steel.[87]

Barter was common in the conduct of wartime trade. British steel was supplied to the Pierce plant in Wexford in exchange for agricultural machinery. British coal was provided to the cement factories in exchange for cement. Britain had imposed restrictions on Irish access to coal in the early years of the Emergency in an attempt to secure the return of the Treaty ports. Ireland had responded with a cement embargo. The dispute was resolved when cement was needed for airfield construction north of the border.[88]

---

[85] Peter Rigney, *Trains, Coal and Turf: Transport in Emergency Ireland* (Irish Academic Press, 2010), 55.
[86] Department of Industry and Commerce, *Trade and Shipping Statistics* (Dublin: Stationery Office), various years.
[87] Rigney, *Trains, Coal and Turf: Transport in Emergency Ireland*, 83.
[88] Ibid., 92.

Though the arrival of large numbers of US troops in Northern Ireland in January 1942 provoked protests from the Irish government, it strengthened its bargaining position. Provisioning the troops from Britain would require the deployment of scarce shipping resources. The alternative was to provision them from the South. A threatened embargo on Guinness exports from St James's Gate led to the British Ministry of Food authorizing an exchange of 30,000 tons of American wheat for a million barrels of beer. The US minister in Dublin looked unfavourably on the deal as shipping was being used to supply a neutral country while the commodity obtained in exchange was 'at best a luxury and at worst poison'.[89] 'The requirements of US troops', as Rigney notes, 'remained a priority for British civil servants'.[90]

Irish Steel's attempts to secure government assistance at the outbreak of the war had been rebuffed twice by McEntee, who had become Minister for Industry and Commerce in 1940 when Lemass moved to the new Department of Supplies. An internal departmental investigation had raised serious concerns about some of Frame's business practices. It concluded that the company had provided a false estimate of the initial cost of the undertaking and that the money loaned to the company by the government had been 'squandered', that one Frame company had sold the plant to another of his companies at an inflated price, and that the steel plant would be totally dependent on another related company for all of its scrap metal requirements.[91] McEntee's 'unfavourable opinion of the efficiency and creditworthiness of the Board of the Company and its advisers' was shared by the new Minister for Finance Seán T. O'Kelly.[92] In spite of this, the drying up of steel imports led to the company's remaining in production on a limited basis until finally, in 1946, with its cash resources exhausted, it went into receivership. Lemass argued that some production capacity needed to be maintained in case of a future national emergency. The Minister for Finance remained 'worried about financing this uneconomic high-cost industry which, even though it enjoys the protection of a 25% duty, has been able to produce only at a very substantial loss'.[93] Lemass again won the day. Irish Steel Holdings was formed in 1947 and provided with a loan from the Department of Finance to purchase the assets held by the receiver. It would remain a semi-state

---

[89] Cited in ibid., 86.
[90] Ibid., 85.
[91] National Archives of Ireland (NAI), TAOIS/S 11603 A: Department of Industry and Commerce Memorandum concerning the present position of Irish Steel, Limited, 16 October 1940.
[92] Ibid.
[93] Cited in Liam Cullinane, *Working in Cork, Everyday Life in Irish Steel, Sunbeam Wolsey and the Ford Marina Plant, 1917–2001* (Cork: Cork University Press, 2020), 59.

company until its sale in 1995 and was loss-making throughout most of its existence.[94] Its workforce remained in the low hundreds until the 1950s.

The immediate post-war years witnessed a strong economic recovery as pent-up consumer demand was released onto the market.[95] Employment in each of the industry groups listed in Table 5.3 expanded between 1945 and 1948. The largest increase in percentage terms was in motor vehicle assembly. Across most classes of commodities, the spending boom was reflected in a sharp increase in imports. The deterioration in the balance of payments and the austerity this triggered would lead to the major transformative economic and industrial policy initiatives of the 1950s—the Whitaker Report of 1958 and the strategy of 'industrialisation by invitation'.

5.4 Industrial Location

Strong localist pressures were brought to bear on both the Cumann na nGaedheal and Fianna Fáil governments to try to influence industrial location.[96] Most protected industries were reliant on imported inputs however and preferred to site their plants at or close to the major ports. Mary Daly concludes on the basis of the aggregated data provided by the CIP that 'the more intensive drive for decentralization in the late thirties appears to have been ineffective'.[97] These data are extended out to 1948 in Table 5.4. As will be seen in later chapters, there was little change in the regional distribution of industry until the 1960s.

It should be noted, however, that the cities, particularly Dublin, were expanding as a share of the population, while the shares of both Connacht and Ulster were declining. Industry was counteracting this trend to at least some modest extent. Plant-level characteristics are also of significance, as average earnings are generally positively related to establishment size. The CIP provides no information on regional distribution by establishment size.

As seen earlier in Chapter 1, there had been nine establishments with workforces of 500 or more in 1929. Four further factories met the criterion in 1938. Two were in Dublin: the Rowntree chocolate factory in Kilmainham

---

[94] Ibid., 64.
[95] There had been a substantial build-up in personal savings over the war years, both for precautionary reasons and because of the non-availability of goods. This was unwound over the post-war period: John Fitzgerald, Seán Kenny, and Alexandra L. Cermeño, 'Household Behaviour under Rationing'. *National Institute Economic Review* (2022): 1–21.
[96] Daly, *Industrial Development and Irish National Identity, 1922–1939*, 106–16.
[97] Ibid., 112.

Table 5.4 Regional distribution of industrial employment, 1931–1948

	1931	1938	1948
Dublin City	42	43	42
Rest of Leinster	18	19	20
Cork City	7	7	9
Limerick City	3	3	3
Waterford City	2	2	2
Rest of Munster	16	13	13
Connacht	7	8	7
Three-county Ulster	5	5	5

Note: These data include other industries such as building and construction in addition to manufacturing. Columns may not sum to 100 due to rounding.
Source: CIP.

and the new Hely print works at East Wall. The other two—the factories of Sunbeam–Wolsey and Irish Dunlop—were in Cork. There was, however, some decentralization of establishments with workforces of 100–499.

Nationally, the number of these second-tier establishments increased from 121 to 211. The number in Connacht increased fivefold.[98] The only such establishments in Connacht in 1929 had been the woollen mills in Galway and Foxford. By 1938, Mayo also hosted Irish Sewing Cotton and Reliable Shoe. Galway hosted, among others, the Tuam Sugar factory, the French-owned hatmaker Les Modes Modernes, and a McDonagh company, the Galway Foundry, which produced agricultural implements that benefited from tariff protection. Sligo hosted Sligo Shoe.

Sewing cotton had been declared a 'reserved commodity' in 1935. As Lemass told the Dáil, this was to 'secure the development of the sewing cotton industry in the West of Ireland'.[99] He was said by one of his senior departmental officials to have 'compelled' a hat factory—presumably Les Modes Modernes—to locate in Galway.[100] The location of the sugar plant was clearly in the government's gift. In these cases, at least, the hand of government is clearly visible.

[98] Michael Scholz, 'Location of Large Manufacturing Establishments in Ireland'. M.Sc. Business Analytics dissertation, Trinity Business School, 2022.
[99] PDDE, Vol. 58, No. 8, 19 July 1935.
[100] Daly, *Industrial Development and Irish National Identity, 1922–1939*, 111.

5.5 Largest Manufacturing Employers of the Late 1940s

Table 5.5 provides details of the largest manufacturing firms (as distinct from establishments) towards the end of Fianna Fáil's first unbroken sixteen-year period in office. There were more than twice as many firms with workforces of 500+ in 1948 as there had been in 1929. Four foreign-owned firms established since 1932—Salts, Polikoff, Irish Dunlop, and footwear manufacturer John Rawson & Sons—appear on the list. Large indigenous employers established over the period include the state-owned Irish Sugar Company, General Textiles, Clondalkin Paper Mills, and Irish Cement. Motor vehicle assembler G. A. Brittain probably briefly employed 500 at this time as a consequence of the demand for cars that had been unleashed at the end of the war.[101] Its workforce would decline to a slightly lower level in the 1950s.

The others on the list, apart from Mitchelstown Co-operative, were already employing close to or in excess of 500 by the late 1920s. As recently as 1939, Mitchelstown had employed only 162. A large part of its workforce was by now engaged in cheese production, though it would lose its monopoly in 1947 when Golden Vale was allowed to enter the market. By 1948, it also hosted a grain mill, a saw mill, a cattle-breeding station, and a range of other agricultural and services activities. It also ran the largest pig-rearing operation in the country, having entered the sector as an alternative disposal method for the cheese by-products that had been polluting local rivers. Over the coming years, it would become one of the largest bacon producers in the state.

Table 5.5 Firms employing 500+, c. 1948

Industry	Firm name	Employment, late 1940s
Meat	Denny (UK)	500
Dairy	Dairy Disposal Company	c. 800
	Mitchelstown Co-operative	500
Milling, bread, and biscuits	Ranks (UK)	≥ 500
	Jacobs	2,000
	Bolands	600
	Johnston, Mooney & O'Brien	600
	Kennedys	540

---

[101] The CIP reports that there were three establishments of this size in the vehicle assembly sector in 1947. Brittain is likely to have been the third, along with Ford and the state transport company CIÉ.

Chocolate, sugar, and confectionery	Irish Sugar	1,200
	Crosse & Blackwell (UK)	700
	Rowntree (UK)	800–900
Brewing	Guinness (UK)	*c.* 3,000
Tobacco	Players–Wills (UK)	1,370
Textiles, clothing, and hosiery	Goodbody Jute	750
	Greenmount & Boyne	760
	General Textiles (including subsidiary Naas Cotton Mills)	700
	Blarney Woollen Mills	700
	Dwyers	500 (excluding footwear)
	Sunbeam–Wolsey (including subsidiaries)	1,600
	Salts (UK)	500
	Polikoff (UK)	530
Footwear	Rawson (UK)	625
	Halliday/Clarks (UK)	631
	Lee Boot & Hanover Shoe	550
Paper and print	*Irish Independent*	800
	Alexander Thom	500
	Helys	500
	Clondalkin Paper	513
Vehicles	Ford (US)	1,000
	Brittain	500
Other metals and engineering	Hammond Lane Group	800
Clay, glass, and cement	Irish Cement Ltd	682
Fertilizer	Gouldings	600
Miscellaneous	Irish Dunlop (UK)	1,200

Source: author.

6

The Post-War World and Dual-Track Reform

Ireland's growth performance up to 1939 was close to what might have been expected for an economy at its level of development: it grew slightly more rapidly on average than richer neighbouring countries and slightly less rapidly than poorer ones.[1] Irish economic policies had not been substantially different from those pursued elsewhere across Europe in the 1920s and 1930s, and though the justification for protectionism differed between advanced and less advanced economies, the policy itself may not have been inappropriate in either case in the era of the Great Depression. Keynes had begun to reconsider his adherence to free trade in British policy debates, though he considered the decline in the value of sterling following the United Kingdom's departure from the Gold Standard an adequate substitute for tariff protection.

Statistician R. C. Geary had attended Keynes's lecture in Dublin in 1933 in the company of 'the two Georges'—Professors George O'Brien of University College Dublin (UCD) and George Duncan of Trinity College Dublin (TCD). On his way to the venue, he would later recount, 'I heard a remark which influenced me all my life (by Duncan, I think)'—that a well-known Swedish economist 'has shown that the classical optimality argument in favour of free trade is valid only when the factors of production are fully engaged.'[2]

Ireland's subsequent growth performance up to 1973—and particularly up to the early 1960s—was much less favourable in comparative terms. Its growth record in 1950–1958 was the worst in Western Europe and the emigration-fuelled decline in population over these years was nearly twice as great as over the entire preceding period since independence.[3] The delay in abandoning protectionism meant that the country not only missed out on

---

[1] That poorer countries can import best-practice technologies developed elsewhere is one reason why some such convergence in income per capita might be expected over the medium term. Ireland's relative growth performance over the various phases since independence is charted in Kevin O'Rourke, 'Independent Ireland in Comparative Perspective'. *Irish Economic and Social History* 44, 1 (2017): 19–45.

[2] R. C. Geary, 'Review of George O'Brien: A Biographical Memoir by J. Meenan'. *Economic and Social Review* 12, 2 (1981): 67–70.

[3] Cormac Ó Gráda, 'Five Crises'. Annual T. K. Whitaker Lecture, Central Bank of Ireland, 2011.

Industry and Policy in Independent Ireland, 1922–1972. Frank Barry, Oxford University Press.
© Frank Barry (2023). DOI: 10.1093/oso/9780198878230.003.0006

the post-war European boom but also remained overly dependent on what was now an underperforming UK economy.

How is the delay to be explained? Ó Gráda and O'Rourke suggest that 'policy-makers had simply been slow to learn that [the policy] was mistaken'.[4] For more advanced economies however, for which the protectionism of the 1930s had been 'defensive', the coordinated nature of the easing of trade restrictions under the aegis of the Marshall Plan made liberalization easier. For less advanced economies, import substitution remained the cornerstone of their development strategies.[5] Most of the other newly established states of the inter-war period were now part of the Eastern bloc. The less developed countries of Western Europe—Greece, Spain, Portugal, and Ireland—would have to forge their own individual paths towards outward reorientation.

There were two dimensions to the bind in which such countries found themselves. The most obvious was the massive industrial disruption that liberalization would entail. The Fiscal Inquiry Committee of 1923 had warned that the industrial structure that would emerge under protectionism would make it more difficult to reverse course later. By 1948, as seen in Chapter 5, almost half of the largest manufacturing operations owed their existence to the import-substitution policy. The Department of Industry and Commerce would suggest, in the internal civil service policy debates of the late 1950s, that up to two-thirds of the country's manufacturing jobs could be lost if trade barriers were completely dismantled.

The second constraint was more subtle. Protectionism enhances the 'discretionary interventions, patronage resources and rent-seeking opportunities for politicians in electoral democracies'.[6] Tom Kettle had written in the pre-independence era of the danger it raised of the 'profound corruption of [...] national political life'.[7] Cormac Ó Gráda observes that the tariff regime created 'a role for the politician as broker'; Mary Daly notes that alternative systems 'would have deprived the government party of potentially beneficial political support'; Tom Garvin surmises that, under the Lemass regime, 'a lot of well-connected people became rich'.[8]

[4] Cormac Ó Gráda and Kevin O'Rourke, 'Irish Economic Growth, 1945–88'. In *Economic Growth in Europe Since 1945*, ed. Nicholas Crafts and Gianni Toniolo (Cambridge: Cambridge University Press, 1996), 414.

[5] H. Liepmann, *Tariff Levels and the Economic Unity of Europe: An Examination of Tariff Policy, Export Movements and the Economic Integration of Europe, 1913–1931* (London: George Allen and Unwin, 1938).

[6] John Waterbury, 'The Long Gestation and Brief Triumph of Import-Substituting Industrialization'. *World Development* 27, 2 (1999): 323–41.

[7] Tom Kettle, 'The Economics of Nationalism', in *The Day's Burden* (Dublin, London: Maunsel, 1918), 143.

[8] Cited in Anna Devlin and Frank Barry, 'Protection versus Free Trade in the Free State Era: The Finance Attitude'. *Irish Economic and Social History* 46, 1 (2019): 3–21.

The politics of exiting such an equilibrium are notoriously difficult. The experience of the developing world since the 1970s is illustrative in this regard. The trade liberalization measures adopted when balance-of-payments difficulties are encountered are frequently reversed once the immediate crisis has passed. Reversal is particularly common in the case of externally imposed programmes which pay inadequate attention to local political economy considerations. This casts doubt on the hypothesis advanced by observers such as Denis O'Hearn and John Kurt Jacobsen that the Irish process was largely scripted in Washington.

O'Hearn asserts that the Irish regime change was 'dominated and redirected by a third force: a world capitalist political economy dominated by the institutions of First World capital'.[9] Jacobsen posits that 'the state elite, and the new cadre of economic consultants, transmitted economic ideas [which] actually emanated from powerful exogenous actors'.[10] The archival evidence demonstrates that the policy initiatives of the period emerged largely from within the Irish policymaking system; that significant components of the advice emanating from the United States were rejected; and that the US authorities and other external agencies, in criticizing the Irish process, failed to understand the political economy difficulties it was designed to surmount. Jacobsen's assertion that '[not] much inventiveness was displayed in adapting [the US advice] to Irish conditions' does not stand up to scrutiny.[11]

Development economist Dani Rodrik suggests:

> New ideas about what can be done can unlock what otherwise might seem like the iron grip of vested interests [. . .] Just as we think of technological ideas as those that relax resource constraints, we can think of political ideas as those that relax political constraints, enabling those in power to make themselves (and possibly the rest of society) better off without undermining their political power.[12]

Ireland's receptivity to new policy ideas was enhanced by the intensified electoral competition of the post-war years. After an unbroken sixteen-year period in office, Fianna Fáil was unseated in the 1948 general election. Each of the next three general elections would institute a further change

---

[9] Denis O'Hearn, 'The Road from Import-Substituting to Export-Led Industrialization in Ireland: Who Mixed the Asphalt, Who Drove the Machinery, and Who Kept Making Them Change Directions?'. *Politics & Society* 18, 1 (1990): 1–38.

[10] John Kurt Jacobsen, *Chasing Progress in the Irish Republic* (Cambridge: Cambridge University Press, 1994).

[11] Ibid. Nor did US consultancy firms and the US administration necessarily speak with one voice, as will be seen below.

[12] Dani Rodrik, 'When Ideas Trump Interests: Preferences, Worldviews, and Policy Innovations'. *Journal of Economic Perspectives* 28, 1 (2014): 189–208.

of government. Lemass himself would later admit that 'it was not until our second period in opposition that we really got down to [. . .] preparing our minds for a comprehensive approach' to the post-war economic problems of the country.[13] Policymakers of all political parties inched each other towards the new export-oriented foreign direct investment (FDI) strategy. The Industrial Development Authority was established by the first Fine Gael-led (Inter-Party) government in 1949; Ireland's low corporation-tax regime originated with the measures introduced by the second Inter-Party government in 1956. Fianna Fáil would prove particularly adept politically however. It would return to office for a further unbroken sixteen-year period in 1957.

'New states', it has been noted, 'generally sought to bypass old masters when seeking technical guidance on industrialisation and development.'[14] Fianna Fáil's value system in particular 'was more politically reconcilable with an opening to the west than with one to the east'.[15] That the United States had overtaken the United Kingdom as the major global source of FDI by the late 1940s facilitated a shift in attitudes towards foreign ownership. The Fianna Fáil newspaper, the *Irish Press*, had consistently promoted the Ford enterprise in Cork, and Lemass had explicitly exempted it from his claim in 1929 that much of the foreign capital operating in Ireland was of little value to the nation. As he said in parliament in 1948, suspicions pertaining to British FDI 'do not necessarily apply to capital from other countries'.[16] From the opposition benches, he asked the new Minister for Industry and Commerce about reports that the US government's European Recovery Programme planned to encourage US business investments in Europe. Both agreed that US investments were to be encouraged.[17] It is not coincidental that all of the external reports on industrial policy from Stacy May in 1952 to Telesis in 1982 were commissioned from US consultancies.

The strategy of 'industrialization by invitation' was particularly suited to Irish circumstances. It exploited the advantages that Ireland's extensive access to the UK market afforded while minimizing, to the extent possible, the costs of the industrial disruption inevitably associated with the dismantling of protectionist barriers. It also provided a way around the historical difficulty that, because of the ease of emigration, 'cheaper labour could do little

---

[13] Cited in Paul Bew and Henry Patterson, *Seán Lemass and the Making of Modern Ireland 1945–66* (Dublin: Gill and Macmillan, 1982), 86.

[14] Eunan O'Halpin, 'Ireland Looking Outwards, 1880–2016', in *Cambridge History of Ireland Volume IV: 1880–2016*, ed. Thomas Bartlett (Cambridge: Cambridge University Press, 2018), 834–35.

[15] John Horgan, *Seán Lemass, The Enigmatic Patriot* (Dublin: Gill and Macmillan 1999), 146.

[16] Cited in Frank Barry and Clare O'Mahony, 'Regime Change in 1950s Ireland: The New Export-Oriented Foreign Investment Strategy'. *Irish Economic and Social History* 44, 1 (2017): 46–65.

[17] Ibid.

to compensate for Ireland's relative backwardness and isolation, or to generate the investment necessary for faster economic growth'.[18] That the new FDI strategy predated the trade liberalization of the Whitaker–Lemass era identifies it as an early example of what has come to be known since the Chinese outward-reorientation process of the late 1970s as 'dual-track reform'.[19] By creating a new source of industrial employment without threatening existing import-substituting interests, it helped to establish the preconditions for the later abandonment of protectionism.[20]

6.1 Developments in Non-IDA-Sponsored Sectors

The adoption of the new export-oriented FDI regime was the economic policy change of most significance over the period 1948–1961. Its emergence is frequently conflated with the publication of the Whitaker report *Economic Development* in 1958 and the trade liberalization of the following decade. These were separate developments. *Economic Development* would provide a framework for broad economic policy in the 1960s and help prepare the country psychologically for the reduction in tariff barriers that began in earnest only in 1963. Discussion of the document and its consequences is for these reasons largely left to Chapter 7.

Before turning to the emergence of the new regime, several other processes that impacted on industrial structure over the period are identified. The 1948 Anglo-Irish Trade Agreement played a role in the birth of Irish beef and footwear exports. Developments in other sectors were more a consequence of post-war conditions than of trade or industry policy per se. The following account tracks the consequences of these various processes up to European Economic Community (EEC) accession.

Sixty per cent of the population had no access to electricity when rural electrification commenced in 1946. By 1965, when the first phase ended, some 80 per cent of rural areas had been connected. Agricultural production processes were transformed as electric water pumps, milking machines, grain dryers,

---

[18] Cormac Ó Gráda, *A Rocky Road: The Irish Economy since the 1920s* (Manchester: Manchester University Press, 1997), 217.

[19] See, e.g. Justin Yifu Lin, *Demystifying the Chinese Economy* (Cambridge: Cambridge University Press, 2012).

[20] There are clear parallels with the case of Mauritius as described by Rodrik, who notes that the creation of an export-processing zone 'generated new opportunities of trade and of employment, without taking protection away from the import-substituting groups. There were no identifiable losers. This in turn paved the way for [later] more substantial liberalizations': Dani Rodrik, 'Institutions for High-Quality Growth: What They Are and How to Acquire Them'. *Studies in Comparative International Development* 35, 3 (2000): 3–31.

and infrared lamps came into common usage. The market for electrical goods increased almost seven-fold. While most electrical machinery continued to be imported, domestic production of other electrical items, which had been negligible before the war, accounted for half of Irish sales in 1961 and 65 per cent of sales in 1969.[21] The most significant new firm to emerge in the electrical equipment sector was Unidare, which was established in 1949 to produce equipment for the state-owned Electricity Supply Board.[22] By 1960, Unidare had a workforce of 1,500 and a substantial export trade (Table 6.1).[23]

Other electrical equipment producers included US company Irish Driver-Harris, which had been producing electric wires and cables in New Ross since the 1930s, UK company Ward & Goldstone, which opened the first of several Irish factories in 1949, and Belgian company ACEC, which commenced operations in Waterford in 1952. UK firm Plessey opened the first of its Dublin factories in 1948 to make components for the Department of Posts and Telegraphs and the Irish radio trade.

Table 6.1 Employment in selected appliance and equipment producers

Unidare	1,500 (1960), 1,883 in Ireland + 300 in UK (1971)
Pye	139 (1948), 650 (1960), 480 (1972)
Irish Driver Harris	78 (1948), 137 (1960)
Ward & Goldstone (including General Plastics)	200 (1963), 300 (1973)
Bush	80 (1953), 450 (1972)
Solus	177 (1948), 220 (1960), 650 (1972)
ACEC	250 (1962), 350 (1970)
Electrical Industries of Ireland/AET/British GEC	57 (1948), 450 (1960), 850 (1972)
Plessey (Ireland)	50 (1948), 150 (1955), 400 (1971)
Philips (Ireland)	500 (1962), 820 (1970)

Source: author.

[21] Committee on Industrial Organisation, Report of Survey of Electrical Equipment and Apparatus Industry (Dublin: Stationery Office, 1964), 18.; Committee on Industrial Progress, Report on Electrical Machinery, Apparatus and Appliances Industry (Dublin: Stationery Office, 1971), 13.

[22] Unidare was initially known as Aberdare Electric. The name was changed to avoid confusion with the Welsh firm Aberdare Cables from which some of its technical knowledge derived.

[23] Unidare was Irish-owned until 1964 when it was taken over by Pye. Ownership later passed to the Dutch company Philips.

Sales of consumer products surged. The first wave of purchases included cookers, radios, kettles, lights, irons, fires, and clocks. Television sets, refrigerators, washing machines, and vacuum cleaners followed later. Pye, a branch of the Cambridge electronics firm controlled by the same Irish-emigrant industrialist as Unidare, had been assembling radio sets in Ireland since 1936. It began to produce TVs and record players in the 1950s. Another UK producer of radios and TVs, Bush, commenced production in Ireland in 1952. Both firms employed close to 500 people in 1972, by which time Bush had become part of the Smurfit Group. Dutch firm Philips began producing for the domestic market in 1957 and already employed 500 by 1962. It would initiate a separate export-oriented operation later in the decade.

The largest producer of domestic appliances at EEC accession was Electrical Industries of Ireland. Established as Aibhleisi Éireannacha Teoranta (AET) at Dunleer in County Louth in 1937, it was acquired by the British General Electric Company (GEC) in 1959. It employed almost 500 in 1960 and 850 in 1972. The British company also took a substantial share in Solus, a domestic firm that been producing electrical lights and bulbs in Bray since 1935. Solus was also a substantial employer by 1972.[24]

Post-war shortages of milk and sugar in the United Kingdom led to the emergence of a substantial new Irish export industry beyond the major urban centres. The large British confectionery firms that had been servicing the Irish market from Dublin since the tariffs of the 1920s and 1930s established plants in the dairying regions of the country to produce chocolate crumb and other related ingredients, most of which went to supply their UK confectionery operations. These were the first substantial *export-oriented* foreign ventures since Ford opened in Cork in 1919. Rowntree initiated production at the Ballyclough cooperative creamery site in Mallow in 1946, Cadbury opened a factory in Rathmore, County Kerry in 1948, and Miloko was established as a joint venture between other British producers and several dozen local cooperatives in Carrick-on-Suir in 1950. UK company John Terry participated in a joint venture in Dungarvan and Nestlé opened a plant in Letterkenny.

Though less labour-intensive than confectionery, chocolate crumb generated substantial export earnings and used vast quantities of local milk. Ireland was referred to by the Chairman of Fry–Cadbury in 1960 as 'the largest exporter of chocolate products by tonnage in the world'.[25] High-season employment at Rathmore grew from around 100 in the late 1940s to almost

---

[24] That Solus had an export–output ratio of 70 per cent in 1972 suggests that there were different motivating factors behind the two acquisitions: *Irish Times*, 28 December 1972.

[25] *Irish Times*, 25 May 1960.

200 in 1960 and 300 in 1972. The Rowntree operation in Mallow employed more than 400 in 1973.

The confectionery producers themselves expanded massively over this period. Cadbury terminated its outsourcing arrangement with Clarnico-Murray when it opened a major new factory in Coolock in 1957, from which it now began to export confectionery. Rowntree's production, other than of chocolate crumb, remained focused on the domestic market. By 1973, Cadbury's workforce had grown to exceed that of Rowntree–Mackintosh by a substantial margin (Table 6.2).

Chocolate crumb was just one example of the diversification that would prove of major long-term significance for the structure of the cooperative creamery sector. The number of cooperatives fell by one-fifth over the course of the 1950s and 1960s as all of the early innovators expanded by acquisition as well as organically.[26] Some of the diversification was into cheese, for which there was a ready market in post-war Britain. By the 1950s, Mitchelstown was exporting one-third of its cheese output and, as noted earlier, had also diversified into bacon. Galtee, the Mitchelstown brand, became the most popular bacon on the Irish market in the 1960s. Most of the long-established private bacon curers would fade from the scene over the coming decades. Employment at Mitchelstown trebled between 1939 and 1948 and trebled again to 1,600 by 1973.

Linkages with UK firms proved beneficial to all of the most successful creamery cooperatives of the era. Besides Mitchelstown, these included Waterford, Ballyclough, and Golden Vale (Table 6.3). All four participated in a joint venture with Unigate in 1959 to promote the marketing of Irish milk powder in Britain. Dungarvan Co-operative had won a contract from

Table 6.2 Employment in selected confectionery and chocolate crumb producers

	1948	1960	1973
Cadbury	c. 300	c.900	2,050
Rowntree	c. 800	1,150	1,210
Urney	300	600	350 (as part of Unilever)

Source: author.

[26] Employment across the entire creamery sector expanded by only 550 between 1948 and 1961, but the product diversification and increase in concentration over the period laid the groundwork for subsequent developments. This supports Kennedy and Dowling's thesis that the 'learning-by-doing' of the 1950s was crucial to the stronger growth performance of the following decade: Kieran Kennedy and Brendan Dowling, *Economic Growth in Ireland: The Experience since 1947* (Dublin: Gill and Macmillan, 1975).

Table 6.3 Employment in selected cooperative creameries

	Employment
Ballyclough	65 (1939), 300 (1960), 600 (1973)
Mitchelstown	162 (1939), 500 (1948, 1959), 800 (1966), 1,600 (1973)
Golden Vale	20 (1948), 120 (1962), 600 (1971)
Waterford Co-op	500 (1969), 1,000 (1973)
of which: Dungarvan Co-op	62 (1936), 100 (1960)

Source: author.

Unigate's progenitor Cow & Gate to supply milk powder for sale in Britain in the late 1930s. Employment at Waterford, into which Dungarvan merged in 1964, would double between 1969 and 1973 as a result of the enhanced export opportunities afforded by the Anglo-Irish Free Trade Area Agreement (AIFTA).

Cow & Gate opened a factory in Mallow in 1946, shortly after Rowntree. Borden, a major US milk processor, established a factory nearby in 1961. Ballyclough supplied milk powder to all three and opened a cheese factory in a joint venture with Manx Creameries in 1962. Its success has been credited explicitly to its diversification into 'the best paying product lines'.[27] Its workforce grew from 65 in 1939 to 300 in 1960 and would expand to 600 by 1973. The other major cooperative of the era, Golden Vale, had been established in 1947 to market the cheese output of a number of local creameries. Its 1965 agreement with British cheese producer Express Dairies provided it with enhanced access to the UK market.[28] Golden Vale's workforce had expanded to 600 by the early 1970s.

An unrelated event that would ultimately secure a significant premium for primary producers was the development of the Kerrygold brand by the state Milk Marketing Board (Bord Bainne). Kerrygold was launched on the export market in 1962, at a time when there were at least sixty Irish butter brands competing on the home market.[29] The highly successful Danish Lurbrand had been launched some sixty years earlier.

---

[27] *Irish Farmers Journal*, 22 May 1971.

[28] Marketing had long been a problem for the Irish creamery sector, as noted in all of the reports on the industry in the 1960s. One-third of all dairy exports (broadly-defined as including chocolate crumb) was estimated to be sold under foreign brand names in 1971: *Irish Independent*, 25 August 1971.

[29] Butter exports were heavily subsidized by the state as a corollary of the agricultural price supports of the time. As was pithily observed in 1963, 'like all dairy boards throughout the world, [Bord Bainne's] success must lie in cutting losses: the glow of profit-making can never be theirs': *Irish Times*, 3 January 1963.

Table 6.4 Employment in major carpet producers

Irish Ropes	255 (1948), 530 (1960), 812 (1972)
Youghal Carpets	20 (1954), 350 (1962), 2,656 (1972), of whom *c.* 1,500 in Ireland
Navan Carpets	59 (1948), 450 (1963), 810 (1972)

Note: The figure for Navan Carpets for 1963 includes Celbridge Spinning, which was acquired in 1958.
Source: author.

The buoyancy of the post-war recovery in overseas markets facilitated export-led growth in a range of other income-elastic items. The 1957/58 report of the Irish Export Board referred to the dollar earnings generated by the 'outstandingly successful export performance of the cordage, ropes and sisal carpeting industry'.[30] The firm alluded to was Newbridge-based Irish Ropes. Other Irish firms went on to achieve export success in wool carpeting, particularly in the United Kingdom. By the early 1970s, Ireland had a strong revealed comparative advantage in the export category 'carpets and floor coverings'.[31] Employment at Youghal Carpets numbered in the thousands even prior to its acquisition of Navan Carpets in 1972 (Table 6.4).

Irish Mist liqueur and Waterford Glass achieved particular success in the United States over this period. Irish Mist was born of an idea to use up the large stocks of whiskey that had accumulated during the war and was brought to the market by the D. E. Williams Group, producers of Tullamore Dew, in 1947, around the time that wartime restrictions on distillery exports were eased.[32] Sales grew by more than 15 per cent per annum into the 1960s, by which time it accounted for half or more of the dollar earnings of all southern Irish distilleries. Powers, the most innovative of the major distillery companies, took over production of the whiskey component in 1965 and spearheaded the formation of Irish Distillers the following year.[33] Prior to the merger, 'there had been fierce competition between Jameson, Powers and Cork Distillers for dominance of the home market, and none of the three

---

[30] *Córas Tráchtála*, Sixth Annual Report 1957–58, (Dublin: *Córas Tráchtála*, 1958), 18, 25.

[31] The revealed comparative advantage index is generally considered to provide an indication of the change in production structure that might be expected post-trade liberalization: Don Thornhill, 'The Revealed Comparative Advantage of Irish Exports of Manufactures 1969–1982'. *Journal of the Statistical and Social Inquiry Society of Ireland* 25 (1986/87): 91–146.

[32] The distilleries blamed the restrictions on 'the enormous [government] revenue which is derived from whiskey consumed on the home market': cited in Madeleine Humphreys, 'The Decline of the Irish Whiskey Trade in Independent Ireland, 1922–1952'. *Journal of European Economic History* 23, 1 (1994): 93–103.

[33] Irish Distillers was initially called United Distillers of Ireland. The name was changed to avoid association with Rhodesia's Unilateral Declaration of Independence (UDI).

had any time, effort, energy or manpower left over for developing exports'.[34] Though Irish Distillers was miniscule in comparison to Scotland's Distillers Company Ltd (DCL), the merger initiated a resurgence in the industry from this point.[35]

1947 also witnessed the revival of an old tradition of crystal-glass making in Waterford. One of the partners in the project was Charles Bacik, who had fled Czechoslovakia following the confiscation of his glass factories by the new post-war Communist regime. After a faltering start, it was rescued by the Glass Bottle Company in 1950 and bought back in 1966. Employment at Waterford Glass grew to more than 500 by 1957 and would expand massively over the period to 1972.

The Irish beef-processing industry also dates only from the immediate post-war years. Live animals (predominantly cattle) had comprised 50 per cent of Irish exports in 1938. By the early 1970s, beef exports equalled or exceeded live cattle exports in value. Ireland had secured enhanced access to the UK market in 1948 alongside a favourable price arrangement covering the period up to the end of British food rationing in 1954. Competitiveness was boosted by the 30 per cent devaluation of sterling (and hence also of the Irish pound) in 1949, and lucrative contracts were received to supply the US armed forces stationed in Turkey and Western Europe. These contracts gave Ireland the necessary veterinary clearance to benefit when access to the US market was liberalized in 1951.[36] Beef exports expanded dramatically from this time (Table 6.5).

Employment in beef processing doubled between the early 1950s and the early 1960s and doubled again to almost 4,000 by 1972.[37] Though a number of traditional bacon curers entered the industry, newer entrants dominated. The major beef processors by the early 1960s were the Dublin-based International Meat Company, Irish Meat Packers of Leixlip, Clover Meats of Waterford, and Roscrea Meat Products (Table 6.6). The Dublin and Leixlip firms would merge to form International Meat Packers (IMP) in 1967, and IMP would merge with Cork Marts in 1968. Cork Marts–IMP and Clover Meats together

---

[34] J. Ryan, 'Foreword'. In *The Lost Distilleries of Ireland*, ed. Brian Townsend (Glasgow: Neil Wilson Publishing, 1997), 1–2.

[35] Irish Distillers had a workforce of almost 1,000 and exports of £6 million in 1972 (*Irish Times*, 28 December 1972). Scotland's Distillers Company Ltd (DCL) had a UK workforce of 18,700 and exports of around £100 million in 1973. Lionel F. Gray and Jonathan Love, *Jane's Major Companies of Europe*, (London: Samson, Low, Marsden and Co., 1973), B238.

[36] Terence J. Baker, Robert O'Connor, and Rory Dunne, *A Study of the Irish Cattle and Beef Industries* (Dublin: Economic and Social Research Institute, 1973), 75–77. I am grateful to Declan O'Brien, author of a recent Ph.D. thesis on the origins of the beef industry, for helpful discussions on this topic.

[37] These numbers refer to the Census of Industrial Production category 'Slaughtering, preserving etc. of meat other than by bacon factories'.

Table 6.5 Carcase and boneless beef exports (tons), 1950–1970

	Total	*Of which:*				
		UK	*Rest of EEC9*	*US and Canadian forces in Europe*	*US and Canada*	*Rest of world*
1950	6,400	3,123	*	*	419	2,858
1960	51,001	15,266	2,803	3,493	28,795	644
1970	142,840	101,627	4,386	1,446	33,647	1,734

Note: *: Included in 'Rest of World'.
Source: Terence J. Baker, Robert O'Connor, and Rory Dunne, *A Study of the Irish Cattle and Beef Industries* (Dublin: Economic and Social Research Institute, 1973), 78.

Table 6.6 Employment in major meat-processing firms

Denny (primarily bacon)	c. 500 (1960), c. 400 (1972)
Clover Meats (beef and bacon)	150 (1936), 350 (1941), 500 (1960), 1,800 (1972)
Cork Marts–IMP (beef)	2,000 (1973)
of which: International Meat Company	350 (1960),
Irish Meat Packers	300 (1960)
Roscrea Meats (beef)	75 (1936), 420 (1941), 325 (1960), 400 (1970)

Source: author.

accounted for more than half of Irish beef production at the time of EEC accession.

Clover's workforce would reach 1,800 by 1972, by which time it had acquired a number of older bacon curers including Shaws of Limerick, Donnellys of Dublin, and Lunham Bros of Cork. The market share of all of the traditional bacon producers was in inexorable decline. E. M. Denny, the UK parent of the 150-year old Henry Denny & Sons, would be sold along with its Irish and Northern Irish operations to an Australian concern in 1973.

The 1948 Anglo-Irish Trade Agreement also had a substantial impact on the Irish footwear sector. Dundalk firm Halliday had been producing some of the Clarks range for the Irish market since 1938. Following the 1948 trade agreement, which granted Ireland a substantial quota for British imports of women's shoes, Clarks commissioned Halliday to produce one of its women's brands for the UK market. Irish footwear exports had been almost non-existent prior to 1948. By 1960, exports accounted for 25 per cent of output.

Over the following decade, Halliday acquired Padmore & Barnes of Kilkenny and Stedfast Shoes of Carrickmacross before being fully bought out by Clarks in 1971. The Halliday operation in Dundalk had employed 800 in 1960: the Clarks Group employed a workforce of 1,700 in Ireland on the eve of EEC accession.

6.2 Emergence of the New FDI Regime

Notwithstanding the export successes seen in some sectors and among some firms, the balance-of-payments position deteriorated sharply between the end of the war and the mid-1950s.[38] In O'Malley's words, the difficulties

> arose partly from the near exhaustion of the 'easy' stage of import-substituting industrialisation, which meant that there was relatively little further replacement of imports by new domestic production. At the same time, imports of goods which had not been replaced by domestic production, including many capital goods and material inputs, had to continue to grow as long as the economy was growing.[39]

The 'easy' first stage relates to the replacement of imported consumer goods by domestically produced foodstuffs, textiles, clothing, and footwear. The second stage requires replacing imported intermediate inputs, capital goods, and consumer durables. These require complex clusters of specialized industries and production on a scale unsuited to smaller, less advanced countries.[40] As early as 1950, the Department of Industry and Commerce had recognized that Irish Steel would be unable to compete with overseas mills whose weekly output exceeded the Irish company's entire annual production.[41] Ireland's chemicals and metals and engineering industries were particularly underdeveloped.[42]

The pan-European dollar shortages of the immediate post-war period added further to these difficulties. The share of imports coming from the

[38] The deficits of the period 1947–1956 more than offset the surpluses that had accumulated during the war, when imports had been curtailed while exports of food and cattle continued: Department of Finance, *Economic Development* (Dublin: Stationery Office, 1958), 15.

[39] Eoin O'Malley, *Industry and Economic Development: The Challenge for the Latecomer* (Dublin: Gill and Macmillan, 1989), 65.

[40] Bela Balassa, 'The Process of Industrial Development and Alternative Development Strategies'. *Essays in International Finance* 141 (1980): 10–11.

[41] NAI: TAOIS 3/S11603, Department of Industry and Commerce Memorandum for the Government: Irish Steel Industry, 20 April 1950.

[42] Frank Barry, Linda Barry, and Aisling Menton, 'Tariff-Jumping Foreign Direct Investment in Protectionist Era Ireland'. *Economic History Review* 69, 4 (2016): 1285–248.

United States had doubled to 22 per cent between 1938 and 1947. The limiting of sterling convertibility in August 1947 meant that payments for items such as wheat, maize, motor vehicle parts, and tobacco—which largely came from the dollar area—could no longer be made through sterling.[43]

Relaxation of the balance-of-payments constraint over the longer term required an increase in exports.[44] The short-run response typically involved austerity. There were two particularly harsh budgetary episodes in the 1950s—in 1952, under Fianna Fáil, and in 1956 under the second Inter-Party government. These episodes bear recounting as factors in the birth of the Whitaker Report and the introduction of export profits tax relief.

The separation of the government budget into its current and capital components by the first Inter-Party government in 1950 signalled a relaxation in attitudes towards public-sector borrowing. Aggregate government spending more than doubled over the space of a single year.[45] As one government advisor of the time would later remark, 'Keynes had come to Kinnegad'.[46] The Central Bank was trenchant in its criticism of the threat to the balance of payments posed by the expansion in both government and private-sector spending. 'Seldom since the Communist Manifesto', Moynihan remarks of the Central Bank report for 1950–1951, 'has a slim volume produced such a medley of heat and noise.'[47]

Denunciation of the Bank from across the political spectrum led Joseph Brennan to step down as Central Bank Governor in 1953, to be replaced by J. J. McElligott, who had succeeded him as Secretary of the Department of Finance in 1927. T. K. Whitaker took over the Department of Finance position three years later. Even before Brennan's departure from the Central Bank, Fianna Fáil Finance Minister Seán McEntee had introduced a severely contractionary budget. By 1955, with the second Inter-Party government now in power, the economy was recovering, but the balance of payments position was again deteriorating. The austerity measures the new government imposed restored the external balance but at the cost of another severe recession.

---

[43] Ronan Fanning, *The Irish Department of Finance, 1922–58* (Dublin: Institute of Public Administration, 1978), 391, 428.

[44] The volume of exports had fallen substantially since the late 1920s as a consequence of the Great Depression, protectionism, the economic war, and the difficult trading conditions of the Second World War era. The 1929 level of exports would be surpassed only in 1960: *Statistical Abstract* (Dublin: Stationery Office, 1974–1975), 147.

[45] John FitzGerald and Seán Kenny, 'Managing a Century of Debt'. *Journal of the Statistical and Social Inquiry Society of Ireland* 48 (2018): 1–40.

[46] Patrick Lynch, cited in Cormac Ó Gráda and Kevin Hjortshøj O'Rourke, 'The Irish Economy during the Century after Partition'. *Economic History Review* 75, 2 (2022): 336–70.

[47] Maurice Moynihan, *Currency and Central Banking in Ireland, 1922–1960* (Dublin: Gill and Macmillan and Central Bank of Ireland, 1975), 375.

One camp within the bureaucracy—centred in the Department of Industry and Commerce and supported by the recently established Industrial Development Authority—advocated the adoption of financial and tax incentives to increase exports. The other—centred in the Department of Finance—advocated trade liberalization. The victory of the former in the mid-to-late 1950s initiated the strategy of 'industrialization by invitation'.

By 1948, Éamon de Valera had been Taoiseach for sixteen years, making him one of the longest-serving heads of government in Europe. Though nine new Dáil seats had been added in a redrawing of constituencies prior to the 1948 general election, Fianna Fáil exited the election with eight fewer seats. It lost ground in both rural and urban areas. To Fianna Fáil's sixty-eight seats, the five other parties represented in the Dáil—Fine Gael, Labour, Clann na Poblachta, Clann na Talmhan, and National Labour—had a total of sixty-seven. Though they had little in common other than a shared antipathy to Fianna Fáil, they came together with the support of a number of independents to form the first Inter-Party government, the most significant institutional achievement of which was the establishment of the Industrial Development Authority (IDA). The IDA would evolve over time to become one of the most powerful governmental agencies in the state.

Some commentators have represented the IDA Act of 1950 as the Inter-Party government's version of a Prices and Industrial Efficiency bill that Lemass had been preparing in 1947. The two pieces of legislation contrasted sharply in their underlying philosophies however. The Lemass bill was symptomatic of the 'command-and-control' approach typically associated with protectionism.[48] Horgan describes it as 'a legislative statement of his determination to compel industry where he could not cajole it'.[49] Having been forced to recognize the inadequacies of protected industry during his tenure as Minister for Supplies during the war, he proposed to establish an agency to identify inefficiencies and penalize recalcitrant proprietors and managers. This would have required even more intrusive government intervention. High prices and inefficiency are in any case natural concomitants of protectionism, particularly in smaller economies where competition is lacking and the requisite economies of scale cannot be achieved.

The IDA, upon its establishment in 1949, was allocated the tasks of reviewing existing tariffs and initiating proposals for the development of new

---

[48] Waterbury, 'The Long Gestation and Brief Triumph of Import-Substituting Industrialization'.
[49] Horgan, Seán Lemass, The Enigmatic Patriot, 133–34.

industries, responsibilities that had been until then within the remit of the Department of Industry and Commerce. It was to be operated by a non-civil service board supported by a staff of civil servants. As government advisor Alexis FitzGerald would later explain, the 'complete regearing of industrial policy [would have been] difficult for a department which had been going along a particular line—the protection of industry'.[50] The Department of Industry and Commerce resented the diminution of its responsibilities. Fianna Fáil interpreted the move as an attack on Lemass and promised to abolish the new body at the earliest possible opportunity. The Department of Finance feared that the IDA's board of non-civil service personnel might be 'a gang of crack-pot socialist planners', warning that 'it should definitely not be within their scope or function to themselves run or plan industry or any branch thereof'.[51]

Of the tasks with which the IDA was entrusted, the tariff review functions would have appeared to be of most significance at the time. There was an awareness within Fine Gael of the damaging knock-on effects of tariffs on agriculture and downstream industries and of their impact on consumer prices, and the Taoiseach told the Dáil that these effects were to be of fundamental importance to the new body.[52]

The establishment of the original Tariff Commission in the 1920s has been seen as a way of depoliticizing what would have been a contentious issue within Cumann na nGaedheal.[53] Tariff policy would have been at least as contentious within the Inter-Party government. Seán MacBride, the Minister for External Affairs, was as deeply committed to protectionism as Lemass, while James Dillon, the Minister for Agriculture, was fiercely opposed to 'the whole crazy structure of tariff industries'.[54] The IDA's independence would prove crucial to the direction in which it would evolve over the next several years.

Other bodies established by the Inter-Party government included the Dollar Exports Advisory Committee and what would later become the Irish Export Board (Córas Tráchtála Teoranta). All threw their weight behind the campaign for export profits tax relief. The Department of Industry and Commerce had first floated the idea—to apply to exports to non-UK

[50] Cited in Frank Barry and Mícheál Ó Fathartaigh, 'The Industrial Development Authority, 1949–58: Establishment, Evolution and Expansion of Influence'. *Irish Historical Studies* 39, 155 (2015): 460–78.

[51] Cited in ibid.

[52] *Irish Press*, 21 July 1949.

[53] Mary E. Daly, *Industrial Development and Irish National Identity, 1922–1939* (New York: Syracuse University Press, 1992), 29.

[54] Cited in Barry and Ó Fathartaigh, 'The Industrial Development Authority, 1949–58'.

destinations—in 1945, but the proposal had been blocked by the Department of Finance, which described it as 'objectionable in principle'. While accepting that financial assistance from public funds might be necessary to stimulate exports, 'this assistance should take the form either of a direct subsidy which can be effectively measured or of loans and grants analogous to those in operation in Northern Ireland'.[55]

The first interim report of the IDA in late 1949 suggested that financial inducements such as a 'tax remission on profits of export trade, a bonus on currencies arising from exports, or a guarantee against the risk of defaulting debtors' were needed 'to attract products to the export pool'. The second report of the Dollar Exports Advisory Committee, issued in mid-1950, recommended the granting of a tax concession for exports to the dollar area. The Department of Finance and the Revenue Commissioners reiterated their opposition, suggesting that such measures would open the door to other demands for special treatment and might run the risk of a countervailing US duty. The Department of Finance doubted that 'income taxation provided the most suitable channel for concessions of this nature'.[56]

The proposals initially advanced were geared towards domestic industry. The IDA appears to have been aware, from the beginning, that the scheme might prove attractive to foreign investors. Among the parties with which it had been in discussion in advance of its 1949 report were 'Irish-American businessmen, a US agency with connections to leading American industrialists, officials of the Organisation for European Economic Cooperation and a Czechoslovak resident of Ireland who had knowledge of the successful export organisation that had been established in his home country prior to the war'.[57]

The first explicit mention of export-oriented foreign investment in connection with the proposed tax relief came in an exchange of memos between the Department of Industry and Commerce and the Department of Finance in 1950. Noting the predominance of agricultural products in existing exports to North America, the Department of Finance suggested that 'it is in this field rather than amongst our newer, protected industries that one should look for dollar export potentialities'. The rejoinder from the Department of Industry and Commerce remarked that 'it is possible that the granting of the concession *may induce foreign enterprise to establish in this country industries capable of exporting goods to the dollar area*' (italics added).[58]

---

[55] Frank Barry, 'Foreign Investment and the Politics of Export Profits Tax Relief 1956'. *Irish Economic and Social History* 38 (2011): 54–73.

[56] Cited in ibid.

[57] Cited in ibid.

[58] Cited in Barry and Ó Fathartaigh, 'The Industrial Development Authority, 1949–58'.

The US authorities believed at this stage that 'Ireland's main contribution to European recovery will take place through the production of more food for export.'[59] Irish criticism of US proposals for how the country's small endowment of Marshall Aid funding should be allocated led to a tiny fraction being redirected to industrial development.[60] The 1952 'Stacy May' Report (named for its lead author) was commissioned from a New York consultancy firm from this small tranche of funds before aid was terminated following Ireland's refusal to participate in the North Atlantic Treaty Organization (NATO).

The broad thrust of the 100-page report was dismissed by the powerful Departments of Agriculture and Finance. One short passage, however, which drew attention to the case of Puerto Rico, would prove of significance. Puerto Rico had reconfigured its tax system to attract light manufacturing enterprises from the United States with apparently dramatic results. Real per capita incomes on the island were reported to have risen by 70 per cent over the decade to 1950. Though the report made 'no suggestion that the particular formula adopted by Puerto Rico is relevant to Ireland', the parallels between the two cases would have been obvious to those within the Irish bureaucracy who were already thinking along these lines. Indeed, the guardedness with which the view is expressed suggests that it may have been inserted at the behest of the IDA, which had furnished comments on an earlier draft.

The report referred to the US protectorate as having exploited its 'favoured position' of being 'within the US trading market but outside the US tax system'. Under the terms of the 1938 and 1948 Anglo-Irish Trade Agreements, most Irish industrial products had duty-free entry to the British market while, in cases where they were dutiable, they generally enjoyed preferential rates equivalent to those accorded to Commonwealth countries. Ireland also enjoyed preferential access to varying degrees in Commonwealth markets, though it had left the Commonwealth upon becoming a republic in 1949. Puerto Rico's favourable tax concessions would appear prominently in the 1956 IDA report on its recent visit to the United States, which noted that many US firms had enquired whether any such concessions were available in Ireland.[61]

Lemass was still clearly wedded to import substitution when Fianna Fáil returned to power in 1951. He furnished the IDA with a long list of imported

[59] *European Recovery Program* (Washington, DC: US Department of State, 1948), 8792.

[60] Peter Murray, *Facilitating the Future: US Aid, European Integration and Irish Industrial Viability: 1948–73* (Dublin: University College Dublin Press, 2009), 20–21.

[61] The US authorities were also advising in 1955 that financial inducements such as tax remission and import duty exemptions might be necessary to attract US FDI: Anne Groutel, 'American Janus-Faced Economic Diplomacy towards Ireland in the Mid-1950s'. *Irish Economic and Social History* 43, 1 (2016): 3–20.

goods and entrusted it 'with the sole and specific task of endeavouring to formulate proposals for the manufacture of these commodities'.[62] The Undeveloped Areas Act of 1952, however, signified a shift away from the 'command-and-control' approach by offering financial inducements to businesses to locate in certain designated 'undeveloped areas'.[63] There were several foreign-owned operations among the grant recipients. Though none employed a workforce of more than fifty or so, German firm Sligo Models was unusual in that its output was oriented towards the export market.

Unlike the Department of Industry and Commerce, the IDA did not have a legacy client base whose interests it would have to take into consideration. By 1954, it had come to focus primarily on attracting export-oriented FDI. As J. P. Beddy, its first Chairman, noted several years later 'the quickest and most advantageous course was to interest foreign industrialists in the establishment of manufacturing units in Ireland'.[64] Norton, the Minister for Industry and Commerce in the second Inter-Party government, told the Seanad in 1956 that he had asked the body in the previous two years to review the operation of all tariffs but:

> [They] have not been able to devote as much time to it as I originally intended they should, due to the fact that they have had to spend a very considerable amount of time in endeavouring to enlist the co-operation and interest of foreign industrialists to come here to Ireland.[65]

IDA missions had been undertaken to the United Kingdom, the United States, and Continental Europe over these two years and several foreign export-oriented firms—including Faber-Castell in Fermoy and Dutch firm Couper Works in Wicklow—were established even prior to the introduction of the new incentives.

In October 1956, after more than a decade of debate, Department of Finance objections were set aside and Inter-Party Taoiseach John A. Costello announced the introduction of export profits tax relief and the nationwide extension of the 'undeveloped areas' industrial grants scheme. His speech—as emigration reached levels last witnessed in the closing decades of the nineteenth century—was one of the most significant economic policy speeches in the history of the state. It was carefully crafted both to minimize political controversy and avoid raising the ire of protectionist industrial interests.

---

[62] Barry and Ó Fathartaigh, 'The Industrial Development Authority, 1949–58'.

[63] The undeveloped areas were Donegal, Kerry, West Cork, West Clare, and all of Connacht. Other areas were added subsequently.

[64] J. P. Beddy, 'Industrial Promotion 1'. *Administration* 10, 4 (1962): 327.

[65] *PDSE*, 22 March 1956.

Draft notes for the speech 'visualise that many *English* manufacturing concerns' (italics added) would find it worth their while to open export businesses to benefit from the favourable tax rate.[66] The speech as delivered made no mention of British FDI. Indeed, there was no explicit linkage between the tax relief and inward FDI of any type, though some perceptive observers recognized that the relief was likely to be of greater significance to foreign investors.[67]

Fianna Fáil had yet to come to an agreed position on the welcome to be extended to new foreign capital. Lemass's 1953 trip to the United States had been partly aimed at attracting US investment yet his Dáil speeches in the summer of 1955 criticized the coalition government's efforts towards this same end. Another senior Fianna Fáil figure, Erskine Childers, criticized the Minister for giving 'the idea that he looks forward to foreign capital investment as a major contribution to further industrial effort here'. 'We can only adopt a highly critical attitude', he argued, in view of the fact that 'exported interest and profits [...] are of no benefit to us in our efforts to pay for imports' and that 'certain types of capital investments here are likely to be of a fugitive character'.[68] De Valera railed against the government's handing over Irish resources to foreigners 'festooned with tax reliefs'.[69]

A 1956 US diplomatic despatch to Washington noted:

Although obviously speaking partly for political purposes, these comments [. . .] are indicative of the fact this party does not fully share the present Coalition Government's policy of actively seeking foreign investment in Ireland. [The] present favorable attitude toward foreign investment in Ireland may be altered if a change of Government occurs.[70]

The Statist, a leading British news magazine, carried a similar report, and at least one US investment project appears to have been jettisoned as a consequence of such concerns.[71]

The Department of Finance was taken aback by Costello's announcement. Whitaker complained to Sweetman, the Minister for Finance, that the export tax relief would further postpone the day 'when we can bring farming profits within the income tax net'. He argued that 'it is production which should

[66] UCD archives, Costello Papers, P190/713(8), italics added.
[67] See, e.g. Garret FitzGerald, 'Mr Whitaker and Industry'. *Studies: An Irish Quarterly Review* 48, 190 (1959): 138–50.
[68] *PDDE*, 7 March 1956.
[69] Barry, 'Foreign Investment and the Politics of Export Profits Tax Relief'.
[70] Groutel, 'American Janus-Faced Economic Diplomacy towards Ireland in the Mid-1950s'.
[71] Bew and Patterson, *Seán Lemass and the Making of Modern Ireland*, 89; Groutel, 'American Janus-Faced Economic Diplomacy towards Ireland in the Mid-1950s'.

be aided rather than exports'.[72] Following the speech, Sweetman wrote to a cabinet colleague that it had left him 'with a sense of disappointment':

> The Taoiseach's speech, with its great variety of new bodies, with its promises of large grants, striking reliefs from taxation and further assistance [. . .] foreshadows further expansion of the already inflated administrative machinery of the state and new large outlays from public funds and losses of revenue through widespread tax concessions.[73]

The following month, upon being informed that 'legislation must be prepared by the Revenue Commissioners forthwith', Whitaker complained that the bill was being rushed and responded in uncharacteristically tetchy language to the Secretary of Industry and Commerce on the matter:

> I will make only two points on your letter: (i) Even though you got the [Córas Tráchtála] report only on 12 November, it would have made a considerable difference if it were sent to us then, rather than nine days later [. . .] (ii) I might add that we did not and indeed could not have sent to Revenue on 21 November a communication which reached us only on the 22nd. *I do not know why you assume that we have invented a new time machine* (italics added).[74]

Though many believe export profits tax relief to have received the imprimatur of the Whitaker Report of 1958, the relevant sections in fact merely record the measures then in place.[75] As discussed in Chapter 7, the defeat inflicted on the Department of Finance is understood to have been one of the motivating factors behind the production of the report.

The need to placate domestic industry presented further challenges. While the section of the Taoiseach's speech on 'Tax Incentives for Exporters' excluded any mention of foreign industry, the later section on 'External Capital' signals that the Control of Manufactures Acts of the 1930s are to be retained. It notes that foreign industries 'will undertake here to manufacture goods which our own manufacturers are not yet equipped to produce'.[76] While many across the policymaking system—including the Taoiseach— favoured repeal of the acts, the Department of Industry and Commerce warned that this 'would permit of the unfettered investment of outside capital

---

[72] NAI: Fin/F200/10/56.
[73] NAI: Fin/F200/13/56.
[74] NAI: Fin/F200/10/56.
[75] Department of Finance, *Economic Development*, 42, 232.
[76] UCDA, Costello Papers, 1956, P190/781.

in unsuitable as well as suitable cases' and would be seen as 'a breach of faith towards those who had set up factories on the basis of [their] existence'.[77]

Though admitting that the provision of the Acts might look formidable to an outsider, the Department advised that it be brought home to potential foreign investors that they were not operated in a restrictive manner. William Taft, the US Ambassador, was sceptical since 'such a law remains on the books'. He complained that 'we would be promoting the Irish tariff economy rather than liberalization of trade'.[78] A US consultancy report of 1960 commissioned by the new Shannon authority would describe the continuing restrictions as 'most detrimental' and 'difficult to understand in light of Ireland's drive for US investments'. Echoing the US Ambassador, it interpreted the acts as representing a form of continued protectionism, while efficiency, it argued, required further competition—including from new foreign companies.[79] The Organisation for European Economic Co-operation (OEEC)—forerunner of today's Organisation for Economic Co-operation and Development (OECD)—also criticized retention of the foreign-ownership restrictions, which fully ceased to operate only in 1968.[80]

Though their remaining on the statute books complicated the job of the IDA (which differed from the Department of Industry and Commerce in favouring repeal), retention of the restrictions was necessary to avoid triggering the opposition of protectionist interests. A similar motivation dictated how the new industrial grants scheme was operated. A convention was adopted 'which had always been accepted by the grant-giving bodies although it is not expressed in any of the legislation, [that] grants were only to be given to new firms which would not compete in the home market with existing firms'.[81]

Minister for External Affairs Liam Cosgrave had been concerned, as was Whitaker, that export profits tax relief would be in breach of an agreement entered into with the OEEC in 1955 that member countries would discontinue artificial aids to exporters. Special opt-outs had been granted to France, Greece, and Turkey however, and there was a clause in the agreement that allowed it to be waived 'for reasons of national importance'. In the event, the

---

[77] UCDA, Costello Papers, 1954, P190/787/(2); David McCullagh, *The Reluctant Taoiseach: A Biography of John A. Costello* (Dublin: Gill and Macmillan, 2010), 293.

[78] US archives cited in Groutel, 'American Janus-Faced Economic Diplomacy towards Ireland in the Mid-1950s', 11.

[79] NAI: DT S 2850G/94.

[80] 1958 OEEC report on Ireland: NAI, DT S 16446. The restrictions were relaxed in 1958 and 1964 and removed entirely in 1968: *Irish Times*, 19 October 1964; James Meenan, *The Irish Economy since 1922* (Liverpool: 'Liverpool University Press, 1970), 151–52.

[81] Catherine Brock, 'Public Policy and Private Industrial Development', in *Economic Policy in Ireland* ed. John A. Bristow and Alan A. Tait (Dublin: Institute of Public Administration, 1968), 160.

OEEC reacted with approval to the evidence of a shift towards outward orientation. The Deputy Secretary General of the organization stated in December 1956 that though Ireland could not fundamentally be considered an underdeveloped country, he accepted that significant industrialization was required and that this might warrant special treatment.[82] The 1957 OEEC report on Ireland, having recorded without critical comment the export tax measures adopted, continued:

> It is extremely important to avoid stimulating new industrial development by measures which, like tariff increases—and to some extent the import levies—tend to a more permanent system of protection against outside competition. The main criterion for encouraging the establishment and development of industries should [be] their capacity to make use of available domestic resources to the best advantage and, in most cases, to contribute towards external earnings.[83]

With the logjam broken, Fianna Fáil threw itself wholeheartedly behind the new strategy upon returning to power. In 1958, it expanded the tax remission to 100 per cent and increased the exemption period. Though the draft notes for the Costello speech had speculated that 'we would get a lot of extra tax', abolishing the tax entirely for the period of the exemption had been advocated by an influential academic commentator, Professor Charles Carter of Queen's University Belfast. Carter had suggested in 1957 that the best way to get 'good management, technical knowledge and capital all at once is from subsidiaries of large foreign companies; and it would be worth very large inducements indeed, *including complete exemption from taxes for a period*, to get more of them' (italics added).[84] Whitaker, unsurprisingly, disagreed.[85]

UK and Continental European firms, constrained by labour shortages at home, responded enthusiastically to the new incentives. It would take somewhat longer for US firms to follow suit. The Shannon Free Zone was targeted particularly towards them. Shannon Airport was located within relatively easy reach of the US east coast—it had been a major refuelling station for transatlantic flights in the era before jet travel—and Irish labour costs were low not just by US, UK, and advanced Western European economy standards

---

[82] Cited in Barry, 'Foreign Investment and the Politics of Export Profits Tax Relief'. As will be seen again on other occasions, Ireland had to continually balance the advantages and disadvantages of being characterized as 'under-industrialized' in international negotiations: Denis J. Maher, *The Tortuous Path: The Course of Ireland's Entry into the EEC, 1948–73* (Dublin: Institute of Public Administration, 1986), 57, 82–84, 126.

[83] Cited in Barry, 'Foreign Investment and the Politics of Export Profits Tax Relief'.

[84] NAI, DT S 16211: March 1957 address by Professor Charles Carter of Queen's University, Belfast, circulated to government by (Fianna Fáil) Minister for Finance.

[85] NAI, Fin/F049/012/58.

but relative even to those of Puerto Rico.[86] Barry and O'Mahony characterize the plan as Fianna Fáil's response to the Inter-Party government's initiative.[87] The idea was first mentioned in a 1953 Department of Industry and Commerce minute. Following a discussion of the possibility of developing manufacturing industry at the airport, which had been duty-free since 1947, the Irish embassy in London had been requested to seek details from the Panamanian authorities of a similar recent initiative.[88] Two years later, US Commerce Department officials would also advise that consideration be given to 'the establishment of a free port or bonded zone where manufacturing, assembling and processing operations could be carried out without payment of import duties on materials or parts and with a minimum of customs formalities'.[89]

The Shannon export processing zone was established by legislation in 1958, with a twenty-five-year tax exemption for qualifying companies (at a time when the national exemption was for ten years).[90] Though identified by the World Bank as one of the world's earliest and most influential such zones, it was based, as seen above, on Latin American prototypes.[91] Study visits had been made to Panama and Puerto Rico as well as to the Hamburg Free Zone, and the laws relating to the Colón Free Zone had been translated and studied. Air-freightable manufacturing soon became the main focus of the endeavour. The managing authority was formally established as the Shannon Free Airport Development Company (SFADCo) in January 1959.

The results achieved by the IDA in attracting US investment had been disappointing up to this point.[92] The competition for US FDI was intense. Though the formal inducements on offer in the Irish case were generous by European standards and were matched or surpassed only by those available in the South of Italy and the port city of Trieste, many competitors were suspected of offering secret tax deals and agreeing 'to extend their delimitation of "undeveloped areas" whenever convenient'.[93] Ireland was not a participant

[86] John Teeling, 'The Evolution of Offshore Investment'. DBA thesis, Harvard University, 1975, exhibits 1.2 and 1.3.

[87] Barry and O'Mahony, 'Regime Change in 1950s Ireland'.

[88] Ibid.

[89] Groutel, 'American Janus-Faced Economic Diplomacy towards Ireland in the Mid-1950s'.

[90] Many of the incentives offered by other countries were dependent on annual budgetary rounds. Tax holidays provided greater certainty for businesses and were an important component of the Irish regime.

[91] World Bank, *Export Processing Zones* (Washington, DC: World Bank, 1992). Jiang Zemin, president of China from 1993 to 2002, was reportedly strongly influenced by a study visit to Shannon in which he had participated in 1980: Justin Yifu Lin and Célestin Monga, *Beating the Odds: Jump-Starting Developing Countries* (Princeton, NJ: Princeton University Press, 2017).

[92] NAI, DT S 2850 G/94, Memo from Department of Industry and Commerce: 'Attracting External Investment in Ireland', 7 September 1960.

[93] NAI, DT 2001/3/122, Economic Development Branch (Department of Finance), Inducements to Industrialists, July 1960. Other examples of suspected or alleged flexibilities being shown by European tax

in either of the European trading blocs, and many of the major US corporations already had production facilities in the United Kingdom, which negated much of the value of what Ireland had to offer.[94] The Netherlands, a member of the Common Market, was perceived as a particularly successful competitor.[95]

There also appears to have been a widespread perception in the United States at this time that Ireland was culturally unsuited to the requirements of modern industry.[96] Groutel quotes from an internal report by the US Ambassador in 1953 that the Irish had a preference for 'rest, relaxation, sport, or some other non-remunerative pursuit rather than for a higher standard of living'.[97] Teeling comments, with reference to attitudes among the Irish-American business community, that 'these potential investors were not uncertain about an Irish project, they were certain that it would be a disaster'.[98]

One of SFADCo's first acts was to commission US consultancy firm Business International to advise on changes to Irish practices and tax and company law that might facilitate the attraction of US businesses. On the cultural issue, the report recommended initiating a campaign 'playing up Ireland's close relationship with Protestant countries'.[99] The main policy advice offered was that Ireland should consider replicating some of the legal, tax, and regulatory aspects of the Swiss regime.[100] The Washington administration was growing increasingly concerned by the aggressive tax planning practices of US corporations however, and President Kennedy had explicitly mentioned the 'unjustifiable use of tax havens such as Switzerland'.[101] The consultants' recommendations were rejected, both to avoid the stigma of being considered a tax haven and because having to make the case for

authorities are provided in the 1960 Business International consultancy report referred to below: NAI, DT S 2850 G/94.

[94] NAI, DT S 2850 G/94, Department of Industry and Commerce: Attracting External Investment in Ireland, 7 Sep 1960; NAI, FIN 2001/3/121, Industrial Development Authority letter to Whitaker, 25 January 1960.

[95] NAI, DT S 2850 G/94, Memo from Department of Industry and Commerce: 'Attracting External Investment in Ireland'.

[96] In Germany, by contrast, Ireland's under-industrialization was perceived as an advantage in that it ensured the availability of a plentiful supply of labour: Barry and O'Mahony, 'Regime Change in 1950s Ireland'; Survey of Grant-Aided Industry: Survey Team's Report, (Dublin: Stationery Office, 1967), 57.

[97] Groutel, 'American Janus-Faced Economic Diplomacy towards Ireland in the Mid-1950s', 16.

[98] Teeling, 'The Evolution of Offshore Investment', 58, 67.

[99] NAI, DT S/2850G/94. On a similar note, Boston consultancy company Arthur D. Little advised the Northern Ireland authorities to emphasize 'the historical and ethnic differences' between Northern Ireland and the Republic: PRONI Cab/9/F/188/15, 'A Program to Attract American Industry to Northern Ireland', 15 October 1959.

[100] NAI, DT S 2850G/94.

[101] Cited in Joint Committee on Internal Revenue Taxation, 'Tax Effects of Conducting Foreign Business through Foreign Corporations' (Washington, DC: 1961), 19.

special 'underdevelopment concessions' (if the changes to US tax laws then under discussion were to proceed) could complicate possible future negotiations with the EEC. It was determined, furthermore, that adoption of the Swiss regime would not necessarily maximize employment creation, which remained the primary goal of Irish policy.[102]

The cultural concerns of earlier years would dissipate with the passage of time. The *Wall Street Journal* carried a report on recent industrial progress in 1960 under the title 'Why Irish Eyes are Smiling'. *Time Magazine* featured Lemass on its front cover three years later under the heading 'New Spirit in the Ould Sod'.[103] Many of the new foreign firms reported in the 1960s that their original expectations of the efficiency and capabilities of the Irish workforce had been set far too low.[104] By the 1970s, the IDA officials whom Teeling interviewed believed that cultural ties with the United States were responsible for many of the projects undertaken.[105]

6.3 Developments in 'New' Foreign Industry

Manufactured exports increased strongly in 1957 and more than doubled—though from a very low base—between 1956 and 1960. The annual reports of the Irish Export Board ascribe the expansion largely to the new financial and tax incentives that had been introduced. Though the new industries established were substantially more import-intensive in their production processes than existing export industries, the parallel expansion in imports over the coming years was largely a consequence of the relaxation of the balance-of-payments constraint. A visiting US academic would report in 1974 that the directors of the Central Statistics Office, the Economic and Social Research Institute, and the Research and Planning Division of the IDA had all agreed in correspondence that new industry—the bulk of it foreign— was 'the primary causative force in reducing emigration between 1958 and 1971'.[106]

Available estimates suggest that there were around 7,000 jobs in 'new' (post-1955) internationally competitive foreign industrial projects in 1962,

---

[102] Frank Barry, 'Shannon Connections: Aggressive tax planning by US MNCs in the pre-Kennedy era'. Presentation to Central Bank of Ireland Economic History Workshop, December 16, 2016.
[103] *Time Magazine* cover story, 12 July 1963; *Wall Street Journal*, 1 November 1960, clipping contained in NAI, DT S/2850G/94.
[104] *Survey of Grant-Aided Industry: Survey Team's Report*, 90.
[105] Teeling, 'The Evolution of Offshore Investment', 58.
[106] Kevin. A. Kearns, 'Industrialization and Regional Development in Ireland, 1958–72'. *American Journal of Economics and Sociology* 33, 3 (1974): 299–316.

including 1,000 or so at the Shannon Industrial Estate.[107] This was less than half of the overall increase in manufacturing employment over these years. Other drivers of the more general expansion included the normal cyclical recovery from the severe recession of the mid-1950s, a pick-up in economic growth in the United Kingdom, and the bolder approach to aggregate demand management policy adopted from this time.[108] As Kennedy and Dowling observe however, a bolder approach could be taken precisely because the balance-of-payments constraint had been relaxed.[109] From the mid-1960s through to EEC accession, almost all of the increase in manufacturing employment would be in 'new' foreign industry.[110]

Most of the foreign-owned grant-aided projects initiated over the period 1955–1961, though larger on average than Irish-owned projects, employed a workforce of no more than fifty. The largest included the atypical cases of Verolme Dockyard and the Whitegate oil refinery: Verolme (discussed further later) was a brownfield rather than a greenfield project, while Whitegate was a non-manufacturing operation.[111] Others included Liebherr, Wavin Pipes, Kire Manufacturing, and the Fortune 500 company Standard Pressed Steel (SPS) of Pennsylvania (Table 6.7).[112] SPS accounted for almost half of the jobs in the early years of the Shannon Free Zone.

Other early arrivals at Shannon included Lana-Knit, Shannon Diamond & Carbide (later De Beers), and Sony. Sony's establishment in 1959 has been described as 'the first post-war direct manufacturing investment in Europe by any major Japanese corporation'.[113] The operation aroused controversy in Britain, as some of the early German investments in Ireland would also do. The Japanese manager of the plant admitted that the 'Made in Ireland' label would prove advantageous as some European countries still looked

---

[107] See Chapter 7.

[108] Kennedy and Dowling, *Economic Growth in Ireland: The Experience since 1947*, 232; Liam Kennedy, *The Modern Industrialisation of Ireland, 1940–1988* (Dundalk: Dundalgan Press, 1989), 15.

[109] Kennedy and Dowling, *Economic Growth in Ireland: The Experience since 1947*, 232.

[110] CIP (various years); Denis O'Hearn, 'Estimates of New Foreign Manufacturing Employment in Ireland 1956–1972'. *Economic and Social Review* 18, 3 (1987): 173–88.

[111] Eligibility for New Industry grants formally required that plants be internationally competitive rather than export-oriented per se, though most were export-oriented. The 1967 *Survey of Grant-Aided Industry* (which excluded Shannon) found that while non-grant-aided firms had an export-output ratio of 18 per cent, the ratio for grant-aided firms was 74 per cent. New *foreign* industries exported 88 per cent of their gross output in 1973: Dermot McAleese, *A Profile of Grant-Aided Industry in Ireland* (Dublin: Industrial Development Authority, 1977), 30, table 4.2; Dermot McAleese, 'Ireland in the Enlarged EEC: Economic Consequences and Prospects', in *Economic Sovereignty and Regional Policy: A Symposium on Regional Problems in Britain and Ireland*, ed. John Vaizey (Dublin: Gill and Macmillan, 1975), 138.

[112] Kire Manufacturing had established in Kinsale in 1960 and by 1971 had other factories in Bandon, Fermoy, and Newmarket. Employment peaked at 400. Its 1,500 workers in West Virginia had gone on strike over concerns that production was being outsourced to Ireland.

[113] Mark Mason, 'The Origins and Evolution of Japanese Direct Investment in Europe'. *Business History Review* 66, 3 (1992): 435–74. A year after it established at Shannon, Sony opened a regional office in Zug, Switzerland, 'to support the company's European efforts and take advantage of local tax laws'.

Table 6.7 Major 'new foreign industry' employers, *c.* 1961

Firm	Sector	Nationality	Date established	Employment, *c.* 1961
Verolme	Dockyard	Dutch	1959	700
Irish Refining	Oil refining	Anglo-American	1959	300
Liebherr	Crane construction	German	1958	330
Wavin Pipes	Plastic pipes	Dutch	1957	150
Kire Manufacturing	Women's clothing	United States	1960	300
SPS, Shannon	Steel tools	United States	1959	400

Source: author.

unfavourably on imports from Japan.[114] The plant employed fewer than 100 and closed in 1964 when Britain imposed an emergency surcharge on manufactured imports in response to balance-of-payments difficulties it was itself experiencing at this time.

The exports of the earliest grant-aided foreign investors—among which British firms predominated—were directed more towards the United Kingdom than to Continental Europe. Shannon, with its strong North American market orientation, was a special case.[115] The EEC became a more significant destination as the share of US and Continental European firms establishing in Ireland expanded over the course of the 1960s.[116]

Irish exports had declined as a share of national income since the 1930s. The trend would be reversed from this point.[117] Table 6.8 depicts the related shifts in export composition and export destinations.[118] Dermot McAleese would note in 1975 that 'it has been fairly clearly established that most of the last 15 years' export growth, and the attendant diversification of export markets, is attributable to [. . .] new grant-aided enterprises. Thus nearly half

[114] *Irish Times*, 8 July 1960.

[115] The 1967 *Survey of Grant-Aided Industry* found that 'for grant-aided industries operating in 1966 [...] Britain is by far the most important market' (paragraph 2.64). (Shannon enterprises were not included.) On Shannon, see Barry and O'Mahony, 'Regime Change in 1950s Ireland'.

[116] Buckley shows that US and Continental European-owned projects were much more heavily oriented towards the EEC market than UK-owned projects: Peter Buckley, 'The Effect of Foreign Direct Investment on the Economy of the Irish Republic', Ph.D. thesis, Lancaster University, 1975, 148–149. See also Teeling, 'The Evolution of Offshore Investment', 30–32, tables 2.2–2.4.

[117] Kieran Kennedy, Thomas Giblin, and Deirdre McHugh, *The Economic Development of Ireland in the Twentieth Century* (London: Routledge, 1988), 194.

[118] The first detailed breakdown by destination for Shannon is for 1973, when North America accounted for a higher share of exports than the entire EEC, including the United Kingdom.

Table 6.8 Manufactured exports (excluding Shannon), 1956–1972

	1956	1961	1972
Manufactured exports as share of total exports	12	18	40
UK-market share of manufactured exports	81	80	59
EEC6 market share of manufactured exports	4	9	17

Note: Manufactured exports exclude food and drink.
Sources: Irish Export Board (CTT) annual reports.

of Ireland's manufactured exports in 1970 are estimated to have come from firms which were established since 1959.'[119]

6.4 The Largest Manufacturing Employers of the Early 1960s

Details of the largest manufacturing employers at key junctures in the past have been provided in Chapters 2, 4, and 5. Table 6.9 identifies the largest manufacturing employers of the early 1960s.[120] Unsurprisingly, the expansion in employment since the late 1940s was accompanied by a substantial increase in the number of relatively large firms (i.e. with workforces of 500+). None of the export-oriented greenfield FDI firms that had entered as a consequence of the new strategy yet met the criterion for inclusion.[121]

Most of the firms that appeared on the equivalent list for the late 1940s had expanded in the interim. A number of semi-state or state-supported companies—Irish Steel Holdings, Verolme Dockyard, and the Industrial Engineering Company—also entered this size category for the first time (Table 6.10). Given its extremely limited capacity, Irish Steel remained dependent on protection and a monopoly on scrap metal purchases. The nearby Rushbrooke Dockyard, which had been reopened in 1941, was acquired by Dutch company Verolme in 1959. Employment, as at the Liffey dockyard, was sporadic: the relatively large workforce recorded in Table 6.9 reflected

---

[119] McAleese, 'Ireland in the Enlarged EEC: Economic Consequences and Prospects', 138. For a detailed analysis of the period 1966–1973 see John Blackwell, Gerard Danaher, and Eoin O'Malley, *An Analysis of Job Losses in Irish Manufacturing Industry* (Dublin: National Economic and Social Council, 1983).

[120] Employment at milk distributor Merville Dairies and builders' suppliers Dockrells and Brooks Thomas had also expanded to around 500 by this time. Knitwear producer C. Kennedy & Sons of Ardara, County Donegal, was one of the largest employers of out-workers, with around 800 home knitters on its books.

[121] Philips was something of an intermediate case. The output of its Clonskeagh plant was initially directed towards the home market, but exporting had begun by 1962. It opened a fully export-oriented plant at Finglas several years later.

Table 6.9 Firms employing 500+ in the early 1960s

Industry	Firm name	Employment, 1960–1962
Meat	Denny (UK)	500
	O'Mara	500
	Clover Meats	500
Dairy	Dairy Disposal Company	1,296 (1964)
	Mitchelstown Co-operative	600
Milling, bread, and biscuits	Ranks Group (UK)	1,000
	Jacobs	2,400
	Bolands	1,000
	Johnston, Mooney & O'Brien	800
Chocolate, sugar, and confectionery	Irish Sugar	2,000
	Crosse & Blackwell (UK)	950
	Rowntree (UK)	1,150
	Cadbury (UK)	790–1,000
	Urney	600
Brewing	Guinness (UK)	3,700
Tobacco	Players–Wills (UK)	1,500
	Carrolls	500
Textiles, clothing, and hosiery	Goodbody Jute	1,200
	Greenmount & Boyne	800
	General Textiles	830
	Blarney Woollen Mills	740
	Sunbeam–Wolsey	2,500
	Salts (UK)	850
	Seafield Fabrics (including Blackwater Cottons)	800
	Irish Ropes	530
Footwear	Rawson (UK)	700
	Halliday/Clarks (UK)	800
	Lee Boot & Hanover Shoe (Dwyers)	500
Paper and print	*Irish Independent*	900
	Alexander Thom Group	1,000
	Browne & Nolan	530
	Irish Press	900
	Clondalkin Paper	500
	Killeen Paper	670
Vehicles	Ford (US)	800
	Lincoln & Nolan	500
Other metals and engineering	Liffey Dockyard	600
	Verolme Dockyard (Netherlands)	1,000
	Industrial Engineering Company, Dundalk	800

Continued

Table 6.9 *Continued*

Industry	Firm name	Employment, 1960–1962
	Irish Steel	650
	Philips (Netherlands)	500
	Pye (UK)	650
	Unidare	1,500
	Hammond Lane Group	800
Clay, glass, and cement	Cement Ltd	900
	Arklow Pottery	520
	Waterford Glass	600
	Irish Glass Bottle	800
Fertilizer	Gouldings	600
	Gouldings Group	1,200
Miscellaneous	Irish Dunlop (UK)	2,100

Source: author.

completion of a ship launched in 1961. Verolme also engaged in heavy general engineering work for the Irish market. It, too, was heavily subsidized, and the government took an almost 50 per cent stake in the company in 1968.

Industrial Engineering had been formed in 1958 to provide employment for the almost 1,000 workers threatened with redundancy by the closure of the Great Northern rail yards. The largest of its five subsidiaries was Dundalk Engineering Works.[122] Goods produced at the site included Heinkel 'bubble cars', agricultural machinery, steel foundry products, and chassis for heavy-duty road vehicles. Contract work was also carried out for the state transport company CIÉ in relation to the repair and maintenance of rolling stock. This venture also cost the state large sums of money, both directly and through the Industrial Credit Corporation, and was liquidated in 1966.[123]

Two further firm-specific developments of note relate to Guinness and Jacobs, the largest Dublin manufacturers. Guinness opened a brewery in Lagos, Nigeria in the early 1960s. This was the first to have been purpose-built by the company since Park Royal in London. Its brief venture in the post-war United States has been largely forgotten. E. & J. Burke, Guinness's early export bottlers, had been brewing stout and ale on Long Island since the end of Prohibition. Hoping to capitalize on the popularity of its product with the US troops who had been stationed in Northern Ireland during the war, Guinness acquired the brewery from Burke in 1949. It was found, however, that

[122] The others were Heinkel Cabin Scooters, Commercial Road Vehicles, Frank Bonser and Co., and Dealgan Steel Founders.
[123] For an analysis of the failed endeavour, see Charles Flynn, *Dundalk 1900–1960: An Oral History* (National University of Ireland Maynooth, 2000), 189–90.

Table 6.10 Employment in Verolme, Irish Steel, and Dundalk Industrial Engineering

	Employment
Verolme Dockyard	200 (1960), 700 (1961), 800 (1966), 870 (1969), 1,100 (1972)
Irish Steel (Irish Steel Holdings from 1947)	120 (1938), 250 (1946), 450 (1950, 1960), 650 (1961), 800 (1968), 847 (1972)
Industrial Engineering Company, Dundalk	800 (1962), liquidated 1966

Source: author.

the servicemen, upon repatriation, tended 'to go back to their favourite home products'.[124] The New York brewery closed in 1954 and Guinness returned to supplying the US market from St James's Gate.

Jacobs had ceased exporting from Dublin during the Emergency and its entire overseas trade was sold to the UK sister company in 1949. Senior management blamed the government for refusing to sanction the supply of inputs necessary to maintain the overseas trade in order to satisfy domestic demand.[125] The company had been exporting more than two-thirds of its output in the early Free State era. Its export–output ratio in 1972 stood at only 15 per cent.[126]

---

[124] *Irish Times*, 9 August 1954; see also *Irish Times*, 15 June 1949.
[125] Séamus Ó Maitiú, *W. & R. Jacob: Celebrating 150 Years of Irish Biscuit Making* (Dublin: Woodfield Press, 2001), 81.
[126] Largest Irish Industrial Companies, *Irish Times* 28 December 1972.

7

Trade Liberalization and the Road to Europe

T. K. Whitaker would suggest in later life that 'perhaps Ireland owes de Gaulle a vote of thanks for delaying enlargement'.[1] The remark refers to the years that elapsed between Ireland's first application for membership of the European Economic Community (EEC) and eventual accession in 1973. Ireland had scrambled in 1961 to prepare an application when it became clear that Britain was to do so. The French President, Charles de Gaulle, deeply sceptical of Britain's commitment to the European project, blocked the way. This gave Ireland time to get its house in order. Industrial restructuring began, redundancy entitlements were overhauled, education revamped and the Exchequer's dependence on trade taxes reduced.[2] Crucially, the expansion of export-oriented foreign industry would serve as a counterbalance to the job losses experienced as protectionist-era industries went into decline.

7.1 The Whitaker Report: Context and Content

Whitaker's 1958 report *Economic Development* has generally been credited with triggering the dismantling of the trade barriers then in place.[3] As his remark reflects, he underestimated the difficulties involved in adjusting to freer trade. Policy did indeed pivot in the early 1960s, though not as rapidly as—and frequently not in the direction—Whitaker had advocated. The document's true significance can be argued to lie as much in context as in content. Whitaker's macroeconomic views are presented more sharply in the address he delivered to the Statistical and Social Inquiry Society a week before his appointment as Secretary of the Department of Finance in 1956. His thinking

---

[1] Anne Chambers, *TK Whitaker: Portrait of a Patriot* (Dublin: Random House, 2014).
[2] Trade taxes accounted for 41 per cent of tax revenue in 1960. By the time of EEC accession, with the introduction of new forms of taxation, the share had declined to 20 per cent. Most remaining tariffs would be reclassified as excise duties over the next several years: Jonathan Haughton, Trade Agreements and Tax Incentives: The Irish Experience. ITD–INTAL Tax and Integration Series (Washington, DC: Inter-American Development Bank, 2002).
[3] Department of Finance, *Economic Development* (Dublin: Stationery Office, 1958), (hereafter Whitaker Report).

Industry and Policy in Independent Ireland, 1922–1972. Frank Barry, Oxford University Press.
© Frank Barry (2023). DOI: 10.1093/oso/9780198878230.003.0007

on outward reorientation is shown to best effect in the civil service debates of 1959–1960 on policy towards the European Free Trade Association (EFTA), the UK-centred trade bloc then in the process of formation in response to the establishment of the EEC.

The EFTA correspondence would be published many years later under the title *Protection or Free Trade—The Final Battle*.[4] The title is something of a misnomer. The outcome of the battle serves as a reminder of the dominance of agricultural considerations in Irish trade policy. Lemass's 1961 submission to the EEC Council of Ministers stated that 'because of the close inter-relationship of the economy of Ireland and that of the UK, and the vital interest of Ireland in agricultural trade', Ireland hoped that its application would be considered alongside that of the United Kingdom.[5] Agricultural interests favoured not free trade but access to the sheltered European market.

Though the Whitaker Report helped to lift the mood of despondency and prepared the country psychologically for the onset of freer industrial trade, it would be another five years before tariff barriers would begin to be dismantled. The official announcement of the first unilateral tariff cuts in 1963 explicitly stated that the step was taken as part of the campaign to gain entry to the EEC, which could not have been envisaged at the time of the Whitaker Report. To credit the turnaround in trade policy solely or primarily to *Economic Development* is to ignore this crucial factor.

Nor was *Economic Development*, as seen in Chapter 6, responsible for the new export-oriented foreign direct investment strategy. By the time it was written, the new strategy was already in place. Though Whitaker favoured inward investment and removing the restrictions on foreign ownership, only in 1960 did the Department of Finance explicitly accept that 'tax concessions must continue to play a vital role in our industrial promotion campaign'. Revenue continued to withhold its support.[6]

The vast bulk of the sectoral analysis in *Economic Development* was devoted to agriculture and the agri-food industries, which it assumed would be the engine of future growth. Other branches of manufacturing received relatively little attention. The document placed its money, in Liam Kennedy's phrase, 'on the agricultural donkey rather than the industrial horse'.[7] The

---

[4] T. K. Whitaker (ed.), *Protection or Free Trade: The Final Battle* (Dublin: Institute of Public Administration, 2006).

[5] Cited in Gary Murphy, *Economic Realignment and the Politics of EEC Entry: Ireland, 1948–1972* (Bethesda, MD: Academica Press, 2003), 141.

[6] NAI, DT 2001/3/122, Letter from Murray to MacCarthy, 30 September 1960.

[7] Liam Kennedy, *The Modern Industrialisation of Ireland, 1940–1988* (Dundalk: Dundalgan Press, 1989), 14–15.

associated government Programme for Economic Expansion (1958–1963) was welcomed particularly warmly by the farming community.[8]

Publishing the Whitaker report and the government White Paper within weeks of each other provided useful political cover for Fianna Fáil. It indicated that 'the Programme was not, and was not claimed to be, a policy prepared by the government party, but was a national programme, prepared by the head of the civil service'.[9] Lemass, while asserting that protectionism had secured 'a basis of industrial organization [and] a pool of managerial competence and industrial skill', accepted that 'there is a need now to raise our targets and, I believe, also to change our methods'.[10] De Valera claimed that 'we set out these policies in 1926'.[11]

There was no meeting of minds between Whitaker and Lemass on broader economic policy. A later Fianna Fáil minister has suggested that the approach outlined in the documents may have been viewed by the new Taoiseach as overly grounded in traditional Department of Finance orthodoxy.[12] The expansion in government spending and lax wage controls over which Lemass and his successor Jack Lynch presided resulted in a sharp deterioration in international competitiveness just as trade barriers were being dismantled.[13] Though Irish economic growth was substantially higher in the 1960s than in earlier periods, so too was growth elsewhere. The country continued to underperform by international—and by other low-income Western European economy—standards.[14]

The Whitaker Report inaugurated a new era of coordination between private enterprise and the public sector, something that even conservative commentators had hoped for from the establishment of the Industrial Development Authority (IDA) almost a decade earlier.[15] Occasional references to Whitaker's 'Keynesianism', however, inappropriately employ the term as a synonym for economic planning. Protectionism itself was a highly

---

[8] Paul Rouse, *Ireland's Own Soil: Government and Agriculture in Ireland, 1945–65* (Dublin: Irish Farmers Journal, 2000), 139–40.

[9] Garret FitzGerald, *Planning in Ireland* (Dublin: Institute of Public Administration, 1968), 26. See also J. J. Lee, *Ireland 1912–1985: Politics and Society* (Cambridge: Cambridge University Press, 1989), 352.

[10] Cited in James Meenan, *The Irish Economy since 1922* (Liverpool: Liverpool University Press, 1970), 144.

[11] Tim Pat Coogan, *De Valera: Long Fellow, Long Shadow* (London: Arrow Books, 1995), 671.

[12] Cited in Frank Barry, 'Politics and Fiscal Policy under Lemass: A Theoretical Appraisal'. *Economic and Social Review* 40, 4 (2009): 393.

[13] On fiscal policy over the period, see Louden Ryan, 'Fiscal Policy and Demand Management in Ireland, 1960–70'. *Economic and Social Review* 2, 2 (1971): 253–308.

[14] Kevin O'Rourke, 'Independent Ireland in Comparative Perspective'. *Irish Economic and Social History* 44, 1 (2017): 31: figure 7; Frank Barry, 'Economic Integration and Convergence Processes in the EU Cohesion Countries'. *Journal of Common Market Studies* 41, 5 (2003): 897–921.

[15] Frank Barry and Mícheál Ó Fathartaigh, 'The Industrial Development Authority, 1949–58: Establishment, Evolution and Expansion of Influence'. *Irish Historical Studies* 39, 155 (2015): 460–78.

state-directed strategy: decision-making as to which sectors to protect and the extent to which they were to be protected was centralized to a large extent in the hands of the Minister for Industry and Commerce. More formally, the French type of indicative planning, which came into vogue in Ireland and elsewhere in the 1960s, entailed detailed and consistent quantitative targets. The First Programme, which was based on the Department of Finance report, was not a plan in this sense. Indeed, it explicitly stated that 'in an economy in which private enterprise predominates and which is so exposed to fluctuations in external trade, there would be little point in drawing up a detailed plan based on predetermined production targets'.[16] The recovery that followed was read by many however (including Whitaker) as providing an indication of what planning could achieve.[17] Though quantitative targets *were* adopted in the Second and Third Programmes, which covered the periods from 1964 to 1972, in neither case were the targets achieved.

To an economist, Keynesianism refers not to economic planning but to the conduct of macroeconomic policy. On this and many other matters, Whitaker did indeed adhere strongly to traditional Department of Finance orthodoxy. He warned in his 1956 address to the Statistical and Social Inquiry Society of the adverse balance-of-payment consequences of expansionary fiscal spending directed towards goals other than raising productivity. For an economy of Ireland's size, much of the hoped-for stimulus effect would be lost through increased imports.[18] These warnings were reiterated in *Economic Development*.[19]

Patrick McGilligan's 1950 budget was the first to have shown clear evidence of Keynesian influences. McGilligan would later express his regret that he had not accepted the Finance portfolio in the second Inter-Party government as 'he might have avoided some of the mistakes in the finance policy of that time'.[20] Whitaker, by contrast, would remark of Sweetman, who took on the portfolio and implemented the austerity programme, that he was 'singularly unfortunate [. . .] in that his government was overthrown before the ideas which he implemented could bear fruit'.[21] Indeed, in what can only be seen as an implicit criticism of Lemass, he told an interviewer in 1986 that Sweetman

---

[16] *Programme for Economic Expansion* (Dublin: Stationery Office, 1958), 7.

[17] Cormac Ó Gráda, *A Rocky Road: The Irish Economy since the 1920s* (Manchester: Manchester University Press, 1997), 75.

[18] T. K. Whitaker, 'Capital Formation, Saving and Economic Progress'. *Journal of the Statistical and Social Inquiry Society of Ireland* 16 (1955/56): 184–209.

[19] Whitaker Report, 4, 16, 206.

[20] *Irish Times*, 21 February 1973.

[21] Ronan Fanning, *The Irish Department of Finance, 1922–58* (Dublin: Institute of Public Administration, 1978), 19.

'had both the energy and capacity to carry a thing like *Economic Development* through'.[22]

Whitaker's 1956 address outlined the supply-side measures by which he believed industrial development could be best advanced. In its advocacy of education and training, adequate provision of utilities, low taxation, tackling restrictive work practices, and aligning pay with productivity, it bore striking parallels to the memorandum that McElligott had furnished to Finance Minister Ernest Blythe in 1923.

The most substantive difference between *Economic Development* and the government *Programme* was on regional policy. Joseph Brennan, Whitaker's distant predecessor as Secretary of Finance, had been sceptical of the value of any such policy.[23] Less trenchantly, Whitaker argued:

> A realistic appraisal of development prospects indicates that, apart from exceptional cases, industries must be at or near the larger centres of population. Special subsidisation of remote areas by more extensive grants for industrial development is wasteful and retards progress in areas better situated.[24]

Mary Daly describes the First Programme as 'a watered-down version of *Economic Development* that expunged or diluted many of the tougher, politically-unpalatable recommendations'.[25] Whitaker's views on industrial location were not incorporated. The rationale was clearly political, though the political reality is that popular support is required if reform programmes are to be sustained. Responsibility for regional industrial dispersal would ultimately devolve to the IDA.

Whitaker believed that most pre-existing firms and industries would survive outward reorientation. So, too, did Garret FitzGerald, Ireland's leading economic commentator of the time. This expectation would prove hugely overoptimistic. While tariff reductions are of immediate benefit to consumers, the benefits on the production side would accrue only over time through the emergence of new businesses. Most of the protectionist-era firms would have disappeared or downsized dramatically by the mid-to-late 1980s. The industrial transition would be more difficult than either had anticipated.

---

[22] Cited in John F. McCarthy, *Planning Ireland's Future: The Legacy of TK Whitaker* (Dublin: Glendale Press, 1990), 43.

[23] Lee, *Ireland 1912–1985: Politics and Society*, 196.

[24] Whitaker Report, 218.

[25] Mary E. Daly, *Sixties Ireland: Reshaping the Economy, State and Society, 1957–1973* (Cambridge: Cambridge University Press, 2016), 23.

Economic Development's most immediate consequences were in the realm of administrative politics. Lemass had clashed continuously with the Department of Finance during his long tenure as Minister for Industry and Commerce. There was a danger, as Lee notes, that he might, upon becoming Taoiseach, make other departments central to the formulation of economic policy.[26] Already in 1957, Whitaker was urging his assistant secretaries that the department 'should do some independent thinking and not simply wait for Industry and Commerce or the IDA to produce ideas'.[27] This accorded with Lemass's view that all of the organs of government should function as 'development corporations'.[28] Publication of the report signalled that the primacy of the department had been re-established. Though Whitaker largely subscribed to traditional Department of Finance orthodoxy, he differed from his predecessors Brennan and McElligott in his diplomatic nous and his political skills.[29]

7.2 European Trade Liberalization: The Inner Six and the Outer Seven

It was presumed, when *Economic Development* was in preparation, that a Western European Free Trade Area was in the offing. The negotiations sponsored by the Organisation for European Economic Co-operation (OEEC) broke down at the end of 1958 and the region divided into competing trading blocs: the 'inner six' (the original EEC) and the 'outer seven' (the UK-centred EFTA). The formation of these blocs forced a reappraisal of policy across much of the rest of Western Europe.[30]

EFTA's primary focus was on reducing barriers to industrial trade. As Ireland's industrial exports already enjoyed largely tariff-free access to the UK market, the benefits of this privileged position would be eroded no matter what course of action the Irish government chose to pursue. What the policy response should be was debated by a committee of senior civil servants over a period of several months in late 1959 and early 1960. The

---

[26] Lee, *Ireland 1912–1985: Politics and Society*, 343.

[27] Fanning, *The Irish Department of Finance, 1922–58*, 509.

[28] Sean F. Lemass, 'The Organisation behind the Economic Programme'. *Administration* 9, 1 (1961): 4–10.

[29] T. K. Whitaker, 'The Civil Service and Development'. *Administration* 9, 2 (1961): 107–13. Though a planning unit was set up within the department around this time, many of its proposals were stymied by others into whose territories it was perceived to have strayed: Louden Ryan, 'Opening Up to the International Economy: Ireland in the 1950s'. TCD Witness Seminar, Centre for Contemporary Irish History, 8 December 2004.

[30] On the Finnish case, see, e.g. Tapani Paavonen, 'From Isolation to the Core: Finland's Position towards European Integration, 1960–95'. *Journal of European Integration History* 7, 1 (2001): 53–75.

memos exchanged were intended especially for the eyes of Lemass, who had just become Taoiseach. Industry and Commerce had suggested in previous discussions that two-thirds of existing manufacturing jobs could be lost if industrial trade were liberalized across all of Western Europe. Between 20 and 40 per cent would be at risk, it believed, if Ireland were to join EFTA even under the concessionary terms accorded to the Portuguese. As the United Kingdom comprised over half of the entire EFTA economy, it could foresee little prospect of gains to offset the import penetration that would ensue.

Whitaker disagreed. The Industry and Commerce position paid no attention to competitiveness. Increasing competition on the home market was, in Whitaker's view, a better way of improving efficiency than the 'special aids and incentives' of recent years 'to which only the progressive undertakings would respond.'[31] The discipline of tariff reduction would reduce costs and improve quality and would thereby enhance export prospects not only in EFTA but also more broadly. Membership would also encourage further export-oriented inward foreign direct investment (FDI).

The memos exchanged were models of clarity and succinctness. One raised the challenging question of whether—given the freedom of movement of labour between Ireland and Britain—'a setback in industrial production [would] result not in higher productivity and greater competitiveness but in an outflow of redundant manpower'. Whitaker's response was to ask how maintaining the existing regime could be expected to raise living standards sufficiently to reduce emigration.

The crucial intervention came from the Department of Agriculture. It pointed to the likelihood that Irish membership would see pressure brought to bear on the United Kingdom to extend equivalent agricultural access to other EFTA member states. Irish interests would be better served, it suggested, by seeking a Free Trade Area agreement with Britain alone. Whitaker accepted this proposition and EFTA membership was not pursued.[32]

A free trade agreement with the United Kingdom would not resolve the differences between the Department of Finance and the Department of Industry and Commerce. Nor would EEC membership, though this would be far more attractive to agriculture as it offered a route out from under Britain's traditional 'cheap food' policy. The National Farmers' Association saw merit in seeking EEC membership even without the United Kingdom, though the

---

[31] 'Reasons for Reducing Protection': Department of Finance memo, 14 December 1959.

[32] It is not clear in any case that the United Kingdom would have supported Irish membership. As the Secretary of the Department of Agriculture pointed out, to do so 'would [bring] additional competition for her exporters into a market where at present they are predominant'. See also Maurice Fitzgerald, *Protectionism to Liberalisation: Ireland and the EEC, 1957 to 1966* (Aldershot: Ashgate, 2000), 31.

Department of Agriculture judged that the adverse impact this would have on access to the UK market would outweigh any possible benefits. Britain's surprise decision to submit an application to join the EEC in 1961 resolved this dilemma. A further benefit would be that the 'traditional links between the United Kingdom and the Commonwealth would be weakened to the advantage of the Irish'.[33]

When news reached Dublin of the United Kingdom's change of heart, an Irish application for membership was immediately submitted. Commission officials, judging that Irish industry would be unable to withstand the shock of full membership, proposed associate membership instead. This would not have guaranteed full access either to the emerging Common Agricultural Policy or to EEC regional aid. The Irish priority then became to demonstrate a willingness and ability to compete on a level playing field.[34]

The unilateral tariff reductions of 1963 and 1964 were part of this process. The official announcement of the first tariff cut stated that 'in anticipation of our entry to the EEC, the Government has decided to make a unilateral reduction of 10 percent in protective duties on industrial products on 1st January next'.[35] These were the across-the-board tariff cuts that Whitaker had been advocating since at least 1956. The signing of the Anglo-Irish Free Trade Area Agreement (AIFTA) in 1965 was the next step in the process.[36] De Gaulle's veto of the British application in 1963 gave Ireland a further ten years to prepare.

7.3 Policy Developments

Committee on Industrial Organisation

A new tripartite body, the Committee on Industrial Organisation (CIO), was established by government in 1961 to consider how industry might be assisted in preparing for the onset of freer trade. Twenty-six branches of manufacturing were identified as likely to be particularly strongly impacted and were earmarked for careful examination.[37] The Department of Agriculture was tasked with reporting on the issues pertaining to dairy products, grain milling, and fresh meats. The reports published by the CIO over the

---

[33] Murphy, *Economic Realignment and the Politics of EEC Entry*, 215.
[34] Fitzgerald, *Protectionism to Liberalisation*, 121.
[35] Murphy, *Economic Realignment and the Politics of EEC Entry*, 88.
[36] Denis J. Maher, *The Tortuous Path: The Course of Ireland's Entry into the EEC, 1948–73* (Dublin: Institute of Public Administration, 1986), 172, 200; Fitzgerald, *Protectionism to Liberalisation* 2, 292.
[37] On the choice of the branches of industry to be surveyed, see FitzGerald, *Planning in Ireland*, 58–59.

next several years provided clear evidence of the structural defects to which decades of protection had given rise. These included small firm size, excessive diversification, short production runs, and inferior quality. Garret FitzGerald's reading of the reports nevertheless led him to conclude that there was a 'viable industrial base, with individual inefficient firms, rather than a series of industries incapable of withstanding competition'. 'With the possible exception of vehicle assembly work', he believed, 'the industrial activities started in Ireland since 1932 were likely, in one form or another, to survive free trade.'[38]

One of the purposes of the surveys was to 'encourage the businessman himself to start asking more questions and to assess his own position more critically'.[39] Many business leaders soon came to understand the extent of the rationalization required.[40] A 1975 report of the Restrictive Practices Commission records the massive wave of mergers and acquisitions that occurred across all of industry in the years leading up to EEC accession. These developments are discussed towards the end of this chapter and in Chapter 8.

One of the CIO reports was devoted to the role of state aid in promoting the necessary adjustment. A later National Economic and Social Council review suggested that the various types of financial assistance that became available from 1963 were less than adequate.[41] Grant payments do not appear to have been carefully targeted however, and many ended up being extended to business sectors that had not been surveyed by the CIO.

The issue of redundancy payments, the subject of another of the Committee's reports, was tackled more successfully. A Redundancy Payments Act was introduced in the United Kingdom in 1965 as part of the Labour government's efforts to promote industrial modernization. While Irish social security reforms generally followed those in the United Kingdom with a long lag, an Irish act followed in this case within two years. 'From very restricted and ad hoc coverage under protectionism', Murray notes, 'state compensation for redundancy became a basic employment right in the course of adaptation to free trade.'[42]

---

[38] Ibid., 64–65.
[39] Catherine Brock, 'The CIO Industrial Survey'. *Journal of the Statistical and Social Inquiry Society of Ireland* 21, 2 (1964): 184.
[40] See, e.g. the reflections of the former owner of Killarney footwear manufacturer Hilliard, who had overseen its acquisition by UK company G. B. Britton (Ireland) in 1965: *Irish Times*, 25 February 1972.
[41] See, e.g. John Blackwell, Gerard Danaher, and Eoin O'Malley, *An Analysis of Job Losses in Irish Manufacturing Industry* (Dublin: National Economic and Social Council 1983), 47. For details of the incentives and incentive structures of the period, see Eoin O'Malley, *Industrial Policy and Development: A Survey of Literature from the Early 1960s* (Dublin: National Economic and Social Council, 1980).
[42] Peter Murray, *Facilitating the Future: US Aid, European Integration and Irish Industrial Viability: 1948–73* (Dublin: University College Dublin Press, 2009), 96.

Education

The overhauling of the country's education system was a consequence of the change in mindset associated with outward reorientation. Garvin characterizes the education system of the time as designed to reproduce 'a certain social type, pious, familial, loyal to the native acres, culturally ingrown and obedient to clerical guidance in matters moral and intellectual'.[43] Richard Mulcahy had described his role as Education Minister in the mid-1950s as 'a kind of dungaree man [to] take the knock out of the pipes'.[44] The country's increasing contacts with multilateral organizations encouraged it to benchmark itself against international standards. When a suggestion was made at a conference in Washington in 1961 that the Organisation for Economic Co-operation and Development (OECD) examine a number of educational systems in their entirety, Ireland was the first country to volunteer to be surveyed.[45] Whitaker was instrumental in shepherding the potentially divisive proposal through the Irish administrative system.[46]

The resulting report, *Investment in Education*, was published in 1965.[47] Conducted by a team of Irish economists and educationalists under the auspices of the OECD, its central propositions were that a non-meritocratic education system was wasteful of natural talent and that investment in human capital had made a substantial contribution to post-war European growth. The finding that attracted most attention was that one-third of Irish children were leaving school at or before the age of thirteen.[48] An appendix provided information on the educational attainment levels of the populations of seventeen countries across the globe, including seven in Eastern Europe. No equivalent statistics could be produced for Ireland. Questions on educational attainment would be included in the Irish population census from the following year.

The changing industrial environment also influenced the work of the corporatist National Industrial Economic Council. One of its first reports, issued under Whitaker's chairmanship, alluded to the concept known to economists as 'the ladder of comparative advantage': as the average level of skills and technical competence rises, 'the range of economic activity which can be

[43] Tom Garvin, *Preventing the Future: Why Was Ireland So Poor for So Long?* (Dublin: Gill and Macmillan, 2004), 184.

[44] *PDDE*, 19 July 1956.

[45] Tony White, *Investing in People: Higher Education in Ireland from 1960 to 2000* (Dublin: Institute of Public Administration, 2001).

[46] John Walsh, *The Politics of Expansion: The Transformation of Educational Policy in the Republic of Ireland, 1957–72* (Manchester: Manchester University Press, 2009), 64–65.

[47] *Investment in Education* (Dublin: Stationery Office, 1965).

[48] Garret FitzGerald, 'Investment in Education'. *Studies: An Irish Quarterly Review* 54, 216 (1965): 361–74.

carried on efficiently in Ireland will grow and the pace of economic development will be accelerated'.[49] This was the background to Donogh O'Malley's announcement of 'free education' in his first major speech as Education Minister in September 1966. Universal access to free second-level schooling and to free or subsidized school transport was introduced the following year. The school-leaving age was raised shortly afterwards. That O'Malley's announcement had not been approved by the Cabinet caused consternation in the Department of Finance, though any failure to sanction the policy would have been politically disastrous given the enthusiasm with which it had been greeted.[50] In its by-passing of the Department of Finance, it bears similarities to Costello's announcement of export profits tax relief almost exactly ten years earlier.

There was a discernible surge in the numbers attending second-level institutions following the removal of tuition fees, and a particularly sharp increase in the number of girls completing the senior cycle.[51] Overall completions increased by 150 per cent over the decade between the lapse of Ireland's first EEC application and eventual accession. Attendance at third-level educational institutions expanded in tandem, and new types of institutions were created to provide the technical skills necessary to meet prospective industrial requirements. The first five Regional Technical Colleges (RTCs) were established in 1970. Those established later in the decade would be financed to a large extent by the European Social Fund. Many have combined in recent years to form the country's new technological universities.

Industrial Relations and Macroeconomic Policy

Economic Development had advocated that the margin between British and Irish wages and salaries be maintained, at least into the near term.[52] This was not achieved. Compensation per manufacturing employee increased at one-and-a half times the UK rate between 1960 and 1972.[53] Though these wage pressures may have been independent of trade liberalization, the

---

[49] NIEC (National Industrial Economic Council), *Report on Manpower Policy* (Dublin: National Industrial Economic Council, 1964), 19. See also the *Survey of Grant-Aided Industry: Survey Team's Report* (Dublin: Stationery Office, 1967), 98.

[50] Walsh, *The Politics of Expansion*, 190. Whether Lemass had prior knowledge of the announcement and had given it his approval remains unclear: Frank Barry, 'Outward-Oriented Economic Development and the Irish Education System'. *Irish Educational Studies* 33, 2 (2014): 213–23.

[51] Adrian E. Raftery and Michael Hout, 'Maximally Maintained Inequality: Expansion, Reform, and Opportunity in Irish Education, 1921–75'. *Sociology of Education* 66, 1 (1993): 41–62; Thomas Kellaghan and Mary Hegarty, 'Participation in the Leaving Certificate Examination, 1961–1980'. *Irish Journal of Education* (1984): 72–106.

[52] Whitaker Report, 27.

[53] Wage data from European Commission AMECO database.

employment consequences were not. Costs could not be passed on as easily to consumers in a world of freer trade.

Lemass's macroeconomic policies were influenced more by his desire to maintain the support of the trade union movement than by *Economic Development*. Within a year of becoming Taoiseach, 'he had abandoned the cautious economic policy, and budgets began to expand with increased investment in those areas identified by Congress both in policy documents and in its private research'.[54] Tensions over his perceived acquiescence to trade union demands led to the resignation of his agriculture minister in 1964.

Lemass appears to have desired to emulate the social partnership arrangements that prevailed across much of Continental Europe. These involved unions committing to wage moderation in exchange for increased social spending.[55] In 1963 he proposed that 'wages and salaries should [. . .] be adjusted upward at an average rate slightly less than the realised growth of national production' in order to provide a margin 'for social insurance benefits or other desirable social objects'.[56] In the highly fragmented Irish industrial relations system of the time, such a deal could not be secured.[57] Hardiman notes that 'no single bargaining group believed it had to pay any attention to the impact of its activities on the overall state of economic performance'.[58] Lemass's wooing of the unions, in Horgan's estimation, gave them 'a new sense of their industrial strength, which was to usher in unparalleled unrest in 1964 and 1965 and wage settlements that ran quickly out of control'.[59] As a later Fianna Fáil finance minister, Ray MacSharry, would comment of the 'ill-fated' 1977 Fianna Fáil Manifesto, 'all the benefits were front-loaded, and the payback never came'.[60]

Though unemployment was higher and productivity growth lower than in the other less advanced economies to which the Ireland of the time bears

---

[54] Brian Girvin, 'Trade Unions and Economic Development', in *Trade Union Century*, ed. Donal Nevin (Dublin: Mercier Press, 1994), 117–32.

[55] Barry Eichengreen, 'Institutions and Economic Growth: Europe after World War II', in *European Economic Growth*, ed. Nicholas Crafts and Gianni Toniolo (Cambridge: Cambridge University Press, 1996), 38–72.

[56] John Horgan, *Seán Lemass, The Enigmatic Patriot* (Dublin: Gill and Macmillan 1999), 229.

[57] This was also the case in France, Italy, and the United Kingdom, where the industrial relations environment impacted adversely on economic growth: Eichengreen, 'Institutions and Economic Growth: Europe after World War II'.

[58] Niamh Hardiman, 'Pay Bargaining: Confrontation and Consensus', in *Trade Union Century*, ed. Nevin.

[59] Horgan, *Seán Lemass, The Enigmatic Patriot*, 190. Roche, too, concludes that Lemass had 'seriously underestimated the challenge of transforming the Irish industrial relations system': William K. Roche, 'Social Partnership: From Lemass to Cowen'. *Economic and Social Review* 40, 2 (2009): 183–205.

[60] Ray MacSharry and Padraic A. White, *The Making of the Celtic Tiger: The Inside Story of Ireland's Booming Economy* (Cork: Mercier Press, 2000).

comparison, Irish real wage growth was far more rapid. Greece, Spain, and Portugal all converged strongly on Western European living standards over the period 1960–1973. Ireland did not.

Anglo-Irish Free Trade Area Agreement

The Anglo-Irish Free Trade Area Agreement (AIFTA) was signed in 1965 and came into effect the following year. It committed the Irish government to eliminating restrictions on non-agricultural imports from the United Kingdom over the next ten years. Tariffs were to be eliminated in ten equal annual steps. Given the height of the restrictions at the outset of the process, the effects were expected to become apparent only around 1970. The United Kingdom for its part liberalized access to Irish agri-food exports and eliminated its tariffs on products containing man-made fibres, which were among the few items that remained dutiable at this point.[61]

AIFTA was clearly perceived as a trade-off between Ireland's agri-food interests and the interests of protectionist-era industry.[62] To the latter, it was seen as an even greater threat than EEC membership. There would be little gain in market access to compensate for the increase in imports, and Britain's export drive would be concentrated on Ireland rather than dispersed more broadly across the EEC.[63] The share of the market captured by competing imports would have continued to expand in any case as consumption across the developed world was becoming increasingly 'cosmopolitan.'[64] Contemporary analyses that took this into account concluded that the net job losses specifically ascribable to the agreement would be quite modest.[65] The most comprehensive analysis, by McAleese and Martin, suggested that AIFTA would result in around 3,000 job losses alongside a gain of around 1,000 in artificial fibres.[66]

The McAleese and Martin study was focused particularly on quantifying the import effects. It may have underestimated the number of new jobs that would be created. In extrapolating from agriculture it largely ignored the job gains associated with the expansion of agri-food businesses.[67] The dramatic

---

[61] Dermot McAleese and John Martin, 'Irish Manufactured Imports from the UK in the Sixties: The Effects of AIFTA'. *Economic and Social Research Institute (ESRI) Research Series*, 70 (1973): 9, 54–55.

[62] Fitzgerald, *Protectionism to Liberalisation*, ch. 3, 127.

[63] Daly, *Sixties Ireland: Reshaping the Economy, State and Society, 1957–1973*, 31.

[64] McAleese and Martin, 'Irish Manufactured Imports from the UK in the Sixties', 40.

[65] Garret FitzGerald, *Irish Times*, 14 January 1972; McAleese and Martin, 'Irish Manufactured Imports from the UK in the Sixties'.

[66] McAleese and Martin, 'Irish Manufactured Imports from the UK in the Sixties'.

[67] Ibid., 57.

increase in exports of butter, cheese, and beef from 1965 created almost 3,500 new jobs in these sectors by 1972.[68] The impact of AIFTA on inward FDI was also not taken into consideration.[69] Two major AIFTA-related synthetic-fibre projects, 'Pretty Polly' in Killarney and Lana-Knit at Shannon, employed over 1,300 by 1972.[70]

In most industrial sectors—as anticipated—competing imports captured an increased share of the domestic market. The increase in the export share of Irish output was largely ascribable to the increasing presence of new export-oriented foreign firms.[71] For the few existing firms for which data are available, there were particularly large increases in the cases of Sunbeam–Wolsey, Seafield–Gentex and Martin Mahony.[72] Janelle, a recently established indigenous manufacturer of synthetic-fibre garments for British department stores, also expanded strongly as a result of the agreement.[73]

AIFTA was associated, nevertheless, with a striking increase in the number of industrial redundancies. Job losses *per annum* in the early 1970s were multiples of the entire *aggregate* job losses considered likely by McAleese and Martin.[74] The conflict-ridden industrial relations system of the time was at least partly to blame. The emerging 'dual-economy' nature of Irish manufacturing may have further distorted wage-setting behaviour. The much more rapid productivity growth of the era—another consequence of the influx of new modern industries—appears to have driven wage settlements across the entire manufacturing sector.[75] This would have hastened the demise of cost-sensitive traditional industry.[76]

---

[68] Around one-third of the jobs were in beef processing. Beef exports, which had been encouraged by subsidy payments introduced by agriculture minister Charles Haughey, partly substituted for live cattle exports: Terence J. Baker, Robert O'Connor, and Rory Dunne, *A Study of the Irish Cattle and Beef Industries* (Dublin: Economic and Social Research Institute 1973), 75; Declan O'Brien, *The Dublin Cattle Market's Decline, 1955–1973* (Dublin: Four Courts Press, 2021), 27.

[69] Dermot McAleese, 'Anglo-Irish Economic Interdependence: From Excessive Intimacy to a Wider Embrace', in *Ireland and Britain since 1922*, ed. P. J. Drudy (Cambridge: Cambridge University Press, 1986), 96.

[70] Teeling provides evidence that the marketing plans of new foreign companies became increasingly focussed on the United Kingdom in the late 1960s: John Teeling, 'The Evolution of Offshore Investment'. DBA thesis, Harvard University, 1975, 28, tables 2.1.

[71] Dermot McAleese, 'Do Tariffs Matter? Industrial Specialization and Trade in a Small Economy'. *Oxford Economic Papers* 29, 1 (1977): 117–27.; Blackwell et al., *An Analysis of Job Losses in Irish Manufacturing Industry*.

[72] The expansion relates to the period 1966/67–1971/72: *Irish Times*, Fifty largest Irish industrial companies, November–December, various years.

[73] Janelle's workforce grew from less than 50 in 1961 to 622 in 1972.

[74] 'The Disappearing Jobs', *Irish Times*, 11 August 1972.

[75] Lucio Baccaro and Marco Simoni, 'Centralized Wage Bargaining and the "Celtic Tiger" Phenomenon'. *Industrial Relations: A Journal of Economy and Society* 46, 3 (2007): 426–55.

[76] The differential productivity patterns of indigenous and foreign industry continue to complicate the measurement of Irish cost competitiveness: Frank Barry, 'The Central Bank's Harmonised Competitiveness Indicators: Users Beware'. *Administration* 65, 4 (2017): 73–82.

The IDA, 'New Industry', and Regional Development

The IDA expanded in size and significance as its success in attracting for-eign industry became increasingly apparent. Its first overseas office had been opened in New York in the late 1950s. By 1966 it also had offices in London and Cologne. There were six overseas IDA offices in 1970, eight in 1972, and eleven by the end of 1973.

It was restructured twice, in 1959 and 1969, in line in each case with its own recommendations. In the second more substantial restructuring the grant-giving agency (An Foras Tionscal) was merged with the pro-motional and advisory authority and the 'new' IDA was established as an autonomous, state-sponsored body entirely outside the confines of the civil service. IDA staff numbers had increased from around a dozen in the late 1940s to sixty in 1967. The 'new' IDA had a staff complement of 250 in 1972.

One recommendation of the 1967 Arthur D. Little consultancy report that had advised on the second restructuring was not acted upon. This was that the functions of the state rescue agency Taiscí Stáit Teoranta be transferred to the new body. It was instead reconstituted as Fóir Teoranta in the early 1970s. The IDA is unlikely to have coveted such a poisoned chalice. One of the few stains on its reputation had been its experience with the French company Potez Aerospace, which had established a venture at Baldonnel in 1961 to build small executive aircraft. None was ever built and the plant closed in 1968 with significant losses to the Exchequer.[77]

By the eve of EEC accession, post-1955 export-oriented foreign firms accounted for almost 20 per cent of manufacturing employment, with the United States the single most significant source of inward investment.[78] US firms accounted for at least one-third of the jobs among the group.[79] As illustrated in Table 7.1, they continued to comprise the bulk of foreign multinational enterprise employment at Shannon.[80]

---

[77] Potez Industries employed around 100 at a separate plant in Galway over this period.
[78] McAleese provides a figure of 36,000 for 'new' foreign industry employment in 1974 (Dermot McAleese, *A Profile of Grant-Aided Industry in Ireland*, (Dublin: Industrial Development Authority, 1977), table 3.3, 21). The more recent data source upon which Table 7.1 is based suggests a higher figure.
[79] The figure of 12,000 US-firm jobs in 1972 comes from Frank Barry and Clare O'Mahony ('Regime Change in 1950s Ireland: The New Export-Oriented Foreign Investment Strategy'. *Irish Economic and Social History* 44, 1 (2017): 46–65) and is broadly consistent with the numbers reported by the US Chamber of Commerce for 1973 (*Irish Times*, 17 August 1973).
[80] The figure of 750 for Shannon in 1962 refers to employment at Lana-Knit (a joint US/UK venture) and Standard Pressed Steel.

Table 7.1 Shannon and 'new foreign industry', 1962 and 1972

	1962	1972
Employment in 'new' foreign industry (including Shannon)	7,000	36,000
Of which: US firms	1,700*	12,000
Employment at Shannon Industrial Estate	1,000	4,000
Of which: US firms	750	3,000
	1963	**1973**
Irish manufactured exports other than food, drink, and tobacco	£47 million	£430 million
Shannon share of manufactured exports other than food, drink, and tobacco	11%	11%

Note: *Calculations based on Shannon Free Airport Development Company Ltd (SFADCo) annual reports and Industrial Development Authority lists of principal new industries with foreign participation, 1971 and 1973.
Source: Denis O'Hearn, 'Estimates of New Foreign Manufacturing Employment in Ireland 1956–1972'; Frank Barry and Clare O'Mahony. 'Regime Change in 1950s Ireland'; SFADCo Annual Reports (various years).

Across much of the developing world, export-platform foreign investment of this type led to a large increase in the female share of employment. In Ireland, the female share of new grant-aided industry did not differ significantly from that of existing industry. The Irish authorities, with the support of the trade unions, focussed heavily on projects that would provide jobs for male workers.[81] The low status of factory work for women, furthermore, meant that it could be difficult to attract and retain female labour.[82] The Shannon Free Airport Development Company (SFADCo) announced in 1963 that:

> In order to maintain the balance in favour of male employment, and to ensure that the demand for women workers by firms already established and engaged in expanding their operations will be met, [...] the Company's current promotional campaign is being directed towards firms such as those in the light engineering industry who would require male employees predominantly.[83]

[81] Jean L. Pyle, 'Export-Led Development and the Underemployment of Women: The Impact of Discriminatory Development Policy in the Republic of Ireland", in *Women Workers and Global Restructuring*, ed. Kathryn Ward (New York: Cornell University Press, 1990).

[82] Damien Hannan, *Rural Exodus: A Study of the Forces Influencing Large-Scale Migration of Irish Rural Youth* (London: Geoffrey Chapman, 1970); Mary Muldowney, 'We were conscious of the sort of people we mixed with: the state, social attitudes and the family in mid twentieth century Ireland', *History of the Family*, 13, 4 (2008): 402–415; *Survey of Grant-Aided Industry: Survey Team's Report*, 97.

[83] SFADCo Report and Accounts for Year ended 31st March 1963 (Shannon: Shannon Free Area Development Company Ltd., 1963), 18.

The Industrial Development Authority noted in 1973 that the male-female employment ratio of roughly 3-to-1 associated with the projects it had approved for grant aid over the previous year was 'in line with our target'.[84]

The IDA had not been an integral part of the planning process initiated under the First Programme for Economic Expansion. This changed from 1966, when it was granted responsibility for evaluating and promoting new indigenous industrial projects as well as those from overseas sources.[85] Though the quantitative targets set out in the Second and Third Programmes were not achieved, the practice of quantitative targeting, paradoxically, would become part of the modus operandi of the 'new' restructured IDA.

Its rise within the policymaking hierarchy would also see it assume responsibility for regional industrial development. O'Farrell comments that 'no single development problem in Ireland has generated so much controversy and emotion as the concept of spatially polarised growth'.[86] The Committee on Industrial Organisation and the National Industrial Economic Council had both largely concurred with the Department of Finance that industry should be concentrated rather than dispersed, as did the most thorough regional policy document of the era, the Buchanan Report of 1969.[87] Neither of the major political parties could afford to adopt this position. The Industrial Development Authority Act of 1969 formally assigned the IDA a regional development mandate, imparting an added impetus, as one senior IDA manager put it, 'to an activity that had been underway for some time'.[88] Its Small Industries Programme was launched on a pilot basis in 1967 and extended across the country two years later. IDA offices were opened in eight of the country's nine planning regions in 1971. (Responsibility for the Mid-West region, which included Shannon, had been allocated to SFADCo.) The IDA's Regional Industrial Plans for 1973–1977 set out manufacturing job targets for large numbers of grouped towns and villages. Only 50 per cent of the new jobs envisaged were to be located in the nine growth centres recommended by Buchanan.[89]

[84] IDA Annual Report 1972/73 (Dublin: Industrial Development Authority, 1973), 12.

[85] FitzGerald, *Planning in Ireland*, 240; *Survey of Grant-Aided Industry: Survey Team's Report*, 98.

[86] Patrick N. O'Farrell, 'The Regional Problem in Ireland: Some Reflections upon Development Strategy'. *Economic and Social Review* 2, 4 (1971): 453.

[87] NESC (National Economic and Social Council), *Regional Policy in Ireland: A Review* (Dublin: National Economic and Social Council, 1975).

[88] *Irish Times*, 20 November 1973. Though grants had been available for industrial projects located in the 'undeveloped areas' since 1952, their relative efficacy had been eroded by the introduction in 1956 of grants for investments elsewhere in the country.

[89] NESC, *Regional Policy in Ireland: A Review*, 48; Industrial Development Authority, Regional Industrial Plans 1973–1977, (Dublin, Industrial Development Authority, 1972), 16.

The period since 1961, and particularly since 1966, had already witnessed substantial industrial dispersal.[90] The Census of Industrial Production data presented in Chapter 5 showed that 42–43 per cent of industrial employment had been located in Dublin in the 1930s and 1940s. The proportion remained around the same in 1961. It had fallen to 31 per cent by 1972. Redundancies were highest in the capital. New export-oriented industries were choosing or being induced to locate elsewhere.[91]

The developing pattern is presented to best effect in Table 7.2, which is based on data for 1974. It compares the regional distribution of 'new industry' employment and overall manufacturing employment.[92] As revealed in the final column, the Mid-West/SFADCo region performed best by this measure, followed by the group of least-developed planning regions. The relatively low share of new industry locating in the advanced Eastern region is immediately apparent.

The planning regions referred to in Table 7.2 had been established under the Local Government (Planning and Development) Act of 1963. There was not an exact overlap between the least developed of these regions (Donegal, Sligo–Leitrim, Mayo–Galway and the Midlands) and the 'designated areas' which were eligible for preferential grant treatment.[93] Westmeath,

Table 7.2 Regional distribution of manufacturing and 'new industry' employment, 1974

	Share of total manufacturing employment (I) (%)	Share of 'new industry' employment (II) (%)	Ratio (II/I)
Least-developed regions	13.1	19.1	1.5
Mid-West	7.7	12.9	1.7
East	46.4	23.6	0.5
Rest of the country	32.8	44.4	1.4
Total	100	100	1

Source: derived from Dermot McAleese. *A Profile of Grant-Aided Industry in Ireland*, (Dublin: Industrial Development Authority, 1977), Table 3.4, 23.

[90] See Table 1, 'Regional industrial development', *Irish Times*, 20 November 1973.
[91] As pointed out earlier, almost all of the manufacturing employment increase between 1966 and 1972 was in 'new' foreign industry.
[92] Dermot McAleese. *A Profile of Grant-Aided Industry in Ireland*, (Dublin: Industrial Development Authority, 1977), table 3.4, 9, 23. 'New industries' refer to projects supported by SFADCo and by 'new industry grants' (as opposed to 'small-industry' or 're-equipment grants') from the IDA.
[93] For a map of these regional groupings, see Patrick N. O'Farrell (1976) 'An Analysis of Industrial Closures: Irish Experience 1960–1973'. *Regional Studies* 10, 4 (1976): 433–448, Figure 1.

for example, was in one of the least developed regions—the Midlands—but was not a designated area, while Kerry, which was not in one of the least developed regions, *was* a designated area.

Among the largest of the new foreign industries to have established in the latter areas by 1972 were Snia in Sligo; Pretty Polly and Liebherr in Kerry; and Digital, Standard Pressed Steel, Potez, and Steinbock/Crown Controls in Galway. These firms were of diverse nationalities. Snia was Italian; Potez was French; Steinbock and Liebherr were German; Pretty Polly was British. Digital, Standard Pressed Steel, and Crown Controls, which took over Steinbock in 1968, were American.

7.4 Sectoral and Firm-Level Developments

The primary focus of both SFADCo and the IDA was on new 'greenfield' investment projects. 'Brownfield' FDI, entailing the acquisition and restructuring of existing businesses, is another common feature of the adjustment to freer trade.[94] It too would have been enhanced by the relaxation of foreign-ownership restrictions and the introduction of export profits tax relief. The acquisitions by Guinness and Halliday/Clarks have been discussed in earlier chapters. Other major brownfield investors included the US firms Grace Brothers and St Joe Paper, and British firms Courtaulds, Lyons, and Bond Worth. Unilever would expand further by acquisition. Each would be among the seventy or so largest manufacturing employers in the state in 1972.

Florida firm St Joe Paper had had a management agreement with National Board and Paper Mills in Waterford since 1958. National Board bought out Killeen Paper Mills in 1963 and both companies were acquired by St Joe Paper the following year.[95] Grace & Co. bought out the indigenous chocolate confectionery firm Urney in 1963, acquiring a number of other smaller confectionery producers in the process. Its acquisition of the large Dublin milk distribution company Hughes Brothers in 1964 triggered the formation of Premier Dairies, upon which Hughes Brothers' milk distribution business was swapped for Premier's ice cream interests. Anglo-Dutch Unilever had acquired the long-established fertilizer and animal feed producer Paul &

[94] As explained by the former owner of Killarney footwear manufacturer Hilliard, it was hoped that the sale of the company to the British group G. B. Britton would allow the Killarney operation to narrow its product range and gain export market sales (*Irish Times*, 25 February 1972).

[95] St Joe's expansion into Europe was a consequence of the restrictions on price competition imposed by the US export cartel of which it was a member. These restrictions did not apply to trade between associate companies. This also explains US firm Continental Can's acquisition of a 20 per cent share in Smurfit in 1972: Michael Smurfit, *A Life Worth Living* (Dublin: Oaktree Press, 2014), 93.

Vincent in 1966 and would acquire both H. B. Ice Cream and Urney (which had been renamed H. B. Chocolates) from Grace & Co. in 1973.

British industry was also restructuring over this period.[96] Man-made fibre producer Courtaulds, already a major employer in Northern Ireland, acquired several assets south of the border as part of its takeover of UK companies Symington & Co. and Ashton Brothers in the late 1960s. Dundalk Textiles had been part of Symington & Co. since 1941. Pre-independence linen and cotton producer Robert Usher, which had since diversified into rayon, had been acquired by Ashton Brothers in the mid-1960s, as had several of its suppliers and associated companies. The takeover of the British parent companies yielded Courtaulds an Irish workforce of over 1,000 by 1972.

Batchelors, the largest Irish vegetable processor after Erin Foods, was acquired by British Oxygen in 1969 and would be sold to Beechams in 1974. Gateaux, whose fruitcakes had established a foothold in the United Kingdom in the deprived conditions of the immediate post-war era, was acquired by tea-blender Lyons Irish Holdings in 1970. English carpet firm Bond Worth took over Kincora Carpets and O'Brien Brothers (Spinners) in 1967, Donegal Carpets and Dublin furniture and bedding manufacturer O'Dea in 1969, and Slumberland in 1972. It also held a large shareholding in G. T. Carpets of Donegal. Table 7.3 provides details of some of the major brownfield FDI acquisitions of the period.

There were numerous significant mergers and acquisitions within indigenous industry also.[97] Selected developments in sectors other than food and drink are outlined in Table 7.4. Cement Roadstone Holdings (CRH) was formed through the merger of Irish Cement and Roadstone in 1970. Cement Ltd's workforce had doubled over the course of the 1960s; Roadstone's had expanded by a factor of six. The latter was by far the larger of the two by the time of the merger. With a workforce in excess of 5,500, CRH was, along with the Guinness group, the largest manufacturing employer in the state at the time of EEC accession.[98]

---

[96] Alan Hughes, 'Mergers and Economic Performance in the UK: A Survey of the Empirical Evidence, 1950–1990', in *European Mergers and Merger Policy*, ed. Matthew Bishop and John Kay (Oxford: Oxford University Press, 1993), 9–95.

[97] Many of the mergers and acquisitions are documented in Restrictive Practices Commission, *Report of Studies into Industrial Concentration and Mergers in Ireland* (Dublin: Stationery Office, 1975); Louis P. F. Smith and Gerard Quinn, *A Study of the Evolution of Concentration in the Irish Food Industry 1968–1973* (Brussels: EU Commission, 1975).

[98] Technically, quarrying—in which Roadstone was primarily engaged—is not included within the definition of manufacturing.

Table 7.3 Selected Brownfield FDI acquisitions, 1960–1972

Acquiror	Workforce prior to acquisition	Acquired companies	Workforce at time of acquisition	Employment, c. 1972
Grace Brothers	–	HB Ice Cream, HB Confectionery (formerly Urney), Liam Devlin & Sons, Old Dutch Confections, and others	300 670 150	1,500 (1973)
St Joe Paper	–	National Board and Paper Mills, Killeen Paper Mills	450 670	c. 1,000 (1972)
Courtaulds	300 (sold to Sunbeam, 1965)	Robert Usher, Slane Manufacturing, Loughrea Cottons, Dundalk Textiles	400 450 100 160	950 (1972)
Unilever (Castleforbes Soap Factory and McDonnells Margarine)	640	Paul & Vincent	250	900 (1972)
Lyons Irish Holdings	150	Gateaux	660	538 (1972)
Bond Worth	–	Kincora Carpets, O'Brien Brothers (Spinners) Ltd, Donegal Carpets, O'Dea, and others	c. 500	c. 500 (1972)
British Oxygen	–	Batchelors	c. 500	c. 500 (1972)

Source: author.

Smurfit, too, had expanded hugely over the course of the decade, when it vied with Clondalkin Paper Mills for control of the print, paper, and packaging sector. Gibson, Guy & Smalldridge, formed from an earlier merger in 1964, employed around 1,000 when acquired by Clondalkin in 1969.

Table 7.4 Selected mergers and acquisitions (M/A) in indigenous industry, 1960–1972

Company	Workforce prior to major M/A	Merged or acquired companies	Workforce c. M/A	Employment, 1972
Irish Cement Group	900 (1962), 1,843 (1970)	Roadstone Holdings	3,491 (1970)	CRH: 5,578 (1972)
Smurfit post-acquisition of Browne & Nolan	300 (1964), 920 (1970)	Hely Group (1970)	2,300 (1970)	Smurfit Group: 3,884 (1972)
Clondalkin Paper Mills	620 (1969)	Swift Brook (1969), Gibson, Guy and Smalldridge (1969)	200 (1970), 1,000 (1964)	1,460 (1972)
Sunbeam–Wolsey	2,500 (1960)	Salts (1965), Mulcahy Bros (1970)	850 (1960), 610 (1970)	4,000 (1972)
Seafield Fabrics (including Blackwater Cottons, acquired in 1962)	800 (1962)	Castleguard Textiles (1965), General Textiles (1965)	400 (1965), 830 (1964)	Seafield–Gentex: 2,100 (1972)
Plunder & Pollock	330 (1960)	Gorey Leather (1967), Irish Tanners (1969), Dungarvan Leathers (1972–1973)	200 (1966), 400 (1966), 250 (1972)	Irish Leathers: 1,300 (1972)
G. A. Brittain	400 (1963)	Lincoln & Nolan, Philip Pierce, Booth Poole	500 (1960), 450 (1960), 140 (1971)	Brittain Group: 1,878 (1972)
P. J. Carroll (tobacco)	840 (1968)	Murray (pipe tobacco) (1960), Dakota (print and packaging) (1971), P. C. Cahill (wholesale chemist & distributor) (1972)	100 (1961), 170 (1971), 520 (1972)	1,540 (1973)
Glen Abbey	250 (1963)	Bradmola Mills (1964), Dublin Hosiery (1968)	150 (1964), c. 500 (1968)	919 (1972)
Doreen	200 (1965)	Jack Toohey (1972)	400 (1972)	650 (1973)

Continued

Table 7.4 *Continued*

Company	Workforce prior to major M/A	Merged or acquired companies	Workforce c. M/A	Employment, 1972
A. H. Masser, Dublin	170 (1960)	Allied Ironfounders (Ireland)/Waterford Ironfounders (1955)	110 (1954)	Masser-Waterford Ironfounders: 600 (1972)

Source: author.

Michael Smurfit ascribed his loss in the acquisition battle, despite apparently having made a higher offer, to a desire among the firms involved to maintain control in Protestant hands.[99] Smurfit's packaging materials business had benefited from the rapid growth in manufactured exports of the era. Its acquisition of both Browne & Nolan and the (Protestant) Hely Group in 1970 saw its workforce increase more than tenfold over the course of a decade.

There were major consolidations also in textiles, clothing, and leather. Seafield–Gentex was formed from the merger of Seafield Fabrics and General Textiles in 1965. It employed more than 2,000 across its eleven factories in 1966.[100] Major acquisitions by Sunbeam–Wolsey included the buy-out of UK company Salts in 1965 and indigenous producer Mulcahy Brothers in 1970. Its workforce increased from 2,500 in 1960 to almost 4,000 by 1972. Most of the leather tanneries also merged over this period. Carrick-on-Suir firm Plunder & Pollock acquired New Ross Tanning in 1955, Gorey Leather in 1966, and Irish Tanners of Portlaw in 1969. Known for a period as Industrial and Commercial Holdings, it was renamed Irish Leathers in 1972. Plunder & Pollock had employed a workforce of 300 in 1960; Irish Leathers had a workforce of 1,300 in 1972.[101] The acquisition of Dungarvan Leathers would be completed in 1973.

Consolidation in the vehicle assembly sector was associated with the formation of British Leyland in the United Kingdom. G. A. Brittain and Lincoln & Nolan, the main assemblers of Morris and Austin vehicles respectively,

[99] Smurfit, *A Life Worth Living*, 79.
[100] Youghal Carpets and Navan Carpets merged in 1972 but continued to be reported upon as separate companies until 1973.
[101] Irish Leathers also had other minor interests in Ireland and owned a small UK manufacturer of chemical finishes.

merged to form Brittain, Lincoln & Nolan in 1966. Wexford agricultural machinery manufacturer Philip Pierce & Co. was subsequently acquired, as was vehicle assembler Booth Poole, and the Brittain Group was awarded the contract to assemble Datsuns in 1972. Of the group's workforce of 1,878 at this time, around 1,000 were engaged in vehicle assembly, 300 were employed at the Pierce plant, and the remainder worked in sales and distribution. Ford's assembly operation remained larger.

Acquisitions by tobacco company P. J. Carroll of Dundalk doubled the size of its workforce over this period. Carrolls had taken over the leading pipe tobacco manufacturer Murray in 1960 and transferred production to Dundalk. Carrolls also integrated across the supply chain, acquiring a print and packaging company in 1971 and a distribution company in 1972. The formation of Masser-Waterford Ironfounders and acquisitions by clothing companies Glen Abbey and Doreen also saw the workforce at these firms expand to 500 or more by 1972.[102]

7.5 Erosion of the Sectarian Divide in Irish Business Life

Though sectarian divisions in the workplace had diminished over time, many firms continued into the 1960s to be known to the public as either Protestant or Catholic.[103] Paradoxically, while protectionism had led to a large increase in the number of Catholic firms, it facilitated the survival of older Protestant enterprises.[104] As Stephen Odlum recounts in his history of the Odlum flour milling family, the quota system introduced in the 1930s had effectively banished competition: 'With the market carved up between the participants, and penalties imposed on those who exceeded their production quota', the family was left 'with more time for pursuits such as hunting, fishing and yachting'.[105] Trade liberalization made such cartels unsustainable. Increased scale was necessary for survival in the new more competitive environment, and most Irish firms were tiny by international standards. Family firms were perceived

---

[102] Waterford Iron Founders had been established as Allied Iron Founders (Ireland), a subsidiary of a large UK company, in 1936.

[103] Tony Farmar, *Heitons—a Managed Transition: Heitons in the Irish Coal, Iron and Building Markets, 1818–1996* (Dublin: A. & A. Farmar, 1996), 34.

[104] Many of the most significant companies of the pre-independence era remained among the largest Irish industrial companies traded on the Dublin Stock Exchange in 1966: *Irish Times*, 8 November 1966.

[105] Stephen Odlum, *Flour Power, the Story of the Odlum Flour Milling Families* (Dublin: Zest Publications, 2015), 6.

as particularly problematic.[106] The determination among some Protestant businesses to keep control in the hands of a shrinking body of co-religionists had become a source of acute weakness.[107]

The mergers and acquisitions of the era paid no heed to the religious associations of earlier times. The earliest high-profile developments in this regard were in banking. To avoid the threat of foreign takeover, the Bank of Ireland merged with the Hibernian Bank in 1958, a development that 'would have astounded the Hibernian's founders'.[108] The National Bank, another of the traditionally Catholic banks, joined the group in 1966. A similar fusion of traditions occurred with the formation of Allied Irish Banks later that year.

In manufacturing, the entry of foreign firms frequently acted as a catalyst. Beamish & Crawford was sold to Canadian Breweries in 1962. By the middle of the decade, many of the other Irish breweries, including Catholic-owned Macardles and Smithwicks, had been acquired by Guinness. The milk distribution companies that merged in the wake of the entry of Grace & Co. included traditionally Protestant and Catholic firms. The year 1966 witnessed the formation of Irish Distillers and the merger of Jacobs and Bolands Biscuits. The Hely Group had been formed from the merger of the largest print, paper, and publishing firms of the 1920s. It was acquired by Smurfit in 1970. By 1972, Gouldings and Dockrells had been acquired by a consortium controlled by Catholic entrepreneur Tony O'Reilly.[109]

An anecdote recounted by Tony Farmar illustrates the broader changes taking place in Irish society. Asked in the 1960s to recommend a new company secretary for an old-style Protestant building firm, Craig Gardner felt obliged to point out that the candidate 'dug with the other foot'. They were informed that this was of no significance as long as the candidate was competent.[110] Stokes Brothers & Pim merged with the Catholic firm Kennedy Crowley in 1972. Craig Gardner became part of the worldwide network of UK firm Price Waterhouse later in the decade.

Not all of the imbalances in recruitment and management had been ascribable to sectarianism. As Cullen observes in his study of Easons:

---

[106] Garret FitzGerald, *Irish Times*, 3 July 1968; Committee on Industrial Progress, *General Report* (Dublin: Stationery Office, 1973), 37–38.

[107] James Quinn, 'Industry Evolution: A Comparative Study of Irish Wholesaling'. Ph.D. thesis, Dublin City University, 2002.

[108] F. S. L. Lyons, 'Reflections on a Bicentenary'. In *Bank of Ireland 1783–1983, Bicentenary Essays*, ed. F. S. L. Lyons (Dublin: Gill and Macmillan, 1983), 209.

[109] Frank Barry, 'The Life and Death of Protestant Businesses in Independent Ireland', in *Protestant and Irish: The Minority's Accommodation with Independent Ireland*, ed. Ian d'Alton and Ida Milne (Cork: Cork University Press, 2019), 155–70.

[110] Tony Farmar, *The Versatile Profession: A History of Accountancy in Ireland since 1850* (Dublin: Chartered Accountants Ireland, 2013), 119.

Staff were recruited from the immediate circle of the principal, and since many recruits were accepted on the recommendation of the senior people in the firm, continued recruitment tended to be slanted in that direction.[111]

By the time of EEC entry, the era of tightly controlled family businesses was coming to an end, many of the traditionally Protestant and Catholic firms had merged, denominationally distinct workplaces had all but disappeared, and educational credentials were eroding the significance of personal connections in recruitment and promotion.

[111] Louis M. Cullen, *Eason & Son: A History* (Dublin: Eason & Son, 1989), 111.

8

The Industrial Landscape of 1972 and Beyond

With the overwhelming endorsement of the electorate, as expressed in a constitutional referendum in May 1972, Ireland joined the European Economic Community along with the United Kingdom and Denmark on 1 January 1973. The most important issues pertaining to industry in the final stages of the accession negotiations had been the length of the transition period and the acceptability to the Community of Ireland's export profits tax incentives. The government had hoped for a significantly extended transition period. Motor vehicle assembly was accorded a special dispensation, with safeguard measures to remain in place until January 1985. For all other industrial goods, remaining restrictions on intra-Community trade would be eliminated by mid-1977.

Article 98 of the Treaty of Rome prohibited the use of export incentives such as Ireland's without the prior approval of EEC member-state governments. The country's economic underdevelopment had been taken into account in how the Organisation for European Economic Co-operation had responded to the introduction of the measure a decade and a half earlier. In a reprise of these earlier developments (and 'contrary to the Irish Government's fears', as the semi-official account of the negotiations informs us), 'the law relating to tax relief on export profits would be applied less rigorously than was suggested by the wording of Article 98'.[1] The country's entire industrial incentives package would be adjudicated upon by the Commission when a review of state aids had been completed. The export profits tax exemption would survive until 1980, when it was replaced by a new (low) 10 per cent rate of corporation tax on all manufacturing enterprises.

The government view, as accession approached, was that 'the main tasks which Irish industry has to tackle are essentially the same in kind, though not in degree, as those identified in the early 1960s'.[2] Ongoing developments in cost competitiveness were judged to remain inconsistent

[1] Denis J. Maher, *The Tortuous Path: The Course of Ireland's Entry into the EEC, 1948–73* (Dublin: Institute of Public Administration, 1986), 314.
[2] *Accession of Ireland to the European Communities* (Dublin: Stationery Office, 1972), 33–34.

Industry and Policy in Independent Ireland, 1922–1972. Frank Barry, Oxford University Press.
© Frank Barry (2023). DOI: 10.1093/oso/9780198878230.003.0008

with the requirements of freer trade.[3] In a best possible scenario (i.e. 'if full advantage is taken by all those engaged in industry of the period of transition'), 'there should be no net redundancy in existing industry'.[4] As discussed below, the scenario that emerged was far from the best that might have been hoped for.

8.1 The Largest Manufacturing Employers of 1972

Food

Bacon curing had been the only large-scale meat-processing sector at the foundation of the state. By 1972, the traditional bacon curers had been displaced by larger, more diversified food producers such as Mitchelstown Co-operative and Clover Meats. Denny had moved much of its production to Northern Ireland and employment at the Bacon Company of Ireland (formerly O'Maras) had fallen below 300. The beef processors that had emerged over recent decades were by now by far the largest employers in the industry.

The amalgamation of dairy cooperatives was already well under way. Mitchelstown was the only cooperative with a workforce of 500 or more in 1960. By 1972 it had been joined by Ballyclough, Waterford, and Golden Vale. These had been the earliest to diversify out of butter, and each had benefited from the marketing relationships established with UK partners such as Unigate and Express Dairies. The state-owned Dairy Disposal Company, which had been formed from the remains of the massive Condensed Milk Company of Ireland in the 1920s, has been credited with having integrated West Kerry and County Clare into the province's dairying heartlands. It was the main early-stage supplier of butter to Bord Bainne to be marketed under the Kerrygold brand.[5] The major manufacturing firms in the meat and dairy sectors in 1972 are listed in Table 8.1. In the cognate milk distribution sector, Premier Dairies employed a workforce of some 1,500.

The bread and grain milling sectors had integrated over time, as was also the case in the United Kingdom. UK company Ranks–Hovis was the largest integrated employer in Ireland, though the Odlums Group—which included

---

[3] *Membership of the European Communities: Implications for Ireland* (Dublin: Stationery Office, 1970), 25.
[4] 1972 Government of Ireland White Paper, as cited in NESC (National Economic and Social Council), *Ireland in the European Community* (Dublin: National Economic and Social Council, 1989), 99.
[5] Mícheál Ó Fathartaigh, *Irish Agriculture Nationalised: The Dairy Disposal Company and the Making of the Modern Irish Dairy Industry* (Dublin: Institute of Public Administrations, 2014).

Table 8.1 Major employers, meat and dairy, 1972

Company	Main activities	Key dates	Ownership	Employment, c. 1972
Cork Marts–International Meat Packers	Meat	1967 amalgamation	Domestic	2,000 (1973)
Clover Meats Group	Meat	Established 1936	Domestic	1,600 (1973)
Mitchelstown Creameries	Dairy	Established 1919	Domestic	1,600 (1973)
Dairy Disposal Company	Dairy	Established 1927	State	1,192 (1972)
Waterford Co-op	Dairy	1964 amalgamation	Domestic	1,000 (1973)
Ballyclough Co-operative	Dairy	Established 1908	Domestic	700 (1973)
Golden Vale Food Products	Dairy	Established 1948	Domestic	600 (1971)

Source: author.

W. & G. T. Pollexfen, Waterford Flour Mills, National Flour Mills, and Dublin Port Milling among others—exceeded it in milling capacity.

Bread consumption had declined sharply since the 1950s, and the rise of supermarkets—many of which produced their own bread brands—put further pressure on the long-established bakers. Dublin bakery chain Peter Kennedy Ltd closed in 1971 with a loss of 300–400 jobs. Johnston, Mooney & O'Brien had been acquired by Odlums in 1956. It continued to employ around 500. Other Dublin bakers of significance included Rourkes, which was part of the Ranks group, and Joseph Downes, originator of the Butter-crust brand, which was part-owned by the Dock Milling Company. Bolands, Downes, Cork firm F. H. Thompson, and Johnston, Mooney & O'Brien would all cease production in the 1980s.

Bolands had responded to the decline in bread consumption by diversify-ing into biscuits. Its biscuit division was bought out by Jacobs in 1970. The integrated firm, Irish Biscuits, employed over 2,000 in 1972 across its three plants: the Bolands factory in Deansgrange, the long-established Jacobs fac-tory in inner-city Dublin, and a new factory in Tallaght at which production would be centralized over the coming years. Many other industries were also in the process of moving to the suburbs.

The acquisition of cake maker Gateaux by UK tea blender Lyons in 1970 brought the Lyons Irish Holdings' workforce to more than 500.

Vegetable processor Batchelors, which had been acquired by British Oxygen in 1966, also employed around 500. Its use of a British brand name required that it export under a different label. (Other Irish companies, including W. & R. Jacob, which was part-owned by its former British branch plant, were similarly constrained: the Dublin firm sold in Britain under the Irish Biscuits or Bolands labels.)

Erin Foods, the other main fruit and vegetable processor, had been established as an export marketing subsidiary of the state-owned Irish Sugar in 1958. It initiated processing operations in the 1960s and formed a joint UK marketing venture with US firm Heinz in 1965. Though Erin was a substantial employer, it remained loss-making throughout the period. Irish Sugar's plants were in Mallow, Carlow, Tuam, and Thurles; Erin also had plants in Middleton, Skibbereen, Limerick, and Glencolumbcille. The three main jam producers were the former Northern Ireland company Lamb Brothers and British firms Chivers and R. & W. Scott. Each had a year-round workforce of 200–300, with substantially higher employment in the high season, as was the case also with Erin Foods and Irish Sugar. Lambs predated the establishment of the state. Scott had initiated production in Dublin in 1927, Chivers in 1932.

There were several major employers in chocolate and sugar confectionery. Crosse & Blackwell had acquired the leading Dublin company Williams & Woods in 1928. Its UK parent was taken over by Swiss firm Nestlé in 1960. Williams & Woods had since been overtaken by both Cadbury Ireland (formerly Fry–Cadbury) and Rowntree–Mackintosh. Cadbury, Rowntree, and a number of other British firms had begun to produce chocolate crumb for export in the late 1940s. Cadbury had begun to export confectionery from Ireland around a decade later. Rowntree–Mackintosh's confectionery production remained focused on the domestic market. Urney, the sole large indigenous confectionery producer, had been acquired by US firm Grace & Co. in 1963 and rebranded as H. B. Chocolates. It would be sold, along with Grace's ice cream interests, to Unilever in 1973.[6] The major employers in food sectors other than meat and dairy in 1972 are listed in Table 8.2.

Drink and Tobacco

Guinness had begun to buy up much of the Irish drinks sector from the late 1950s. New foreign entrants included Canadian Breweries, which acquired

---

[6] Unilever was already a substantial employer by this time, with 400 employed at its Castleforbes soap factory, 240 in McDonnell's margarine, and 250 in fertilizer company Paul and Vincent.

Table 8.2 Major employers, other foods, 1972

Company	Main activities	Key dates	Ownership	Employment, c. 1972
Irish Sugar Company (including Erin Foods)	Sugar; fruit and vegetable processing	Established 1933	State	4,464 (1973), of which: Erin Foods: 1,300
Irish Biscuits (W. & R. Jacob)	Biscuits	Established 1851	Domestic	2,500 (1972)
Cadbury (Ireland)	Confectionery and chocolate crumb	Established 1932	UK	2,000 (1972)
Nestlé	Confectionery and jams	Crosse & Blackwell (1928); acquired by Nestlé (1960)	Switzerland	526 (1971)
Ranks–Hovis	Bread and flour	Bannatyne; acquired by Ranks (1930); becomes Ranks–Hovis (1962)	UK	1,500 (1972)
Rowntree-Mackintosh	Confectionery and chocolate crumb	1926, 1925; merged 1960	UK	1,210 (1973)
Odlum Group	Bread and flour	Established 1845	Domestic	1,200 (1973)
H. B. (Grace & Co.)	Chocolate confectionery and ice cream	H. B. acquired by Grace (1963)	US	1,500 (1973)
Lyons Irish Holdings	Diversified, including flour confectionery from 1970	Established 1962, >500 (from 1970)	UK	810 (1971)
Bolands	Bread and flour	Established 1823	Domestic	750 (1972)
Batchelors	Vegetable processing and canning	Established 1935	UK	550 (1973)

Source: author.

Beamish & Crawford in 1962, and UK company Watney Mann, which acquired Murphys in 1967. Guinness acquired and closed a number of smaller breweries and converted the Great Northern Brewery in Dundalk, which it had purchased from Smithwicks, to the production of Harp Lager.

Other Guinness acquisitions were in conjunction with UK industry partners. One of the brands produced by Cherry Bros, which Guinness had acquired, was in competition with a British brand produced by Macardle Moore by arrangement with the UK company Ind Coope. As the managing director of Cherrys explained, the formation by Guinness and Ind Coope of the holding company Irish Ale Breweries in 1961 would 'wipe out the intensive competition of the past'.[7] The Smithwicks brewery in Kilkenny came under the Irish Ale Breweries umbrella in 1964.

After a complex series of transactions, Guinness acquired just under a half share of Cantrell & Cochrane (C&C), the largest soft drinks producer in the country. Popular brands under its control included Club Orange and Club Lemon, MiWadi, Sláinte, and Taylor-Keith. Around half of C&C's workforce of some 1,200 was located south of the border. Together with Irish Ale Breweries, C&C acquired the former Magners/Bulmers cider operation in Clonmel. Cantrell & Cochrane, Irish Ale Breweries, and a number of other smaller enterprises are included as part of the Guinness Group in Table 8.3.

Irish Distillers was the other major enterprise in the drinks sector. Over the six years since its formation in 1966, its workforce had trebled to 900 and its export share of output had doubled to 25 per cent. It acquired a quarter-share in the 'Old Bushmills' distillery in Antrim in 1972 and would complete

Table 8.3 Major employers, drink and tobacco, 1972

Company	Main activities	Key dates	Ownership	Employment, *c.* 1972
Guinness Group, Irish operations	Brewing, soft drinks	1759	UK	*c.* 5,000 (1972), of which:
	Stout			St James's Gate Brewery: 3,500 (1971)
Irish Distillers	Distilling	Amalgamation (1966)	Domestic	900 (1972)
P. J. Carroll	Tobacco and miscellaneous	Established 1824	Domestic	1,360 (1972) >500 (since 1950s)
Imperial Tobacco/ Players–Wills	Tobacco	Established 1924	UK	800 (1972) >500 (since 1920s)

Source: author.

[7] *Cork Examiner*, 9 January 1961.

the acquisition by the end of the decade. Northern Ireland had been the predominant export destination for southern Irish distilleries in 1960. By the early 1970s, its share of export sales had declined from a quarter to less than one-tenth, and it had been overtaken in importance as an export destination by the United States, Britain, and Germany.

The major tobacco manufacturers in 1972 remained Carrolls of Dundalk and UK company Players–Wills, which had been the first major foreign direct investor in the newly established Irish Free State. Their tobacco operations were of a broadly similar size, but recent diversification by Carrolls left it with a substantially larger workforce.

Textiles and Clothing

The industries in the textiles and clothing sector in 1972 included significant employers from every era of Ireland's industrial history (Table 8.4). Blarney Woollen Mills predated the establishment of the state, as did J. & L. F. Goodbody, whose operations by the early 1970s had transitioned from jute to polypropylene sacking. Sunbeam, Seafield, and Glen Abbey

Table 8.4 Major employers, textiles and clothing, 1972

Company	Main activities	Key dates	Ownership	Employment, c. 1972
Sunbeam	Textiles	Established 1928	Domestic	4,000 (1972), c. 3,900 in Ireland
Youghal Carpets Group	Carpets	Established 1954	Domestic	2,656 (1972), c. 1,500 in Ireland
Seafield–Gentex	Textiles	1965 merger of firms dating from 1936 and 1946	Domestic	2,100 (1972)
J. & L. F. Goodbody	Jute and polypropylene sacking	Established 1865	Domestic	975 (1972)
Glen Abbey	Textiles and clothing	Established 1939	Domestic	919 (1972)
Courtaulds	Towels and related products	Established 1954, >500 (from 1968)	UK	950 (1972)
Jonathan Logan Ltd	Fashion garments	Lana Knit, Shannon, established 1960	US	600 (1972)

		Butte-Knit, Shannon, established 1968		250 (1972)
Irish Ropes	Carpets	Established 1933	Domestic	812 (1972)
Navan Carpets	Carpets	Established 1937	Domestic	810 (1972), *c.* 800 in Ireland
Thomas Tilling Company/ Killarney Hosiery	'Pretty Polly' stockings	Established 1967	UK	750 (1972)
Doreen	Clothing	Established 1946, major acquisition 1972	Domestic	650 (1973)
Janelle	Clothing	Established 1952	Domestic	622 (1972)
Blarney Woollen Mills	Woollen and worsteds	Established 1820s	Domestic	510 (1972)
Bond Worth	Carpets	Acquisitions from 1967	UK	*c.* 500 (1972)

Source: author.

were protectionist-era indigenous companies, the first two of which had been established by members of the extended Dwyer family. Major carpet producers included Youghal, Navan, and Irish Ropes. UK firms Bond Worth and Courtaulds had entered as part of the wave of mergers and acquisitions of recent decades. Post-1955 export-oriented foreign firms included Killarney Hosiery and US firm Jonathan Logan, owner or part-owner of two significant Shannon enterprises. Indigenous companies Doreen and Janelle had emerged or expanded through their export success in the UK market over recent decades.

Footwear and Leather

The expansion of the Halliday Group and its acquisition by Clarks Shoes in 1971 have been discussed in previous chapters. Halliday had developed a significant export trade as a consequence of the Anglo-Irish Trade Agreement of 1948. Its main competitors in Ireland over the decades had been other tariff-jumping operations Woodingtons and Rawsons and the Dwyer family firms Lee Boot and Hanover Shoes.

Woodingtons, too, had shifted into women's footwear in the 1940s when its market for workmen's boots was eroded by the growing popularity of

Table 8.5 Major employers, footwear and leather, 1972

Company	Main activities	Key dates	Ownership	Employment, *c.* 1972
Halliday/Clarks (Ireland) Group	Footwear	Established 1928, 1938	UK	1,700 (1971)
Irish Leathers	Leather	Established 1938; becomes Irish Leathers in 1972	Domestic	1,300 (1972)

Source: author.

rubber wellingtons (made by Irish Dunlop in Cork). It had disposed of its interest in Gorey Leather in 1949. Its acquisition of Munster Shoes and the Birr Shoe factory in the late 1960s proved unsuccessful and employment had declined to around 100 by 1972. Rawsons, for many decades the largest footwear operation in the state, was already in decline when its main factory was destroyed by fire in 1967. The company was liquidated shortly afterwards. Lee Footwear, into which the two Dwyer family footwear firms had merged in 1965, retained a workforce of 370 at European Economic Community (EEC) accession.

Most of the leather tanneries had merged under the umbrella of Plunder & Pollock of Carrick-on-Suir by the end of the 1960s. Known for a period as Industrial and Commercial Holdings, the name Irish Leathers was adopted in 1972. Most of its output was exported to the United Kingdom. Details of the largest employers in footwear and leather are provided in Table 8.5.

Clay, Glass, and Cement

The largest merger of the era had resulted in the formation of Cement Roadstone Holdings (CRH) in 1970. Irish Cement had been formed in 1936 with the backing of the recently established Industrial Credit Company (ICC) and the participation of British and Danish interests attracted by the monopoly of the cement market that the firm had been granted. Roadstone was a sand and gravel haulage company in which the ICC had also taken a large share in 1950. CRH would expand over the following decades to become one of Ireland's leading indigenous multinationals.

Table 8.6 Major employers, clay, glass, cement, and other building materials, 1972

Company	Main activities	Key dates	Ownership	Employment, *c.* 1972
Cement Roadstone Holdings	Cement and related products	1970 merger of firms established 1936 and 1949	Domestic	5,578 (1972), *c.* 4,850 in Ireland
Waterford Glass	Fine cut glass	Established 1947	Domestic	4,000 (1972), *c.* 2,000 in manufacturing in Ireland
Irish Glass Bottle Company	Glass bottles	Re-established 1932	Domestic	823 (1972)
Arklow Pottery	Pottery, giftware, and ceramic products	Established 1935	Domestic	500 (1972)

Source: author.

More than 90 per cent of CRH's sales were on the home market. The Irish Glass Bottle Company was also largely home market-oriented, with an export-output ratio of less than 20 per cent. Waterford Glass, by contrast, was strongly export-oriented. Its workforce expanded from 500 in 1960 to 4,000 in 1972, around 2,000 of whom were employed in the firm's Irish manufacturing operations and a further 1,000 in the Dublin department store, Switzers, that had been acquired to facilitate the company's retail sales. The firm also had subsidiary companies in the United States and the United Kingdom.

Arklow Pottery remained almost exclusively home market oriented at this time. The other pottery firms, Carrigaline Pottery in Cork and Royal Tara China Ltd in Galway, were very much smaller. There were a number of significant employers in the cognate builders' providers sector, which is not included in Table 8.6. Heitons, Dockrells, and Concrete Products of Ireland (Chadwicks) each employed around 700 at EEC accession. Brooks Thomas employed over 1,000.

Metals and Engineering

Ford remained by far the most significant vehicle assembler in 1972. The remainder of the Irish market had been serviced by a large number of much smaller assemblers, many of which had merged into the Brittain Group following the formation of British Leyland in the 1960s. The Brittain Group had substantial engineering, sales, and service divisions and a somewhat larger overall workforce than Ford (Table 8.7). About 300 of Brittain's total workforce were employed at the Philip Pierce plant in Wexford.[8]

Most of the firms in the other traditional (and largely non-exporting) segments have been discussed already. Railway engineering was included under Other Metals, Engineering and Implements in the Census of Industrial Production (CIP) for 1972, so the large workforce at the CIÉ engineering works at Inchicore would form part of the total in the CIP for that year.

Metals and engineering attracted a particularly large share of new export-oriented foreign-owned projects.[9] Tables 8.8 and 8.9 provide details of the largest employers in these two segments. German crane manufacturer Liebherr, Shannon-based US firms General Electric and Standard Pressed Steel (SPS), and Dutch firm Philips had been the earliest substantial employers among the latter group. By 1972, General Electric and SPS had established further operations beyond Shannon—General Electric in Dundalk, SPS in Galway—and had been joined by other substantial employers from Germany, the United States, and the Netherlands.

Table 8.7 Major employers, vehicle assembly, 1972

Company	Main activities	Key dates	Ownership	Employment, c. 1972
Brittain Group	Vehicle assembly, engineering, sales and service	Established 1913, >500 (continuously from 1960s)	Domestic	1,878 (1972)
Ford Motor Company	Vehicle assembly	Established 1919; vehicle assembly from 1932	US	1,500 (1973)

Source: author.

[8] The Pierce plant had been retained by Brittain when the latter's 1968 merger with the Smith Group was unwound in 1970. Only a small minority of the Cavan-based Smith Group's post-demerger workforce of 1,200 was engaged in production. McCairns Motors, which mainly assembled Vauxhall cars and Bedford trucks for General Motors, also had a workforce in excess of 500 from the mid-1960s, only around half of whom were engaged in production. Neither of these firms, for these reasons, are included among the largest manufacturing employers.
[9] Denis O'Hearn, 'Estimates of New Foreign Manufacturing Employment in Ireland 1956–1972'. *Economic and Social Review* 18, 3 (1987): 173–88.

Table 8.8 Major employers, other metals and engineering ('traditional'), 1972

Company	Main activities	Key dates	Ownership	Employment, c. 1972
Unidare	Electrical equipment	Established 1949; name changed to Unidare in 1957	Dutch/Irish; acquired by Philips (Ireland) in 1966	1,640 (1972), c. 1,300 in Ireland
Hammond Holdings	Metal products	Established as Hammond Lane Foundry (1902)	Domestic	1,359 (1972)
Verolme, Cork Dockyard	Shipbuilding and general engineering	Established 1959	Originally Dutch; latterly semi-state	1,100 (1972)
Electrical Industries of Ireland	Domestic electrical appliances	Established 1938; new name adopted 1966	Originally domestic; British from 1959	850 (1972)
Irish Steel	Steel	Established 1938; semi-state from 1947	State	847 (1972)
Solus Teoranta	Electrical appliances	Established 1935	Domestic, with substantial British participation from 1957	650 (1972)
Masser–Waterford	Domestic appliances and hardware	Established as Allied Iron Founders (Ireland) 1936; becomes Masser–Waterford 1955	Initially UK; later, domestic	600 (1972)

Source: author.

Paper, Printing, and Packaging

The three major newspaper groups—the *Independent*, the *Press*, and the *Irish Times*—were among the significant employers in the paper and printing sector in 1972 (Table 8.10). Florida firm St Joe Paper has been discussed in previous chapters. The largest firms in the sector were the Smurfit and Clondalkin Groups.

Clondalkin was the largest of the paper mills to have reopened as a consequence of the tariffs of the 1930s. It diversified by acquisition in the 1960s

Table 8.9 Major employers, 'new' export-oriented metals and engineering, 1972

Company	Main activities	Key dates	Ownership	Employment, c. 1972
General Electric Company of America	Electronic components	E.I. established at Shannon 1960 Ecco established at Dundalk 1966	US	c. 2,000 (1972), of which: E.I. 900 (1972), Ecco, 900 (1970)
Ferenka	Steel cord for automotive industry	Established 1972	Dutch	1,000 (1972)
Becton Dickinson	Medical equipment	Established at Drogheda 1963, Dun Laoghaire, 1970	US	900 (1972–1973), of which: Drogheda, 500 (1973)
Philips	Consumer electronics and components	Established 1957, 1962; consolidated 1967	Dutch	820 (1970)
Krups Engineering	Domestic electrical appliances	Established 1964	German	700 (1973)
Standard Pressed Steel (SPS)	Metal components and precision tools	Shannon 1960, Galway 1967	US	600 (1972)
Technicon	Medical equipment	Established 1966	US	500 (1972)
Liebherr	Cranes	Established 1959	German	500 (1972)

Source: author.

when it vied with Smurfit for control of the domestic industry. Employment at the Clondalkin Group grew from 500 in 1960 to almost 1,500 by 1972. Its acquisition of the printing firm Gibson, Guy and Smalldridge in 1969 had increased its workforce by almost 1,000.

Smurfit had originated in the largely non-traded (packaging) segment of the industry.[10] Though the potential for import competition had grown, the company benefited from the packaging demands of the expanding manufacturing sector of the 1960s and the partnerships it established, particularly with its US raw materials supplier, which gave it access to the

[10] Committee on Industrial Organisation, *Survey Report on the Paper Products Industry* (Dublin: Stationery Office, 1964), 12.

Table 8.10 Major employers, paper and printing, 1972

Company	Main activities	Key dates	Ownership	Employment, c. 1972
Smurfit Group	Packaging and printing	Established 1934	Domestic	3,884 (1972), of which: c. 3,400 in Ireland
Clondalkin Paper Group	Paper, packaging, and printing	Established 1936	Domestic	1,460 (1972)
Independent Newspapers	Newspaper publishing	Established 1905	Domestic	1,408 (1972)
Irish Press Ltd	Newspaper publishing	Established 1931	Domestic	c. 1,000
St Joe Paper	Paper	Acquisitions, mid-1960s	US	c. 1,000
Irish Times	Newspaper publishing	Established 1859	Domestic	c. 500

Source: author.

most up-to-date processes and equipment. Understanding that trade liberalization would result in the rationalization of the industry, Michael Smurfit had determined at an early stage to try to ensure that his company emerged in a dominant position.[11] Smurfit's workforce expanded from 250 in 1962 to almost 4,000 ten years later. From 1973, it would begin to make substantial overseas acquisitions.

Chemicals and Miscellaneous

The chemicals and miscellaneous sector is also best considered in terms of traditional and modern segments. Details of the largest firms in these two groups are provided in Tables 8.11 and 8.12. Firms of significance in the traditional segment included the long-established fertilizer company Gouldings, protectionist-era tariff jumper Irish Dunlop, and the state nitrogenous fertilizer company Nítrigin Éireann. Unilever, whose workforce would double with the acquisition of the chocolate and ice-cream manufacturer H. B. in

---

[11] Michael Smurfit, *A Life Worth Living* (Dublin: Oaktree Press, 2014), 47.

Table 8.11 Major employers, chemicals and miscellaneous ('traditional'), 1972

Company	Main activities	Key dates	Ownership	Employment, c. 1972
W. & H. M. Goulding (Group)	Fertilizer	Established 1856	Domestic	1,400 (1972)
Irish Dunlop	Tyres and rubber products	Established 1934	UK	2,000 (1971)
Nítrigin Éireann Teo. (1961)	Fertilizer	Established 1961	State	c. 800 (1972)
Unilever	Diversified (margarine, soap, and fertilizer)	In operation in Free State area since 1910	Anglo-Dutch	900 (1972)

Source: author.

Table 8.12 Major employers, 'new' export-oriented chemicals and miscellaneous, 1972

Company	Main activities	Key dates	Ownership	Employment, c. 1972
Pfizer Group (including Howmedica and Quigley), chemicals and pharma	Pharma	Pfizer (1972) Howmedica (1972), Quigley (1971 and 1972)	US	c. 900 (1972), of which: Pfizer, 550 (1972); Howmedica, 200 (1972); Quigley, c. 140 (1972)
Semperit	Tyre manufacturing	Established 1969	Austrian	700 (1972)
Snia	Man-made fibres	Established 1972	Italian	550 (1973)
De Beers Industrial Diamonds/Shannon Diamond and Carbide	Industrial diamonds	Shannon Diamond established 1961; other group companies over the next few years	South African, with Anglo-American participation	550 (1972)

Source: author.

1973, contained divisions that dated from diverse earlier eras. Around half of its 1972 workforce was employed in the soap factory it had established in the 1920s, with the other half divided between its margarine, animal feed, and fertilizer interests.

The firms in the modern segment were recently established foreign subsidiaries. De Beers Industrial Diamonds was one of the first companies to commence operations at Shannon in the early 1960s. The opening of the Pfizer plant at Ringaskiddy some ten years later was described by the long-term managing director of the Industrial Development Authority, Padraic White, as a 'major coup'.[12] Pfizer's Ringaskiddy operations employed 550 in 1972.[13] Two other US companies—Quigley in Dungarvan and medical devices company Howmedica in Limerick—were also part of the Pfizer group at this time.

8.2 Firm-Level Developments in the Wake of EEC Accession

The 1972 government White Paper on EEC accession had envisaged a net increase of 50,000 manufacturing jobs between 1970 and 1978, practically all of which were anticipated to come from new foreign industry. The eventual outcome fell far short of this. New foreign industry added only half the number of jobs than had been hoped for, and existing industry contracted significantly.[14]

The world economy had been severely affected by the dramatic oil price increases of the 1970s, and Ireland would perform particularly poorly over the following decade as a consequence of the inappropriate fiscal policies that had been pursued at the time.[15] By 1987, the country was in severe economic crisis. When account is taken of the change in coverage in the CIP (which added an extra 10,000 manufacturing jobs to the number included in 1979),

[12] Ray MacSharry and Padraic A. White, *The Making of the Celtic Tiger: The Inside Story of Ireland's Booming Economy* (Cork: Mercier Press, 2000), 189.

[13] Among the earliest export-oriented pharmaceutical companies to establish operations in Ireland in the early-to-mid 1960s were the Danish company Leo Laboratories and US company Squibb Linson. Both of these operations were much smaller than Pfizer's.

[14] On the number of jobs in new foreign industry over the period, see O'Hearn, 'Estimates of New Foreign Manufacturing Employment in Ireland 1956–1972'.

[15] Reprising his arguments of the 1950s, Whitaker—by now a Senator—complained in the early 1980s of how 'expansionary budgetary policies [had lost] much of their impact by spilling over into imports, creating huge deficits in the balance of payments and destabilising our public finances rather than raising productive activity at home': cited in Cormac Ó Gráda, 'Five Crises'. Annual T. K. Whitaker lecture, Central Bank of Ireland, 2011.

there was a net decline of more than 30,000—some 15 per cent of the total—between EEC entry and 1987.[16]

Though the economic crisis was severe, it was no deeper than others that had been experienced since independence.[17] The contrast in terms of the attrition of leading businesses, however, was stark. By the mid-1970s, almost a dozen were in receipt of support from the state rescue agency Fóir Teoranta. These included Electrical Industries of Ireland, Arklow Pottery, Clover Meats, Irish Biscuits, Irish Dunlop, Martin Mahony, Masser-Waterford, Seafield, Semperit, and Verolme.[18] Other than Irish Biscuits and Semperit, all had closed or downsized dramatically by 1987.

A 1989 report by the National Economic and Social Council categorized industries into three groups in terms of how they had been affected by trade liberalization.[19] Though the analysis paid relatively little attention to the cost competitiveness issues discussed in previous chapters, the classification serves as a useful organizing framework. The first group consisted of the sectors into which Ireland specialized as a consequence of new export-oriented foreign direct investment (FDI) inflows. These included office and data-processing machinery, pharmaceuticals, and medical and optical devices. Some of these sectors were already populated by pre-1972 foreign firms, though the new sectoral classifications only came into use in 1973.

The second group consisted of industries which benefited from some form of natural protection. Transportation costs or customized service requirements served to protect small-scale manufacturing and segments of paper, print, and packaging and clay, glass, and cement. Proximity to raw material inputs yielded Ireland a comparative advantage in meat and dairy products. Long-established brand loyalty insulated the drink and tobacco sectors.

Industries other than in these two groups fared particularly poorly. The discussion that follows tracks what became of the leading firms identified above over the first decade or two of European Community membership. Discussion of the 'new' FDI-dominated sectors is left to the end.

[16] Though manufacturing was declining as a share of employment across the developed world, Ireland was experiencing particularly high unemployment at this time. Fears of 'jobless growth' would persist into the 1990s: NESC, *The Association between Economic Growth and Employment Growth in Ireland* (Dublin: National Economic and Social Council, 1993).
[17] Ó Gráda, 'Five Crises'.
[18] *Irish Times*, 12 May 1977.
[19] NESC, *Ireland in the European Community*, 76–89, 134–35.

Food, Drink, and Tobacco

O'Malley characterizes much of the Irish food industry of the 1980s as 'low value-added basic processing of local primary products'.[20] This provides a reasonably accurate description of the meat-processing segment. Cork Marts–IMP would exit the industry in the 1980s and Clover Meats would go into receivership in 1984. The vacuum created would eventually be filled by the Goodman Group, which was still in its infancy in the early 1970s.

The major creameries of the time, by contrast, would survive and thrive, and a number would evolve into highly sophisticated multinational producers. Mitchelstown and Ballyclough would merge to form Dairygold in 1990; Waterford Co-op and Avonmore would merge to form Glanbia in 1997.[21] The disposal of the assets of the state-owned Dairy Disposal Company in the 1970s would contribute to the emergence of the Kerry Group, into which Golden Vale Foods would ultimately be subsumed.

There was a diversity of experiences among the 'other foods' categories. Ice cream and chocolate confectionery producer H. B. was sold to Unilever in 1973. The confectionery factory (the former Urneys) would close a decade later. Rowntree–Mackintosh's Dublin factory closed in 1986. Two of the four sugar factories also closed in the 1980s, and Erin Foods was wound up over the course of the decade. Irish Sugar would be privatized and renamed Greencore in 1991. Ranks (Ireland) would be liquidated in 1983. The Odlum Group would be partly acquired by Irish Sugar and later fully acquired by Greencore: its workforce had declined to 280 by 1992. The major bakery chains that had survived into the 1960s had all long since closed.

Cadbury (Ireland) stands out as the only significant 'tariff jumper' to remain in operation to the present day. Its chocolate crumb factory in Kerry had been export-oriented from the start. Confectionery had initially been produced only for the local market but, with the opening of a major new plant in Dublin in the late 1950s, it also began to be produced for export. Both plants remain in operation in 2022. The major drink and tobacco companies of 1972 emerged unscathed into the 1990s.

Textiles, Clothing, Footwear, and Leather

Textiles, clothing, footwear, and leather were among the sectors to experience the most dramatic job losses and company closures. Blarney Woollen

---

[20] Eoin O'Malley, *Industry and Economic Development: The Challenge for the Latecomer* (Dublin: Gill and Macmillan, 1989), 115.
[21] Established in the 1960s, Avonmore employed a workforce of 300 in 1972.

Mills ceased production in 1974. The Goodbody jute factories in Clara and Waterford both ceased production around this time, and the firm went out of business in 1984. Doreen and Janelle both closed in the early 1980s. Seafield–Gentex ceased manufacturing later that decade. Sunbeam closed in 1990.

Irish Leathers went into receivership in 1985. The Halliday/Clarks factory in Dundalk also closed in 1985, and the last remaining Clarks (Ireland) footwear operation shut down two years later. Glen Abbey was broken up and sold off. Irish Ropes exited the carpet industry. Youghal Carpets, having been acquired by the state rescue agency, was sold to a British company in 1987. Both Youghal and Navan had already shed substantial numbers of jobs by then. The foreign-owned companies in the sector fared no better. Bond Worth was liquidated in 1977. Courtauld's Irish operations downsized substantially before closing in 1993. The US fashion garments operations at Shannon—Lana Kit and Butte Knit—closed in the early 1980s. 'Pretty Polly' closed in 1995. None of the large employers of 1972 survived in anything close to their original form.

Clay, Glass, and Cement

Consistent with the NESC analysis, developments in the clay, glass, and cement sector were generally more benign. Cement Roadstone Holdings would become a major indigenous multinational, and Waterford Glass would prosper for several more decades. The Irish Glass Bottle Company was still a substantial employer when it was acquired in 1992: its main plant in Ringsend would survive for another decade. Arklow Pottery was bought out by a Japanese firm in 1977. Efforts to develop an export trade failed to ensure its survival, however, and it ceased production in 1985.

Vehicle Assembly and 'Traditional' Metals and Engineering

The Ford plant in Cork closed in 1984 as the safeguard measures agreed at EEC accession approached their expiry date. The Philip Pierce plant in Wexford had been sold as a going concern when the Brittain Group went into liquidation in 1977; it closed in 1980. Unidare vacated its massive Finglas campus in 1995; it would survive as a shadow of its former self until liquidated in 2006. Hammond Holdings and Masser-Waterford were both acquired by the Tonge-McGloughlin (TMG) Group in the 1970s. Hammond Lane Foundry closed in 1973; Masser-Waterford went into receivership in

1982. Electrical Industries of Ireland closed in the 1970s, Solus Teoranta and Verolme Dockyard in the 1980s. Irish Steel remained on life support until sold to the Indian multinational Ispat in 1995. It closed six years later.

Paper and Printing, 'Traditional' Chemicals and Miscellaneous

All three of the newspaper groups survived into the 1990s, though the *Irish Press* would close in 1995. Even by 1972, Smurfit was on the verge of becoming a significant multinational. St Joe Paper had sold its Irish interests in 1979. Both of its former mills would close by 1982. The Clondalkin paper mills also closed in 1982. Irish Dunlop's Cork factory closed in 1983, as did Unilever's Dublin soap factory. By 1984, the workforce at Goulding Chemicals had fallen below 100. The heavily indebted Nítrigin Éireann Teoranta (NET) would become a holding company for Irish Fertilizer Industries, a joint venture with British group ICI, in 1987.

'New' FDI-Dominated Sectors

Overall outcomes in the 'new' (export-oriented) FDI-dominated sectors were more benign, though there was substantial churn even within this segment. Standard Pressed Steel closed its Galway plant in 1977. Philips closed one of its Dublin plants several years later. Other of their Irish plants remained in operation. Ferenka and Snia both exited with the closure of their respective plants in 1977 and 1983.[22]

Ecco was sold in 1988, Technicon in 1989, and Krups in 1991. In these cases, the transition to new ownership was relatively seamless and the plants remained in operation. The Technicon plant, subsequently Bayer Diagnostics and now part of Siemens, remains in operation to this day. So, too, do the Irish operations of Pfizer, Liebherr, Becton Dickinson, and De Beers (now Element Six).

Export-oriented foreign MNC *entrants* post-1973 were concentrated in chemicals and pharmaceuticals; computer, electronic and optical products;

---

[22] Snia was a synthetic fibres producer, as was Ferenka's Dutch parent, Enka. Synthetic fibres had been viewed as a potential growth sector by the Industrial Development Authority but was particularly hard hit by the oil-price shocks of the 1970s. So too was the motor vehicles sector, which was of relevance to Ferenka. Its parent company was restructuring its global operations at the time the Limerick plant— which had been bedevilled by industrial relations problems—was closed.

and medical devices. These sectors accounted for almost half of employment in 'new' (post-1955) foreign multinational companies (MNCs) in 1986, up from one-quarter in 1973.[23] They were the major merchandise export sectors of the 'Celtic Tiger' era, and they remain so to this day.

Each of these segments was already dominated by high-profile US MNCs on the eve of EEC accession. Computer assembly would become a major growth industry over the following decades. Digital Equipment Corporation, which opened in Galway in 1972, was the first computer assembler to commence operations in the country. It would meet the criterion for inclusion on the list of major manufacturing employers within a year of Ireland's joining the EEC.

Appendix 8.1 Largest Manufacturing Establishments of 1972

The primary focus of the book has been on firms rather than establishments. Analysis of the regional distribution of industry, however, depends on where establishments are located. Identifying workforce numbers at this level is generally more difficult than at the level of the firm. Table 8.13 provides what is considered to be a reasonably comprehensive list of the factories or establishments employing 500 or more in 1972. Other than the several in Kerry, none are in the 'designated areas' which were eligible for preferential grant treatment.

Table 8.13 Manufacturing establishments employing workforces of 500+ in 1972

Establishment	Location	Establishment	Location	Establishment	Location
Arklow Pottery	Arklow, County Wicklow	Glen Abbey	Dublin	Navan Carpets	Navan, County Meath
Ballyclough Co-operative Creamery	Mallow, County Cork	Golden Vale	Cork	Nítrigin Éireann Teo	Arklow
Batchelors	Dublin	Goodbody	Waterford	Pfizer	Cork
Becton Dickinson	Drogheda, County Louth	Guinness brewery	Dublin	Philips Electrical	Dublin
Blarney Woollen Mills	Blarney, County Cork	H. B. Ice Cream	Rathfarnham, Dublin	Players–Wills	Dublin
Bolands	Dublin	Independent Newspapers	Dublin	Pretty Polly	Killarney, County Kerry
Bush (Smurfit)	Dublin	Irish Dunlop	Cork	Roadstone (CRH)	Dublin

[23] Frank Barry, 'Foreign Direct Investment and Institutional Co-evolution in Ireland'. *Scandinavian Economic History Review* 55, 3 (2007): 266: table 2.

C&C (included under Guinness Group)	Dublin	Irish Glass Bottle Company	Dublin	Roscrea Meats	Roscrea, County Tipperary
Cadbury (Ireland)	Dublin	Irish Meat Packers	Leixlip, County Kildare	Rowntree–Mackintosh	Dublin
Carrolls	Dundalk, County Louth	Irish Press	Dublin	Semperit	Dublin
Cement Ltd (CRH)	Drogheda, County Louth	Irish Ropes	Newbridge, County Kildare	Smurfit	Walkinstown, Dublin
Clarks Shoes	Dundalk, County Louth	Irish Steel	Cork	Snia	Sligo
Clondalkin Paper Mills	Dublin	Irish Sugar	Mallow, County Cork	Solus Teo.	Bray, County Wicklow
Clover Meats	Waterford	Irish Sugar	Carlow	Sunbeam	Cork
De Beers	Shannon	*Irish Times*	Dublin	Sunbeam	Tullamore, County Offaly
Ecco (General Electric)	Dundalk, County Louth	W. & R. Jacob	Dublin	Technicon	Swords, County Dublin
EI Electronics (General Electric)	Shannon	Johnston, Mooney & O'Brien	Dublin	Unidare	Dublin
Electrical Industries of Ireland	Dunleer, County Louth	Killeen Paper Mills (St Joe Paper)	Dublin	Verolme Dockyard	Cork
Ferenka	Limerick	Krups	Limerick	Waterford Crystal	Waterford
Ford	Cork	Lana Knit	Shannon	Williams & Woods (Nestlé)	Dublin
Galtee Meats	Mitchelstown, County Cork	Liebherr	Killarney, County Kerry	John A. Wood (CRH)	Cork
Gateaux	Dublin	National Board & Paper (St Joe Paper)	Waterford	Youghal Carpets	Cork

Source: author.

Epilogue

Ireland's overall growth performance from independence until well into the European Economic Community (EEC) era was poor by international standards. The early decades of the state's existence had been dominated by issues of legitimacy, sovereignty, and security, leading Kieran Kennedy and his co-authors to suggest that 'it was not until 25 years after the achievement of independence that economic development could receive the degree of attention that might otherwise have been expected from the start'.[1]

More recent research dates Ireland's underperformance primarily to this later period. Growth rates were low generally across Europe in the 1920s and 1930s. The Cumann na nGaedheal governments of the years to 1932 had achieved some success in agricultural and infrastructural development as well as in expanding the boundaries of independence, and the industrial expansion of the time is likely to have been more substantial than has generally been supposed. De Valera was more generous than most on the losing civil war side in recognizing their achievements, reportedly remarking to his son Vivion after coming to power that 'when we got in and saw the files [. . .] They did a magnificent job, Viv. They did a magnificent job'.[2]

Though the contemporary economics community had been highly critical of Fianna Fáil policy in the 1930s, governments of all political dispositions became more protectionist and interventionist with the onset of the Great Depression, and debt default was widespread. The land annuities dispute with Britain caused significant hardship, but the terms of the settlement were such that, in the judgement of quantitative economic historians, 'Ireland under Fianna Fáil rule may not have lost the economic war'.[3]

The problem with the extensive protectionism of the time was the path dependence to which it gave rise, as the Fiscal Inquiry Committee of 1923 had warned. The large number of jobs that had been created—and that

---

[1] Kieran Kennedy, Thomas Giblin, and Deirdre McHugh, *The Economic Development of Ireland in the Twentieth Century* (London: Routledge, 1988), 255.

[2] Tim Pat Coogan, *De Valera: Long Fellow, Long Shadow* (London: Arrow Books, 1995), 426.

[3] J. Peter Neary and Cormac Ó Gráda, 'Protection, Economic War and Structural Change: The 1930s in Ireland'. *Irish Historical Studies* 27, 107 (1991): 250–66. See also Kevin O'Rourke, 'Burn Everything British But Their Coal: The Anglo-Irish Economic War of the 1930s'. *Journal of Economic History* 51, 2 (1991): 357–66.

Industry and Policy in Independent Ireland, 1922–1972. Frank Barry, Oxford University Press.
© Frank Barry (2023). DOI: 10.1093/oso/9780198878230.003.0009

remained dependent on protection for their survival—made it difficult to dismantle the tariff regime when external circumstances changed. The strategy of 'industrialization by invitation' provided a route through the difficult interest-group politics of outward reorientation.

Comparison with the performance of other independent states may in any case entail the application of an overly taxing standard. Sidney Pollard, in his major work on the process of European industrialization, suggests that Ireland's problems—rather than stemming from independence—'were more akin to those of the major non-industrialized regions inside advanced countries, like the Italian South, Corsica, and the French South-West.'[4] Ireland was unusual among independent states in that it continued to share a common labour market with its larger and more prosperous neighbour. Economies of this type can expand more dramatically when circumstances are advantageous and decline more precipitously when they are not.[5] Even within the United Kingdom, regional policy achieved only limited success in counteracting the gravitational forces drawing economic activity towards London and the surrounding South East region.

The 1926 Banking Commission had recognised that the Free State 'is now, and will undoubtedly long continue to be, an integral part of the economic system at the head of which stands Great Britain.'[6] The new export-oriented foreign investment strategy of the mid-1950s initiated the process of decoupling Ireland from the UK market. The latter still served as destination for 90 per cent of Irish merchandise exports in 1955. The figure had fallen to 73 per cent by 1960 and to 55 per cent by 1973. It would fall much further over subsequent decades.[7]

Outward reorientation had been a major determinant of the erosion of the sectarian divide in Irish business life and of the change in mindset that led to the expansion in educational attainment. EEC membership brought dramatic changes on a number of other fronts. The adjustment of Irish agricultural prices to Western European levels saw real agricultural incomes rise by 40 per cent over the years to 1978, though the prosperity of rural Ireland today compared to the position prior to EEC membership owes much to off-farm employment in local towns, regional hubs, and nearby cities.

[4] Sidney Pollard, *Peaceful Conquest: The Industrialization of Europe, 1760–1970* (Oxford: Oxford University Press, 1981), 324.

[5] Frank Barry, 'The Celtic Tiger Era: Delayed Convergence or Regional Boom?' *ESRI Quarterly Economic Commentary* 21 (2002): 84–91.

[6] Banking Commission, Final Reports (Dublin: Banking Commission, 1927), s. 6.

[7] Indigenous firms, however, remain much more heavily oriented towards the United Kingdom than Ireland's foreign-owned industrial sector: Frank Barry, 'From the Treaty to Brexit: The Evolution of Ireland's Export Dependence on the UK Market'. *History Ireland* (2021): 93–96.

Unimpeded access to a vastly broader market increased Ireland's attractiveness as an export platform for foreign multinational corporations. The *Investment in Education* report of 1965 had pointed to the waste of natural talent associated with a non-meritocratic education system: the ending of the marriage bar and the increase in female employment further expanded the pool of talent available to the economy, as well, of course, as enhancing the opportunities for individual fulfilment.

Ireland continued to underperform in comparative terms however until the confluence of circumstances that led to the dramatic growth spurt of the 1990s. EEC accession had come at a particularly difficult time. The two major oil shocks of the 1970s had thrown the industrialized world into deep recession. Prospects for convergence on broader Western European living standards were further damaged by the inappropriate Irish fiscal response of the time. The eventual resolution of the debt crisis that ensued coincided with the coming into being of the Single European Market. Ireland's share of European-bound US foreign direct investment (FDI) had contracted in the 1980s. It expanded dramatically over the following decade, strengthening the country's export concentration in cyclically resilient sectors such as pharmaceuticals, medical devices, and information technology-enabled services.

Ireland's aggregate trade and production statistics are today dominated by the activities of these foreign corporations. Irish-owned firms are much more labour-intensive and much less import-dependent than their foreign-owned counterparts however.[8] Their contribution to economic performance is substantially more significant than the aggregate data might suggest.

Indigenous-dominated agri-food sectors were among those in which Ireland displayed a strong revealed comparative advantage in the years leading up to EEC accession. By 1992, businesses such as the Kerry Group, Avonmore Foods, Waterford Foods, Dairygold, and Goodman International had global workforces numbering in the thousands. So too did the Smurfit Group and Cement Roadstone Holdings. The former employed 15,000 in 1992, the latter almost 12,000. Most of these firms have expanded massively since then, in many cases beyond the European Union's borders.

Ireland had also displayed a revealed comparative advantage in textiles, clothing, and footwear, though the number of foreign-owned export-oriented firms in these sectors would have impacted on the usefulness of the index as a predictor of subsequent developments. Job numbers in these

---

[8] *Per €1 million of merchandise exports,* Irish-owned companies today employ more than three times as many workers as foreign-owned firms and spend twenty times as much on Irish raw materials: ibid.

sectors halved by 1987 and would continue to decline thereafter. Rather than being reallocated within the EEC, which might have benefited Irish industry had cost competitiveness been maintained, production and employment shifted to the developing world. The vast bulk of the job losses were in Irish-owned companies.

The revival in Irish indigenous industry from the late 1980s is an often-forgotten element in analyses of the 'Celtic Tiger' phenomenon.[9] That it occurred alongside an increase in the export intensity of the sector is likely to have been a reflection less of the transformation of existing enterprises than of their replacement by newer ones.[10] Industrial adjustment is not frictionless.[11] In the case of indigenous industry, it may have taken a decade-and-a-half to complete.

The demise of large numbers of major employers over this period, as charted in Chapter 8, tells one part of the story. The experience contrasts sharply with that of the previous half-century. All of the major employers of 1929 remained in operation at the time of EEC accession, though Bannatyne & Co. had been acquired by Ranks in 1930. Of the major employers of 1948, though several had merged or been acquired, only two had closed. The globalized trade environment of the EEC era would prove much less forgiving. Of the approximately 70 firms employing workforces of 500 or more in 1972, half had disappeared or contracted massively by the late 1980s. The high rate of attrition of long-established firms would continue into the future.[12] The other part of the story—the emergence of new export-oriented indigenous businesses—is a project for the future.

Finally, to return to one of the questions raised at the outset of this research: what was the share of foreign-owned industry in manufacturing employment over the first half-century of independence? According to the data compiled by the Industrial Development Authority, the foreign share in 1972 stood at a little over one-third. Estimates for earlier periods are

[9] Eoin O'Malley, 'The Revival of Irish Indigenous Industry 1987–1997'. *ESRI Quarterly Economic Commentary* April (1998): 35–57.

[10] Ciara Whelan and Patrick P Walsh, 'The Importance of Structural Change in Industry for Growth'. *Journal of the Statistical and Social Inquiry Society of Ireland* 29 (2000): 1–32. As suggested by Frances Ruane and Eoin O'Malley in the ensuing discussion, determining the validity of this hypothesis requires the type of firm-level data employed here.

[11] Textbook analyses of the costs of trade liberalization typically focus on the disruption to employment, the costs of which are known to be borne disproportionately by older, less educated workers with long periods of tenure in their former jobs.

[12] Directly comparable studies of this aspect of the consequences of trade liberalization are rare. In the case of the United Kingdom (which is not the ideal comparator), by far the largest share of the manufacturing firms on the list of 100 largest employers in 1972 remained on the equivalent list for 1992: Martin Fiedler and Howard Gospel, *The Top 100 Largest Employers in UK and Germany in the Twentieth Century. Data (ca. 1907, 1935/38, 1955/57, 1972/73, 1992/95)* (Cologne: University of Cologne, Department of Economic and Business History, 2010).

reliant on educated guesswork. Guinness and Ford were the major foreign-owned industrial employers in 1922, followed in a distant third place by Furness & Withy, the UK owners of Rushbrooke Dockyard. These three firms would have accounted for perhaps 10 per cent of manufacturing employment. Across the entirety of manufacturing (as measured by the Census of Industrial Production) the foreign share may have been in the region of 15 per cent.

By 1929, several UK tobacco firms had established substantial operations in Dublin; Williams & Woods, the largest confectionery and jam producer, had been acquired by Crosse & Blackwell; and employment at Ford was close to an all-time peak. Indigenous industry had expanded too, though not as rapidly, suggesting that the foreign share may have grown to a level of perhaps 20 per cent or so.

The indigenous and foreign segments appear to have kept largely abreast of each other over the next several decades. Among the sectors surveyed by the Committee on Industrial Organisation in the early 1960s, the foreign share was a little in excess of 30 per cent.[13] As several indigenous-dominated sectors were underrepresented, the foreign share across all of manufacturing was probably close to around one-quarter.

By 1972, the tariff factories of the protectionist era and the few externally owned firms that predated independence were complemented by the brown-field and greenfield export-oriented foreign investors that had established in Ireland since the mid-1950s. By the early 2000s, foreign-owned firms comprised close to 50 per cent of manufacturing employment. This remains the case to the present day.

[13] Frank Barry, Linda Barry, and Aisling Menton, 'Tariff-Jumping Foreign Direct Investment in Protectionist Era Ireland'. *Economic History Review* 69, 4 (2016): 1285–308.

References

Adams, Robin. 'The "Made in Ireland" Trademark and the Delineation of National Identity', in *National Brands and Global Markets: An Historical Perspective*, ed. David Higgins and Nikolas Glover (Abingdon: Routledge, 2023), 46–66.

Aldcroft, Derek H. *Europe's Third World: The European Periphery in the Interwar Years.* (Aldershot: Ashgate, 2006).

Baccaro, Lucio, and Marco Simoni. 'Centralized Wage Bargaining and the "Celtic Tiger" Phenomenon'. *Industrial Relations: A Journal of Economy and Society* 46, 3 (2007): 426–55.

Baker, Terence J, Robert O'Connor, and Rory Dunne. *A Study of the Irish Cattle and Beef Industries* (Dublin: Economic and Social Research Institute 1973).

Balassa, Bela. 'The Process of Industrial Development and Alternative Development Strategies'. (Washington, DC: World Bank, 1980).

Banking Commission. *Second, Third and Fourth Interim Reports* (Dublin: Banking Commission, 1926).

Banking Commission. *Final Reports of the Banking Commission* (Dublin: Banking Commission, 1927).

Barnard, Alfred. *The Noted Breweries of Great Britain and Ireland* (London: Joseph Causton & Sons, 1889).

Barry, Frank. 'The Celtic Tiger Era: Delayed Convergence or Regional Boom?' *ESRI Quarterly Economic Commentary* 21 (2002): 84–91.

Barry, Frank. 'Economic Integration and Convergence Processes in the EU Cohesion Countries'. *Journal of Common Market Studies* 41, 5 (2003): 897–921.

Barry, Frank. 'Foreign Direct Investment and Institutional Co-evolution in Ireland'. *Scandinavian Economic History Review* 55, 3 (2007): 262–88.

Barry, Frank. 'Politics and Fiscal Policy under Lemass: A Theoretical Appraisal'. *Economic and Social Review* 40, 4 (2009): 393.

Barry, Frank. 'Foreign Investment and the Politics of Export Profits Tax Relief 1956'. *Irish Economic and Social History* 38 (2011): 54–73.

Barry, Frank. 'Outward-Oriented Economic Development and the Irish Education System'. *Irish Educational Studies* 33, 2 (2014): 213–23.

Barry, Frank. 'Shannon Connections: Aggressive Tax Planning by US MNCs in the Pre-Kennedy Era'. Presentation to Central Bank of Ireland Economic History Workshop, December 16, 2016.

Barry, Frank. 'The Central Bank's Harmonised Competitiveness Indicators: Users Beware'. *Administration* 65, 4 (2017): 73–82.

Barry, Frank. 'The Leading Manufacturing Firms in the Irish Free State in 1929'. *Irish Historical Studies* 42, 162 (2018): 293–316.

Barry, Frank. 'The Life and Death of Protestant Businesses in Independent Ireland', in *Protestant and Irish: The Minority's Accommodation with Independent Ireland*, ed. Ian d'Alton and Ida Milne (Cork: Cork University Press, 2019), 155–70.

Barry, Frank. 'From the Treaty to Brexit: The Evolution of Ireland's Export Dependence on the UK Market'. *History Ireland* (2021): 93–96.

Barry, Frank. 'Business Establishment Opposition to Southern Ireland's Exit from the United Kingdom'. *Enterprise & Society* (2022), 23, 4, 984–1018.

Barry, Frank, and Mary Daly. 'Irish Perceptions of the Great Depression', in *The Great Depression in Europe: Economic Thought and Policy in a National Context*, ed. Michael Psalidopoulos (Athens: Alpha Bank Historical Archives, 2012), 395–424.

Barry, Frank, and Joe Durkan. 'Team Aer Lingus and Irish Steel: An Application of the Declining High-Wage Industries Literature'. *IBAR-Irish Business and Administrative Research* 17 (1996): 58–72.

Barry, Frank, and Mícheál Ó Fathartaigh. 'The Industrial Development Authority, 1949–58: Establishment, Evolution and Expansion of Influence'. *Irish Historical Studies* 39, 155 (2015): 460–78.

Barry, Frank, and Clare O'Mahony. 'Regime Change in 1950s Ireland: The New Export-Oriented Foreign Investment Strategy'. *Irish Economic and Social History* 44, 1 (2017): 46–65.

Barry, Frank, Linda Barry, and Aisling Menton. 'Tariff-Jumping Foreign Direct Investment in Protectionist Era Ireland'. *Economic History Review* 69, 4 (2016): 1285–308.

Beddy, J. P. 'Industrial Promotion 1'. *Administration* 104 (1962): 327.

Berend, Ivan T. 'The Failure of Economic Nationalism: Central and Eastern Europe before World War II'. *Revue économique* 51, 2 (2000): 315–22.

Bew, Paul, and Henry Patterson. *Seán Lemass and the Making of Modern Ireland 1945–66* (Dublin: Gill and Macmillan, 1982).

Bielenberg, Andy. *Cork's Industrial Revolution 1780–1880* (Cork: Cork University Press, 1991).

Bielenberg, Andy. *Ireland and the Industrial Revolution: The Impact of the Industrial Revolution on Irish Industry*, 1801–1922 (London, New York: Routledge, 2009).

Bielenberg, Andy, and David Johnson. 'The Production and Consumption of Tobacco in Ireland, 1800–1914'. *Irish Economic and Social History* 25, 1 (1998): 1–21.

Blackwell, John, Gerard Danaher, and Eoin O'Malley. *An Analysis of Job Losses in Irish Manufacturing Industry* (Dublin: National Economic and Social Council, 1983).

Bolger, Patrick. *The Irish Co-operative Movement: Its History and Development* (Dublin: Institute of Public Administration, 1977).

Bowen, Kurt Derek. *Protestants in a Catholic State: Ireland's Privileged Minority* (Dublin: Gill and Macmillan, 1983).

Boylan, Shaun. 'Cleeve, Sir Thomas Henry', in *Dictionary of Irish Biography* (Cambridge: Cambridge University Press, 2009).

Brannick, Teresa, Francis Devine, and Aidan Kelly. 'Social Statistics for Labour Historians: Strike Statistics, 1922–99'. *Saothar* 25 (2000): 114–20.

Broadberry, Stephen N. 'Manufacturing and the Convergence Hypothesis: What the Long-Run Data Show'. *Journal of Economic History* 53, 4 (1993): 772–95.

Brock, Catherine. 'The CIO Industrial Survey'. *Journal of the Statistical and Social Inquiry Society of Ireland* 21, 2 (1964): 176–88.

Brock, Catherine. 'Public Policy and Private Industrial Development', in *Economic Policy in Ireland* ed. John Bristow and Alan Tait (Dublin: Institute of Public Administration, 1968).

Browne, R. F. 'The Electricity Supply Board'. *Journal of the Statistical and Social Inquiry Society of Ireland* 18 (1947): 564–584.

Brown, Terence. *The Irish Times: 150 Years of Influence* (London: Bloomsbury, 2015).

Buckland, Patrick. *Irish Unionism 1: The Anglo-Irish and the New Ireland, 1885–1922* (Dublin: Gill and Macmillan, 1972).

Buckley, Peter. 'The Effect of Foreign Direct Investment on the Economy of the Irish Republic'. Ph.D. thesis, Lancaster University, 1975.

Campbell, Fergus. *The Irish Establishment, 1879–1914* (Oxford: Oxford University Press, 2009).

Chambers, Anne. *T.K. Whitaker: Portrait of a Patriot* (Dublin: Random House, 2014).

Childers, Erskine. *The Framework of Home Rule* (London: Edward Arnold, 1911).

Clavin, Patricia. *The Great Depression in Europe, 1929-1939* (New York: Macmillan, 2000).

Commission of Inquiry into Banking, Currency and Credit. Reports (Dublin: Stationery Office, 1938).

Committee on Industrial Organisation. *Report on the Motor Vehicle Assembly Industry* (Dublin: Stationery Office, 1962).

Committee on Industrial Organisation. *Report of Survey of Electrical Equipment and Apparatus Industry* (Dublin: Stationery Office, 1964).

Committee on Industrial Organisation. *Survey Report on the Paper Products Industry* (Dublin: Stationery Office, 1964).

Committee on Industrial Organisation. *Report on Survey of the Woollen and Worsted Industry* (Dublin: Stationery Office, 1965).

Committee on Industrial Progress. *Report on Electrical Machinery, Apparatus and Appliances Industry* (Dublin: Stationery Office, 1971).

Committee on Industrial Progress. *General Report* (Dublin: Stationery Office, 1973).

Coogan, Tim Pat. *De Valera: Long Fellow, Long Shadow* (London: Arrow Books, 1995).

The Condensed Milk Co. of Ireland (Cleeve Bros.): A Monster Irish Industry Reviewed (Limerick: McKerns Printers, 1898).

Cork Incorporated Chamber of Commerce & Shipping. Cork: Its Trade and Commerce (Cork: Guy & Co., 1919).

Cromien, Seán. 'Brennan, Joseph'. In *Dictionary of Irish Biography* (Cambridge: Cambridge University Press, 2009).

Cullen, Louis M. *Princes & Pirates: The Dublin Chamber of Commerce, 1783-1983* (Dublin: Dublin Chamber of Commerce, 1983).

Cullen, Louis M. *Eason & Son: A History* (Dublin: Eason & Son, 1989).

Cullinane, Liam. *Working in Cork, Everyday Life in Irish Steel, Sunbeam Wolsey and the Ford Marina Plant, 1917-2001* (Cork: Cork University Press, 2020).

Daly, Mary E. 'An Irish-Ireland for Business?: The Control of Manufactures Acts, 1932 and 1934'. *Irish Historical Studies* 24, 94 (1984): 246-72.

Daly, Mary E. *Dublin: The Deposed Capital, 1860-1914* (Cork: Cork University Press, 1984).

Daly, Mary E. 'Government Finance for Industry in the Irish Free State: The Trade Loans (Guarantee) Acts'. *Irish Economic and Social History* 11, 1 (1984): 73-93.

Daly, Mary E. 'The Employment Gains from Industrial Protection in the Irish Free State during the 1930s: A Note'. *Irish Economic and Social History* 15, 1 (1988): 71-75.

Daly, Mary E. *Industrial Development and Irish National Identity, 1922-1939* (New York: Syracuse University Press, 1992).

Daly, Mary E. *The Buffer State: Historical Roots of the Department of the Environment* (Dublin: Institute of Public Administration, 1997).

Daly, Mary E. *The First Department: A History of the Department of Agriculture* (Dublin: Institute of Public Administration, 2002).

Daly, Mary E. 'The Irish Free State and the Great Depression of the 1930s: The Interaction of the Global and the Local'. *Irish Economic and Social History* 38 (2011): 19-36.

Daly, Mary E. *Sixties Ireland: Reshaping the Economy, State and Society, 1957-1973* (Cambridge: Cambridge University Press, 2016).

Daniel, T. K. 'Griffith on His Noble Head: The Determinants of Cumann na nGaedheal Economic Policy, 1922-32'. *Irish Economic and Social History* 3, 1 (1976): 55-65.

de Cogan, Dominic. 'The Wartime Origins of the Irish Corporation Tax'. *Irish Journal of Legal Studies* 3, 2 (2013): 15-32.

Dempsey, Pauric J. 'Campbell, Charles Gordon', in *Dictionary of Irish Biography* (Cambridge: Cambridge University Press, 2009).

Dennison, Stanley R., and Oliver MacDonagh. *Guinness 1886–1939: From Incorporation to the Second World War* (Cork: Cork University Press, 1998).

Department of Agriculture. Committee of Inquiry on Post-Emergency Agricultural Policy (Dublin: Stationery Office, 1945).

Department of Finance. *Economic Development* (Dublin: Stationery Office, 1958) (Whitaker Report).

Devlin, Anna, and Frank Barry. 'Protection versus Free Trade in the Free State Era: The Finance Attitude'. *Irish Economic and Social History* 46, 1 (2019): 3–21.

Doyle, Pat, and Louis PF Smith. *Milk to Market: A History of Dublin Milk Supply* (Dublin: Leinster Milk Producers' Association, 1989).

Dublin Port and Docks Board. *Dublin Port Yearbook* (Dublin: Dublin Port and Docks Board, 1926).

Dwyer, D. J. 'The Leather Industries of the Irish Republic, 1922–55: A Study in Industrial Development and Location'. *Irish Geography* 4, 3 (1961): 175–89.

Eichengreen, Barry. 'Institutions and Economic Growth: Europe after World War II', in *European Economic Growth*, ed. Nicholas Crafts and Gianni Toniolo (Cambridge: Cambridge University Press, 1996), 38–72.

Eichengreen, Barry, and Douglas A Irwin. 'The Slide to Protectionism in the Great Depression: Who Succumbed and Why?' *Journal of Economic History* 70, 4 (2010): 871–97.

Eichengreen, Barry, and Jeffrey Sachs. 'Exchange Rates and Economic Recovery in the 1930s'. *Journal of Economic History* 45, 4 (1985): 925–46.

European Recovery Program (Washington, DC: US Department of State, 1948).

Fanning, Ronan. *The Irish Department of Finance, 1922–58* (Dublin: Institute of Public Administration, 1978).

Farmar, Tony. *Heitons—a Managed Transition: Heitons in the Irish Coal, Iron and Building Markets, 1818–1996* (Dublin: A. & A. Farmar, 1996).

Farmar, Tony. *The Versatile Profession: A History of Accountancy in Ireland since 1850* (Dublin: Chartered Accountants Ireland, 2013).

Farrell, Mel. '"Few Supporters and No Organisation?" Cumann na nGaedheal Organisation and Policy, 1923–33'. Ph.D. thesis, National University of Ireland Maynooth, 2011.

Fiedler, Martin, and Howard Gospel. *The Top 100 Largest Employers in UK and Germany in the Twentieth Century. Data (Ca. 1907, 1935/38, 1955/57, 1972/73, 1992/95)* (Cologne: University of Cologne, Department of Economic and Business History 2010).

Fiscal Inquiry Committee. Final Report (Dublin: Stationery Office, 1923).

Fishback, Price. 'US Monetary and Fiscal Policy in the 1930s'. *Oxford Review of Economic Policy* 26, 3 (2010): 385–413.

FitzGerald, Garret. 'Mr Whitaker and Industry'. *Studies: An Irish Quarterly Review* 48, 190 (1959): 138–50.

FitzGerald, Garret. 'Investment in Education'. *Studies: An Irish Quarterly Review* 54, 216 (1965): 361–74.

FitzGerald, Garret. *Planning in Ireland* (Dublin: Institute of Public Administration, 1968).

FitzGerald, John, and Seán Kenny. 'Managing a Century of Debt'. *Journal of the Statistical and Social Inquiry Society of Ireland* 48 (2018): 1–40.

FitzGerald, John, and Seán Kenny. '"Till Debt Do Us Part": Financial Implications of the Divorce of the Irish Free State from the United Kingdom, 1922–1926'. *European Review of Economic History* 24, 4 (2020): 818–42.

FitzGerald, John, Seán Kenny, and Alexandra L Cermeño. 'Household Behaviour under Rationing'. *National Institute Economic Review* (2022): 1–21.

Fitzgerald, Maurice. *Protectionism to Liberalisation: Ireland and the EEC, 1957 to 1966* (Aldershot: Ashgate, 2000).

Flood, Finbarr. *In Full Flood: A Memoir* (Dublin: Liberties Press, 2006).

Flora, Peter, Franz Kraus, and Winfried Pfenning. *State, Economy, and Society in Western Europe 1815–1975: The Growth of Industrial Societies and Capitalist Economies*, Vol. 2 (Chicago, IL: St James Press, 1987).

Flynn, Charles. *Dundalk 1900–1960: An Oral History.* Ph.D thesis. National University of Ireland, Maynooth, 2000.

Fogarty, Michael P. 'Irish Entrepreneurs Speak for Themselves'. Economic and Social Research Institute Research Series, ESRI Broadsheet No. 8, 1973.

Fox, P. F., and Proinnsias Breathnach. 'Proprietary Creameries in Ireland', in *Butter in Ireland: From Earliest Times to the 21st Century*, ed. Peter Foynes, Colin Rynne, and Chris Synnott (Cork: Cork Butter Museum, 2014), 67–70.

Garvin, Tom. *Preventing the Future: Why Was Ireland So Poor for So Long?* (Dublin: Gill and Macmillan, 2004).

Geary, Frank, and Tom Stark. '150 Years of Regional GDP: United Kingdom and Ireland', in *The Economic Development of Europe's Regions*, ed. Joan R. Rosés and Nikolaus Wolf (Abingdon: Routledge, 2018), 330–62.

Geary, R. C. 'Irish Economic Development since the Treaty'. *Studies: An Irish Quarterly Review* 40, 160 (1951): 399–418.

Geary, R. C. 'Review of *George O'Brien: A Biographical Memoir* by J. Meenan'. *Economic and Social Review* 12, 2 (1981): 67–70.

Girvin, Brian. *Between Two Worlds: Politics and Economy in Independent Ireland* (Dublin: Gill and Macmillan, 1989).

Girvin, Brian. 'Trade Unions and Economic Development', in *Trade Union Century*, ed. Donal Nevin (Dublin: Mercier Press, 1994), 117–32.

Government of Ireland White Paper. *Programme for Economic Expansion* (Dublin: Stationery Office, 1958).

Government of Ireland White Paper. *Membership of the European Communities: Implications for Ireland.* (Dublin: Stationery Office, 1970).

Government of Ireland White Paper. *Accession of Ireland to the European Communities* (Dublin: Stationery Office, 1972).

Gray, Lionel F., and Jonathan Love. *Jane's Major Companies of Europe* (London: Samson, Low, Marsden and Co., 1973).

Greer, Desmond S, and James W Nicolson. *The Factory Acts in Ireland, 1802–1914* (Dublin: Four Courts Press, 2003).

Grimes, Thomas. 'Starting Ireland on the Road to Industry: Henry Ford in Cork'. Ph.D. thesis, National University of Ireland, Maynooth, 2008.

Groutel, Anne. 'American Janus-Faced Economic Diplomacy towards Ireland in the Mid-1950s'. *Irish Economic and Social History* 43, 1 (2016): 3–20.

Hannan, Damien. *Rural Exodus: A Study of the Forces Influencing Large-Scale Migration of Irish Rural Youth* (London: Geoffrey Chapman, 1970).

Hardiman, Niamh. 'Pay Bargaining: Confrontation and Consensus', in *Trade Union Century*, ed. Donal Nevin (Dublin: Mercier Press, 1994), 147–58.

Haughton, Jonathan. *Trade Agreements and Tax Incentives: The Irish Experience.* ITD–INTAL Tax and Integration Series (Washington, DC: Inter-American Development Bank, 2002).

Honohan, Patrick. 'Currency Board or Central Bank? Lessons from the Irish Pound's Link with Sterling, 1928–79'. *Banca Nazionale del Lavoro Quarterly Review* 50, 200 (1997): 39–67.

Hooker, Elizabeth R. *Readjustments of Agricultural Tenure in Ireland* (Chapel Hill, NC: University of North Carolina Press, 1938).

Horgan, John. *Seán Lemass, the Enigmatic Patriot* (Dublin: Gill and Macmillan 1999).

Hughes, Alan. 'Mergers and Economic Performance in the UK: A Survey of the Empirical Evidence, 1950–1990', in *European Mergers and Merger Policy*, ed. Matthew Bishop and John Kay (Oxford: Oxford University Press, 1993), 9–95.

Humphreys, Madeleine. 'The Decline of the Irish Whiskey Trade in Independent Ireland, 1922–1952'. *Journal of European Economic History* 23, 1 (1994): 93–103.

Industrial Credit Company Ltd. *Twenty-One Years of Industrial Financing, 1933 to 1954.* (Dublin: Industrial Credit Company Ltd, 1954).

Industrial Development Authority, *Regional Industrial Plans 1973–1977.* (Dublin: Industrial Development Authority, 1972).

Investment in Education (Dublin: Stationery Office, 1965).

Irish Unionist Alliance. *30th Annual Report, 1919–1920.* (Dublin: Irish Unionist Alliance, 1920).

Jacobsen, John Kurt. *Chasing Progress in the Irish Republic* (Cambridge: Cambridge University Press, 1994).

Jenkins, William. *Tipp Co-op: Origin and Development of Tipperary Co-operative Creamery Ltd.* (Dublin: Geography Publications, 1999).

Johnson, David. *The Inter-War Economy in Ireland* (Dundalk: Dundalgan Press, 1989).

Johnson, David. 'The Belfast Boycott, 1920–1922', in *Irish Population, Economy, and Society: Essays in Honour of the Late K. H. Connell*, ed. J. M. Goldstrom and L. A. Clarkson (Oxford: Clarendon Press, 1981), 287–307.

Johnston, Joseph. 'An Outlook on Irish Agriculture'. *Studies: An Irish Quarterly Review* 28, 110 (1939): 195–209.

Joint Committee on Internal Revenue Taxation. *Tax Effects of Conducting Foreign Business through Foreign Corporations* (Washington, DC: US Government Printing Office, 1961).

Jones, Geoffrey. 'The Growth and Performance of British Multinational Firms before 1939: The Case of Dunlop'. *Economic History Review* 37, 1 (1984): 35–53.

Kearns, Kevin C. 'Industrialization and Regional Development in Ireland, 1958–72'. *American Journal of Economics and Sociology* 33, 3 (1974): 299–316.

Kellaghan, Thomas, and Mary Hegarty. 'Participation in the Leaving Certificate Examination, 1961–1980'. *Irish Journal of Education* (1984): 72–106.

Kenneally, Ian. 'Nationalist in the Broadest Sense: The Irish Independent and the Irish Revolution', in *Independent Newspapers a History*, ed. Mark O'Brien and Kevin Rafter (Dublin: Four Courts Press, 2012).

Kennedy, Kieran, and Brendan Dowling. *Economic Growth in Ireland: The Experience since 1947* (Dublin: Gill and Macmillan, 1975).

Kennedy, Kieran, Thomas Giblin, and Deirdre McHugh. *The Economic Development of Ireland in the Twentieth Century* (London: Routledge, 1988).

Kennedy, Liam. *The Modern Industrialisation of Ireland, 1940–1988* (Dundalk: Dundalgan Press, 1989).

Kennedy, Liam. *Colonialism, Religion and Nationalism in Ireland* (Belfast: Institute of Irish Studies, 1996).

Kenny, Seán, and Eoin McLaughlin. 'The Political Economy of Secession: Lessons from the Early Years of the Irish Free State'. *National Institute Economic Review* 261, 1 (2022): 48–78.

Kepple, Simon. 'A Survey of Taxation and Government Expenditure in the Irish Free State, 1922–36'. MA thesis, University College Cork, 1938.

Kettle, Tom. 'The Economics of Nationalism', in *The Day's Burden* (Dublin, London: Maunsel, 1918), 129–147.

Keynes, John Maynard. 'National Self-Sufficiency'. *Studies: An Irish Quarterly Review* 22, 86 (1933): 177–93.

Keynes, John Maynard. *The General Theory of Employment, Interest and Money* (London: Macmillan, 1936).

Larkin, Felix M. "'A Great Daily Organ": The Freeman's Journal, 1763–1924'. *History Ireland* 14, 3 (2006): 44–49.

Lavelle, Patricia. *James O'Mara: A Staunch Sinn Féiner, 1873–1948* (Dublin: Clonmore and Reynolds, 1961).

Lee, J. J. *Ireland 1912–1985: Politics and Society* (Cambridge: Cambridge University Press, 1989).

Lemass, Sean F. 'The Organisation behind the Economic Programme'. *Administration* 9, 1 (1961): 4–10.

Liepmann, Heinrich. *Tariff Levels and the Economic Unity of Europe: An Examination of Tariff Policy, Export Movements and the Economic Integration of Europe, 1913–1931* (London: George Allen and Unwin, 1938).

Lin, Justin Yifu. *Demystifying the Chinese Economy* (Cambridge: Cambridge University Press, 2012).

Lin, Justin Yifu, and Célestin Monga. *Beating the Odds: Jump-Starting Developing Countries* (Princeton, NJ: Princeton University Press, 2017).

Lindert, Peter H. 'The Rise of Social Spending, 1880–1930'. *Explorations in Economic History* 31, 1 (1994): 1–37.

Lynch, Patrick, and John Vaizey. *Guinness's Brewery in the Irish Economy 1759–1876* (Cambridge: Cambridge University Press, 1960).

Lyons, F. S. L. 'Reflections on a Bicentenary', in *Bank of Ireland 1783–1983, Bicentenary Essays*, ed. F. S. L. Lyons (Dublin: Gill and Macmillan, 1983).

Macartney-Filgate, William. T. *Irish Rural Life and Industry* (Dublin: Hely's, 1907).

MacDonagh, Oliver. 'The Victorian Bank, 1824–1914', in *Bank of Ireland, 1783–1983: Bicentenary Essays*, ed. F. S. L. Lyons (Dublin: Gill and Macmillan, 1983), 31–53.

MacMahon, Enda. *A Most Respectable Meeting of Merchants, Dublin Chamber of Commerce: A History* (Dublin: Londubh Books, 2014).

MacSharry, Ray, and Padraic A. White. *The Making of the Celtic Tiger: The Inside Story of Ireland's Booming Economy* (Cork: Mercier Press, 2000).

Maguire, Martin. *The Civil Service and the Revolution in Ireland, 1912–38. 'Shaking the Blood-Stained Hand of Mr. Collins'* (Manchester: Manchester University Press, 2013).

Maher, Denis J. *The Tortuous Path: The Course of Ireland's Entry into the EEC, 1948–73* (Dublin: Institute of Public Administration, 1986).

Manning, Maurice, and Moore McDowell. *Electricity Supply in Ireland: The History of the ESB* (Dublin: Gill and Macmillan, 1984).

Mason, Mark. 'The Origins and Evolution of Japanese Direct Investment in Europe'. *Business History Review* 66, 3 (1992): 435–74.

Maume, Patrick. 'Walsh, James Joseph', in *Dictionary of Irish Biography* (Cambridge: Cambridge University Press, 2009).

McAleese, Dermot. 'Effective Tariffs and the Structure of Industrial Protection in Ireland'. Economic and Social Research Institute (ESRI) Research Series, Paper No. 62, 1971.

McAleese, Dermot. 'Ireland in the Enlarged EEC: Economic Consequences and Prospects', in *Economic Sovereignty and Regional Policy: A Symposium on Regional Problems in Britain and Ireland*, ed. John Vaizey (Dublin: Gill and Macmillan, 1975), 133–164.

McAleese, Dermot. *A Profile of Grant-Aided Industry in Ireland*. (Dublin: Industrial Development Authority, 1977).

McAleese, Dermot. 'Do Tariffs Matter? Industrial Specialization and Trade in a Small Economy'. *Oxford Economic Papers* 29, 1 (1977): 117–27.

McAleese, Dermot. 'Anglo-Irish Economic Interdependence: From Excessive Intimacy to a Wider Embrace', in *Ireland and Britain since 1922*, ed. P. J. Drudy (Cambridge: Cambridge University Press, 1986), 88–105.

McAleese, Dermot, and John Martin. 'Irish Manufactured Imports from the UK in the Sixties: The Effects of AIFTA'. Economic and Social Research Institute (ESRI) Research Series, Paper No. 70, 1973.

McCarthy, John F. *Planning Ireland's Future: The Legacy of TK Whitaker* (Dublin: Glendale Press, 1990).

McConnell, James. *The Irish Parliamentary Party and the Third Home Rule Crisis* (Dublin: Four Courts Press, 2013).

McCullagh, David. *The Reluctant Taoiseach: A Biography of John A. Costello* (Dublin: Gill and Macmillan, 2010).

McDowell, R. B. *Crisis and Decline: The Fate of the Southern Unionists* (Dublin: Lilliput Press, 1997).

Meenan, James. 'From Free Trade to Self-Sufficiency', in *The Years of the Great Test 1926–39*, ed. Francis MacManus (Cork: Mercier Press, 1967), 69–79.

Meenan, James. *The Irish Economy since 1922* (Liverpool: Liverpool University Press, 1970).

Meenan, James. 'Irish Industry and Industrial Policy 1921–1943'. *Studies: An Irish Quarterly Review* (1943): 209–18.

Montgomery, Bob. *Motor Assembly in Ireland* (Dublin: Dreoilin Publications, 2018).

Moynihan, Maurice. *Currency and Central Banking in Ireland, 1922–1960* (Dublin: Gill and Macmillan, Central Bank of Ireland, 1975).

Muldowney, Mary. 'We were conscious of the sort of people we mixed with: the state, social attitudes and the family in mid twentieth century Ireland', *History of the Family*, 13, 4 (2008): 402–415.

Murphy, Gary. *Economic Realignment and the Politics of EEC Entry: Ireland, 1948–1972* (Bethesda, MD: Academica Press, 2003).

Murphy, Gary. *In Search of the Promised Land: The Politics of Post-War Ireland* (Cork: Mercier Press, 2009).

Murray, Peter. *Facilitating the Future: US Aid, European Integration and Irish Industrial Viability: 1948–73* (Dublin: University College Dublin Press, 2009).

Nash, Catherine, Lorraine Dennis, and Brian Graham. 'Putting the Border in Place: Customs Regulation in the Making of the Irish Border, 1921–1945'. *Journal of Historical Geography* 36, 4 (2010): 421–31.

Neary, J. Peter, and Cormac Ó Gráda. 'Protection, Economic War and Structural Change: The 1930s in Ireland'. *Irish Historical Studies* 27, 107 (1991): 250–66.

Nesbitt, Ronald. *At Arnotts of Dublin, 1843–1993* (Dublin: A. & A. Farmar, 1993).

NESC (National Economic and Social Council). *Regional Policy in Ireland: A Review* (Dublin: National Economic and Social Council 1975).

NESC. *Ireland in the European Community* (Dublin: National Economic and Social Council,1989).

NESC. *The Association between Economic Growth and Employment Growth in Ireland* (Dublin: National Economic and Social Council, 1993).

Nevin, Edward. 'The Irish Price Level: A Comparative Study'. Economic Research Institute, Paper No. 9, 1962.

NIEC (National Industrial Economic Council). *Report on Manpower Policy* (Dublin: National Industrial Economic Council, 1964).

O'Brien, Declan. *The Dublin Cattle Market's Decline, 1955–1973* (Dublin: Four Courts Press, 2021).

O'Brien, George. 'The Budget'. *Studies: An Irish Quarterly Review* 14, 54 (1925): 177–90.

O'Broin, Leon. 'Joseph Brennan, Civil Servant Extraordinary'. *Studies: An Irish Quarterly Review* 66, 261 (1977): 25–37.

Ó Fathartaigh, Mícheál. *Irish Agriculture Nationalised: The Dairy Disposal Company and the Making of the Modern Irish Dairy Industry* (Dublin: Institute of Public Administrations, 2014).

Ó Gráda, Cormac. *Ireland: A New Economic History 1780–1939* (Oxford: Clarendon Press, 1994).

Ó Gráda, Cormac. 'Money and Banking in the Irish Free State 1921–1939', in *Banking, Currency and Finance in Europe between the Wars*, ed, Charles H. Feinstein (Oxford: Clarendon Press, 1995), 414–433.

Ó Gráda, Cormac. *A Rocky Road: The Irish Economy since the 1920s* (Manchester: Manchester University Press, 1997).

Ó Gráda, Cormac. '"The Greatest Blessing of All": The Old Age Pension in Ireland'. *Past & Present* 175, 1 (2002): 124–61.

Ó Gráda, Cormac. 'Irish Agriculture after the Land War', in *Land Rights, Ethno-nationality and Sovereignty in History*, ed. Stanley Engerman and Jacob Metzer (London: Routledge, 2004), 131–52.

Ó Gráda, Cormac. 'Five Crises'. Annual T. K. Whitaker lecture, Central Bank of Ireland, 2011.

Ó Gráda, Cormac. 'Triocha bliain ag fás: Some Reflections on a Classic'. Contribution to a conference marking the thirtieth anniversary of the publication of J. J. Lee's *Ireland: Politics and Society*, Royal Irish Academy, 24 April 2019.

Ó Gráda, Cormac, and Kevin O'Rourke. 'Irish Economic Growth, 1945–88', in *Economic Growth in Europe since 1945*, ed. Nicholas Crafts and Gianni Toniolo (Cambridge: Cambridge University Press, 1996), 388–426.

Ó Gráda, Cormac, and Kevin Hjortshøj O'Rourke. 'The Irish Economy during the Century after Partition'. *Economic History Review* 75, 2 (2022): 336–70.

Ó Maitiú, Séamus. *W. & R. Jacob: Celebrating 150 Years of Irish Biscuit Making* (Dublin: Woodfield Press, 2001).

Odlum, Stephen. *Flour Power, the Story of the Odlum Flour Milling Families* (Dublin: Zest Publications, 2015)

O'Donoghue, Cathal. 'A Century of Irish Agriculture: A Policy Driven Sector'. *Journal of the Statistical and Social Inquiry Society of Ireland* 51 (2022): 86–127.

O'Donovan, John. 'State Enterprises'. *Journal of the Statistical and Social Inquiry Society of Ireland* 18 (1947): 327–348.

O'Farrell, Patrick N. 'The Regional Problem in Ireland: Some Reflections upon Development Strategy'. *Economic and Social Review* 2, 4 (1971): 453–480.

O'Farrell, Patrick N. 'Analysis of Industrial Closures: Irish Experience 1960–1973'. *Regional Studies* 10, 4 (1976): 433–448.

O'Halpin, Eunan. 'Ireland Looking Outwards, 1880–2016', in *Cambridge History of Ireland Volume IV: 1880–2016*, ed. Thomas Bartlett (Cambridge: Cambridge University Press, 2018), 834–35.

O'Hearn, Denis. 'Estimates of New Foreign Manufacturing Employment in Ireland 1956–1972'. *Economic and Social Review* 18, 3 (1987): 173–88.

O'Hearn, Denis. 'The Road from Import-Substituting to Export-Led Industrialization in Ireland: Who Mixed the Asphalt, Who Drove the Machinery, and Who Kept Making Them Change Directions?' *Politics & Society* 18, 1 (1990): 1–38.

Oliver, Emmet. 'The Business of Dublin in the Early 20th Century: An Overview of the Retail and Financial Sectors'. *Dublin Historical Record* 71, 2 (2018): 236–50.

Ollerenshaw, Philip. 'Businessmen and the Development of Ulster Unionism, 1886–1921'. *Journal of Imperial and Commonwealth History* 28, 1 (2000): 35–64.

O'Malley, Eoin. *Industrial Policy and Development: A Survey of Literature from the Early 1960s* (Dublin: National Economic and Social Council, 1980).

O'Malley, Eoin. *Industry and Economic Development: The Challenge for the Latecomer* (Dublin: Gill and Macmillan, 1989).

O'Malley, Eoin. 'The Revival of Irish Indigenous Industry 1987–1997'. *Quarterly Economic Commentary* (1998): 35–57.

O'Rourke, Kevin. 'Burn Everything British But Their Coal: The Anglo-Irish Economic War of the 1930s'. *Journal of Economic History* 51, 2 (1991): 357–66.

O'Rourke, Kevin. 'Independent Ireland in Comparative Perspective'. *Irish Economic and Social History* 44, 1 (2017): 19–45.

Paavonen, Tapani. 'From Isolation to the Core: Finland's Position towards European Integration, 1960–95'. *Journal of European Integration History* 7, 1 (2001): 53–75.

Plunkett, Horace. *Report of the Proceedings of the Irish Convention* (Dublin: HM Stationery Office, 1918).

Pollard, Sidney. *Peaceful Conquest: The Industrialization of Europe, 1760–1970* (Oxford: Oxford University Press, 1981).

Potter, Matthew. *Limerick's Merchants: Traders and Shakers* (Limerick: Limerick Chamber, 2015).

Press, Jon. 'Protectionism and the Irish Footwear Industry, 1932–39'. *Irish Economic and Social History* 13, 1 (1986): 74–89.

Press, Jon. *The Footwear Industry in Ireland, 1922–1973* (Dublin: Irish Academic Press, 1989).

Pyle, Jean L. 'Export-Led Development and the Underemployment of Women: The Impact of Discriminatory Development Policy in the Republic of Ireland", in *Women Workers and Global Restructuring*, ed. Kathryn Ward (New York: Cornell University Press, 1990).

Quinn, James. 'Industry Evolution: A Comparative Study of Irish Wholesaling'. Ph.D. thesis, Dublin City University, 2002.

Raftery, Adrian E, and Michael Hout. 'Maximally Maintained Inequality: Expansion, Reform, and Opportunity in Irish Education, 1921–75'. *Sociology of Education* 66, 1 (1993): 41–62.

Rains, Stephanie. 'Here Be Monsters: The Irish Industrial Exhibition of 1853 and the Growth of Dublin Department Stores'. *Irish Studies Review* 16, 4 (2008): 487–506.

Regan, John M. 'The Politics of Utopia: Party Organisation, Executive Autonomy and the New Administration', in *Ireland: The Politics of Independence* ed. Mike Cronin and John M. Regan (New York: St. Martin's Press, 2000), 32–66.

Regan, John M. *The Irish Counter-Revolution, 1921–1936: Treatyite Politics and Settlement in Independent Ireland* (Dublin: Gill and Macmillan, 2001).

Restrictive Practices Commission. *Report of Studies into Industrial Concentration and Mergers in Ireland* (Dublin: Stationery Office, 1975).

Rigney, Peter. *Trains, Coal and Turf: Transport in Emergency Ireland* (Dublin: Irish Academic Press, 2010).

Riordan, Edward J. *Modern Irish Trade and Industry* (London, New York: Metheuen, E.P. Dutton, 1920).

Robertson, Nora. *Crowned Harp: Memories of the Last Years of the Crown in Ireland* (Dublin: Allen Figgis and Co., 1960).

Roche, William K. 'Social Partnership: From Lemass to Cowen'. *Economic and Social Review* 40, 2 (2009): 183–205.

Rodrik, Dani. 'Institutions for High-Quality Growth: What They Are and How to Acquire Them'. *Studies in Comparative International Development* 35, 3 (2000): 3–31.

Rodrik, Dani. 'When Ideas Trump Interests: Preferences, Worldviews, and Policy Innovations'. *Journal of Economic Perspectives* 28, 1 (2014): 189–208.

Rosenbaum, Simon, ed. *Against Home Rule: The Case for the Union* (London: F. Warne, 1912).

Rouse, Paul. *Ireland's Own Soil: Government and Agriculture in Ireland, 1945–65* (Dublin: Irish Farmers Journal, 2000).

Ryan, J. 'Foreword', in *The Lost Distilleries of Ireland*, ed. Brian Townsend (Glasgow: Neil Wilson Publishing, 1997), 1–2.

Ryan, Louden. 'Measurement of Tariff Levels for Ireland, for 1931, 1936, 1938'. *Journal of the Statistical and Social Inquiry Society of Ireland* 18 (1947): 109–32.

Ryan, Louden. 'The Nature and Effects of Protective Policy in Ireland, 1922–1939', Ph.D. thesis, Trinity College Dublin, 1949.

Ryan, Louden. 'Protection and the Efficiency of Irish Industry'. *Studies: An Irish Quarterly Review* 43, 171 (1954): 317–26.

Ryan, Louden. 'Fiscal Policy and Demand Management in Ireland, 1960–70'. *Economic and Social Review* 2, 2 (1971): 253–308.

Ryan, Louden. 'Opening Up to the International Economy: Ireland in the 1950s'. TCD Witness Seminar, Centre for Contemporary Irish History, 8 December 2004.

Saorstát Éireann: Irish Free State Official Handbook (Dublin: Talbot Press, 1932).

Shaw, Alexander. 'The Irish Bacon-Curing Industry', in *Ireland: Industrial and Agricultural*, ed. Department of Agriculture and Technical Instruction (Dublin: Brown and Nolan, 1902), 241–257.

Schoen, Lothar. 'The Irish Free State and the Electricity Industry, 1922–1927', in *The Shannon Scheme and the Electrification of the Irish Free State*, ed. Andy Bielenberg (Dublin: Lilliput Press, 2002), 28–47.

Scholz, Michael. 'Location of Large Manufacturing Establishments in Ireland'. M.Sc. Business Analytics dissertation, Trinity Business School, 2022.

Smith, Cornelius F. *The Shipping Murphys: The Palgrave Murphy Shipping Line 1850–1926* (Dublin: Albany Press, 2004).

Smith, Louis PF, and Gerard Quinn. *A Study of the Evolution of Concentration in the Irish Food Industry 1968–1973* (Brussels: European Commission, 1975).

Smurfit, Michael. *A Life Worth Living: Michael Smurfit's Autobiography* (Dublin: Oak Tree Press, 2014).

Society for the Protection of Protestant Interests. *Reply to the Catholic Association and Its Allies, 'the Leader' and 'the Irish Rosary'* (Dublin: Society for the Protection of Protestant Interests, 1903).

Strattens' Dublin, Cork and South of Ireland: A Literary, Commercial and Social Review, with a Description of Leading Mercantile Houses and Commercial Enterprises (London: Stratten & Stratten, 1892).

Survey of Grant-Aided Industry: Survey Team's Report (Dublin: Stationery Office, 1967).

Sweeney, John. 'Foreign Companies in Ireland'. *Studies: An Irish Quarterly Review* 62 (1973): 273–86.

Tariff Commission. 'Report on the Application for a Tariff on Leather', Report No. 11 (Dublin: Stationery Office, 1931).

Teeling, John. 'The Evolution of Offshore Investment'. DBA thesis, Harvard University, 1975.

Thomas, Ryland, and Nicholas Dimsdale. 'A Millennium of Macroeconomic Data for the UK'. *Bank of England's Historical Macroeconomic and Financial Statistics: Version* 3 (2017).

Thornhill, Don. 'The Revealed Comparative Advantage of Irish Exports of Manufactures 1969–1982'. *Journal of the Statistical and Social Inquiry Society of Ireland* 25 (1986/87): 91–146.

Townsend, Brian. *The Lost Distilleries of Ireland* (Glasgow: Neil Wilson Publishing, 1997).

Ulster Year Book (Belfast: H.M. Stationery Office, 1926).

Unionist Convention for Provinces of Leinster, Munster and Connaught. 'Report of Proceedings, Lists of Committees, Delegates', (Dublin: Irish Unionist Alliance, 1892).

Walsh, Brendan M. 'Aspects of Labour Supply and Demand, with Special Reference to the Employment of Women in Ireland'. *Journal of the Statistical and Social Inquiry Society of Ireland* 22, 3 (1971): 88–123.

Walsh, John. *The Politics of Expansion: The Transformation of Educational Policy in the Republic of Ireland, 1957–72* (Manchester: Manchester University Press, 2009).

Waterbury, John. 'The Long Gestation and Brief Triumph of Import-Substituting Industrialization'. *World Development* 27, 2 (1999): 323–41.

Weir, Ron B. 'The Patent Still Distillers and the Role of Competition', in *Comparative Aspects of Irish and Scottish Economic and Social Development, 1660–1900*, ed. Louis M. Cullen and T. Christopher Smout, 1600–900 (Edinburgh: John Donald, 1975), 129–144.

Weir, Ron B. 'In and Out of Ireland: The Distillers Company Ltd. and the Irish Whiskey Trade 1900–39'. *Irish Economic and Social History* 7, 1 (1980): 45–65.

Whelan, Ciara, and Patrick P Walsh. 'The Importance of Structural Change in Industry for Growth'. *Journal of the Statistical and Social Inquiry Society of Ireland* 29 (2000): 1–32.

Whelan, Edward. *Ranks Mills: The Industrial Heart of Limerick City* (Limerick: Limerick City Council, 2012).

Whitaker, T. Kenneth. 'Capital Formation, Saving and Economic Progress'. *Journal of the Statistical and Social Inquiry Society of Ireland* 16 (1955/56): 184–209.

Whitaker, T. Kenneth. 'The Civil Service and Development'. *Administration* 9, 2 (1961): 107–13.

Whitaker, T. Kenneth. 'Opening Up to the International Economy: Ireland in the 1950s'. Witness seminar, Centre for Contemporary Irish History, Trinity College Dublin, 19 January 2005.

Whitaker, T. Kenneth. (ed.) *Protection or Free Trade: The Final Battle* (Dublin: Institute of Public Administration, 2006).

Whitaker's Red Book of Commerce, or Who's Who in Business (London: J. Whitaker and Sons, 1912).

White, Tony. *Investing in People: Higher Education in Ireland from 1960 to 2000* (Dublin: Institute of Public Administration, 2001).

World Bank. *Exporting Processing Zones* (Washington, DC: World Bank, 1992).

Index

For the benefit of digital users, indexed terms that span two pages (e.g., 52–53) may, on occasion, appear on only one of those pages.

Please note that firm names beginning with initials will be sorted under the main part of the name, e.g. John H. Bennett & Co. will be found under 'Bennett'.